CULTURE SHOCK!

Jakarta
At your Door

Derek Bacon

Graphic Arts Center Publishing Company
Portland, Oregon

In the same series

Australia	*Hong Kong*	*Pakistan*	*Chicago at Your Door*
Bolivia	*India*	*Philippines*	*London at Your Door*
Borneo	*Indonesia*	*Singapore*	*Paris at Your Door*
Britain	*Iran*	*South Africa*	*Rome at Your Door*
Burma	*Ireland*	*Spain*	
California	*Israel*	*Sri Lanka*	*A Globe-Trotter's Guide*
Canada	*Italy*	*Sweden*	*A Parent's Guide*
Chile	*Japan*	*Switzerland*	*A Student's Guide*
China	*Korea*	*Syria*	*A Traveller's Medical Guide*
Cuba	*Laos*	*Taiwan*	*A Wife's Guide*
Czech	*Malaysia*	*Thailand*	*Living and Working Abroad*
Republic	*Mauritius*	*Turkey*	*Working Holidays Abroad*
Denmark	*Mexico*	*UAE*	
Egypt	*Morocco*	*USA*	
France	*Nepal*	*USA—The*	
Germany	*Netherlands*	*South*	
Greece	*Norway*	*Vietnam*	

All illustrations and photographs by Derek Bacon,
except photograph on p. 127 by Ian J. Viney

© 1999 Times Editions Pte Ltd

This book is published by special
arrangement with Times Editions Pte Ltd
Times Centre, 1 New Industrial Road, Singapore 536196
International Standard Book Number 1-55868-419-0
Library of Congress Catalog Number 98-87496
Graphic Arts Center Publishing Company
P.O. Box 10306 • Portland, Oregon 97296-0306 • (503) 226-2402

Printed in Singapore

To the memory of Made Irviananta

ACKNOWLEDGMENTS

A thousand 'thank yous' go to the individuals who gave me their time and ideas in helping to realize this book. Sincere thanks go to Ratna Astuti, and Bapak and Ibu Made Suandhe, whose expertise and enthusiasm were an endless resource.

Likewise, I am ever grateful to the following 'misters': to Ian Betts for helping corroborate a seemingly limitless amount of factual information; to Francis Windsor for always being able to supply, when my own brain failed me, the perfect phrase to describe Jakarta; to Eric Birn for his dedicated analysis of Indonesia's social and political concerns.

Finally, I am grateful to Mary Cooksey and Sarah Holland, whose critical eyes made me rewrite the book several hundred times over. I am indebted to everyone who has helped me, in ways small and large, to make this book possible.

CONTENTS

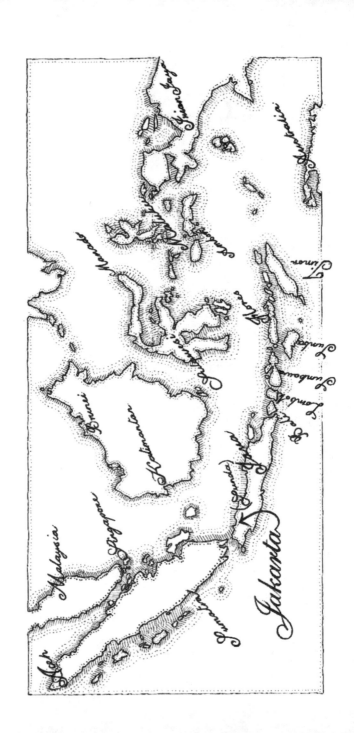

CHAPTER ONE

THE BIGGER PICTURE

INTRODUCTION

Slam! It's the last time I make this journey; last time I take a taxi across this hot mad city — tomorrow I'm gone. Well-rehearsed, I'm saying hello and winding up the window as the driver turns the air-conditioning on. His name is Budi. He's Javanese, brown, glowing and married with six children. We talk. Well I'm from England actually. No I'm not married. Yes I quite like rice. This is what it's been like: Jakarta. Home. Hmm.

We stop at our first traffic lights. Three cars ahead I spot a man in lipstick shaking a tambourine. To avoid fatal eye contact I sink down, but it's too late — he (or she) has made a beeline for us. I'm almost invisible but the stares from the other vehicles and Budi's laughter soon blows my cover and I end up pushing a thousand-rupiah note through the window. And so we are mobbed by a hundred other people performing impossible human tasks: children selling cakes, boys selling themselves and lepers begging for release. A man with a gaping hole for a nose slides past on a trolley. I wish the lights would change. The lights change.

I suppose I might come to miss all this.

By the time I get home I will have grimaced through 26 sets of traffic lights and acquired the following: a hefty woodcarving of a horse, a censored girlie calendar, an inflatable Power Ranger, a chess set, nine boiled sweets, two slices of salted pineapple, a fake Rolex, three kretek cigarettes and a blowpipe.

It's nearly 6 p.m. and the sun is about to go down. It's prayer time: I'm journeying across this great wobbling thug of a city in a Koperasi *taxi; my driver is Budi and I'm not invisible. We pick up speed on a stretch of dual carriageway still whitewashed-white from some VIP's visit. An orange bus, tilting dangerously to one side, tries to overtake us from the inside. For a while we are neck and neck: old folk, pregnant women and knee-high schoolchildren elbowing around with the same blank abandon. Sometimes repairs are made with the bus still in motion. Sometimes the passengers have to get out and push. You see that too.*

Keep your eyes glued to the road at all times and never assume you are going the right way. This road changed overnight recently from a two to a one-way street and, a week later a bus lane appeared, running in the opposite direction. I ask Budi to be "hati-hati" *on this road. But then again: not too careful — we wouldn't want to get pulled over.*

Past air-brushed promises of malls-to-be and hand-painted billboards of the President, we zoom into the home straight, aiming for the middle of the road and swerving only when necessary. Random oil drums and funeral processions are two such necessities.

We arrive. He overcharges me; I overpay him. Thanks. See you again maybe. Slam.

PLANET JAKARTA

"So what's Jakarta like?" I asked the Australian behind me. "Well, mate," he said, breathing in sharply, "it's no oil painting — I'll tell you that for nothing."

It is the worst place in Indonesia — and Indonesia is an amazing place. It is the biggest, most expensive, most polluted, most corrupt, most westernized, most crowded, most lurid, most worldly city in Indonesia. It is the worst you will see of Indonesia. Oh dear.

It's so big, it's in danger of imploding. It can't quite seem to cope, but somehow, despite every overwhelming odd, it always seems to manage. It looks like it *ought* to work — on the surface, that is. It's all there: gloss, fashion, technology, machinery, attitude but ... something's not quite right. Look closely and see that everything is slightly broken, slightly chipped and cracked, slightly skew-whiff. On paper, it shouldn't really work at all. City planners would have given up at the drawing board had someone given them the plans for the city that exists today. It's wonky; lopsided. It's a mutant. It's the wrong shape. There's no apparent logic behind its design — it seems to have just happened this way.

It's a city under constant revision. The signs are everywhere: the endless traffic jams, the super-rich living opposite the very poor, hopelessly struggling telephone and transport systems, a suffocating confusion of red tape, and an increasingly restless young generation, frustrated with the inequalities of their nepotistic society and its rampant corruption.

Jakarta's synopsis is a fragmented one; its map is vast. It doesn't have a centre as such. With nothing to grab hold of, everything hurtles past in a random rush of snapshots. First-time visitors will feel perpetually lost in a maze of never-ending back-streets, broken only by the occasional scrawny patch of grassland, bubbling river, festering rubbish pile and sudden, surprise area of high-walled real estate. It seems at times to be deliberately hiding itself. And people are absolutely everywhere.

Construction work goes on day and night. The bamboo scaffolding, hills of red earth and continuous migration of cheap labourers all confirm to agree that Jakarta is by no means finished. It has been said before, and it's true: Jakarta is all of Indonesia concentrated into a single fat Mother City — *ibukota kita*. Some ten million people call it home, although nearly every one of them originates from somewhere else.

From the air, it is surprisingly green. Genuine efforts in recent years to colour the city and create something of a green belt area are paying off. Basically old in the north, it gets newer as you head south. Yet apart from a tight area of skyscrapers in the centre, the city is still a dishevelled mass of red residential *kampung* roofs. The worst, most poverty-stricken slums are now fewer and further between, but the struggle to make basic ends meet goes on. The railway lines and river banks are still home to some of the worst indications of poverty, but in today's city, much of the urban poor live in brick, or part-brick houses with running water and electricity. And every home has a television. The city has come a moderate way from the Jakarta depicted in *The Year of Living Dangerously*, but it is still mostly *kampung*.

It shouldn't be boring; it depends ultimately on what you find interesting. You see, in this city, there's always something going on, always something slightly shocking to see. It never sleeps. People seem to sit about, hang around, play cards, strum guitars and watch the world at every hour of the day. There's always something going on, always a *warung* open. It may be incredibly frustrating, it may seem like The Last Place on Earth, The End of the World, The Town Where No One Got Off, The Land That the West Forgot … maybe, but it's not boring. It's an entire planet of its own.

Planet Jakarta

When you consider Jakarta, you consider the "problem" of Jakarta. The "problem" of the overcrowded city, the "problem" of what is an impossible city, and the "problem" of trying to live here. It's certainly not an easy place. Indonesians themselves go into culture shock when they come here. On the face of it, it doesn't appear to make any concession to being sympathetic to anyone. But given time and patience, and a certain understanding, Jakarta will lodge itself in the heart of anyone who has lived there. Part of you will hate it, part of you will love it. And part of you will hate yourself for loving it. Ultimately, however, you shouldn't have to gripe about Jakarta — it can't help it after all. It didn't mean to be like this.

For some, those coming from the West, where clean streets, freedom of speech, and equal opportunity are taken for granted, it may seem nothing less than the end of the world. For rural Indonesians, it is only the start — the land of apparent plenty. People flood Jakarta all the year round in search of work. And with them bring a little piece of their home, a little something from the 17,000 or so islands of the world's largest archipelago. This city's personnel is a constantly changing one.

For an Indonesian, Jakarta is the surest place to find work. It's obvious: with so many people concentrated in one place, there's always going to be something to sell; always some kind of service to provide. Unemployment is not necessarily the problem, it's more like *under*employment for the most part. But still, there's always the chance of making that extra rupiah in Jakarta.

They might open a food stall. They might spend the day giving people lifts on their *ojek*, or cleaning people's houses or driving a taxi or *bajaj*. They might find work in a massage parlour or hawking the streets selling something: food, *jamu*, individual cigarettes, kitchen utensils, furniture, paintings, a particular regional variation of a drink. They might offer a service of some sort: sharpening knives, cutting hair, refilling disposable lighters,

11

repairing broken things, unjamming stuck things, weighing and measuring things, re-soling shoes, taking Polaroid photos. They might get work operating a photocopier all day, or paying other people's bribes, or polishing shoes, or working the night market, or running errands in an office, or carrying bags of shopping for people, or digging holes for a construction company, or lending out umbrellas when it rains. They might end up begging for a living.

A great many, however, find the returns much less lucrative than they might have anticipated. And when they do eventually leave the teeming, steaming metropolis that is Jakarta, and *pulang kampung* (go home), most find they are no richer than when they had started — though not necessarily dejected by the experience.

The main benefit for those who stick it out is the prospect of being able to send regular money to their families back home. The returns may be small in comparison to some of the Big Money being made in Jakarta, but *uang* (money) goes further in the villages — everyone agrees on that. This system of sharing-alike is a widespread and unspoken obligation throughout Indonesia. For a country with very little in the way of an effective welfare system, it must be taken for granted that parents will provide for their children, no matter what difficulties arise. And the children, usually the eldest but not always, will be responsible for bearing the burden of the parents in old age. This unwritten agreement extends far beyond the nuclear family. An example of this would be if a particular member of the extended family had attained a certain degree of prosperity. It's quite possible that a distant (and poorer) relative would send one of their children to live with the well-off family, to run errands and generally be an unpaid servant on condition that the family provide an education for the child.

The person coming from the "developed" world will find a world where a contradiction occurs with every other step. A world of improbable extremes. A world where any notion of apparent "logic" is out the window; where saving face outweighs any other obvious course of thought. A world where individual opinions are blurred into a single collective mentality. Where people will actually "lie" rather than risk offending you with what might be the truth. A world where, for the most part, people are forced to accept all manner of conditions, without even a murmur of protest. Where glaringly corrupt policies are implemented and labour forces exploited. Where imported technology gathers dust. Where human error runs high.

Where breakfasts are spicy. Where cats have no tails. Where brothels operate opposite mosques. Where every "respectable" home has a servant. Where pineapples are salted. Where men hold hands. Where courting couples shouldn't. Where cough sweets are small change. Where mosquitoes are hungry. Where endangered species are on sale. Where a glass of beer is expensive. Where hormone-loaded snake blood is drunk. Where the police are bribable. Where the women outnumber the men. Where the days and nights are equal length. It's a place where the people are always smiling.

It's no oil painting, but as the people who live there will usually tell you, "*tidak apa-apa*" — it doesn't matter.

WEATHER

Hot. There are two seasons, both are hot but one is wetter than the other. In the *musim hujan* (wet season), it's definitely a bit cooler, especially elsewhere in Java, but Jakarta's short distance from the equator means it's nothing less than hot and tropical almost all the time.

From time to time, however, strange weather does occur. Brief but intense falls of hailstones have been recorded several times in Jakarta, while on the other extreme, the notorious El Niño weather phenomenon forced the season's rains to move in the opposite direction in 1997, plunging the region into its worst

13

drought for fifty years, and leaving forest fires burning uncontrollably for months on end. These are exceptional weather conditions, however, and although it's true that long-term inmates do become sensitive to subtle variations in the weather, no one need go to Jakarta expecting a variable barometer.

The *musim kering* (dry season) is not without its drawbacks. When rain hasn't fallen for months on end, water supplies get scarce as wells begin drying up. If you don't have air conditioning, the nights are hot and sticky, although you are welcome to try your best with a carefully-angled fan. *Nyamuk* (mosquitoes) are never much fun at the best of times, not least than in the dry season when their quantity and ferocity is at a peak.

The dry season runs from about May to September and is influenced mainly by the Australian continental air masses. The wet season's tendencies are attributed to Pacific Ocean air masses and the Asian continent. But let's not pull any punches: Jakarta is HOT and that's that. Yet it could be hotter, if Java wasn't an island, or was bigger. The warm seas surrounding Java keep temperatures a touch less extreme than they could be. Something to be almost thankful for perhaps.

Rain can be phenomenal in Jakarta — a monsoon no less. On an average day in the middle of the wet season, the sky is heavy with great swollen cumulonimbus clouds. By early afternoon, many of them have already greyed and things start to look ominous. An early indication of impending doom is a vibrating ripple in the water-dispenser, accompanied soon after by the far-off rumble of *guntur* (thunder). You know there's a monster coming and there's nothing you can do about it. Then the *halilintar* (lightning) starts: the sky flashing in one giant Polaroid photo. Several flashes occur on top of one another and the sky goes bright white for a few long seconds. Everyone holds their breath and then says "*aduh*" (blimey). It's cartoon weather, with everything turning to X-ray. Bolts leap from cloud to cloud, before forking violently groundwards. Every building that values its future, not to mention the occupants within, needs to be grounded against lightning. Try watching a storm from the highest storey of a Jakarta skyscraper. While you enjoy the fireworks display, you can play spot-the-biggest-lightning-rod and place bets on which area will blackout next.

By now it's dark and the rain is all around you. What sounds like a bomb goes off above your head as a bolt hits home. You know the time has come. The rain is heavy and the noise tremendous. Conversation, phone calls and TV are put on hold; all other sounds obliterated by the roar. Then leaks start appearing. All round the building the ceiling starts to weep — little drips, dribbles and drops appearing from nowhere. The rain finds its way through ceilings on every floor of a high-rise building. After cooking in the daytime heat, Jakarta's slap-quick skyscrapers are nothing but gap-toothed cavities waiting to be filled when the afternoon rain finally comes. The walls start trickling while inexplicably, a light bulb starts filling with water. A mass exodus of evacuating ants begins to chug its way down one side of one wall, re-enacting a scene from the Old Testament. The floor is cluttered with pots, pans and *ember* (buckets). The toilet belches before the electricity finally gives out.

Outside, the street has become a river. Sewers overflow; street-children start swimming. As any normal concept of "traffic" is out of the question, the street becomes an open-market war. Taxi drivers wholeheartedly refuse to go anywhere near the *banjir* (flood) without hefty payment. Public transport is a free-for-all. People are left to wade single-file through the knee-high slush with everything balanced on their heads, hoping not to fall down a pot hole. Whole areas of *kampung* disappear, submerged by the sudden gush of water, much of it rushed downhill from nearby Bogor (probably the wettest place in the world, incidentally). Household guttering struggles to cope with the deluge; great

15

fountains arching upwards from downpipes; evacuation pipes spouting like geysers on an oil field.

And then of course, the rain clouds pass, the sun comes out and within five minutes everything is dry again. But sometimes the rain is a relief. When it hasn't rained for months on end, when it seems all the air has run out, everyone breathes a sigh when the skies finally let rip. And as the season draws to an end, the rain bursts get less irate. By the beginning of the dry season, the rain is infrequent; isolated cloud bursts appear, sometimes so small only a couple of houses are hit. Getting drenched in Jakarta then becomes as simple as turning the wrong corner.

HEAT

The heat is ever-present, all-year round and rarely lets up. It hits you the instant you leave the airport and stays with you. With an average day and night temperature of around 30°C, you need to learn either to get used to it, or find your own way of keeping cool. If you can't find a parasol big enough, don't be *malu* (shy) about investing in a large umbrella for your outdoor activities. Often the hottest days in Jakarta are the ones with the most umbrellas.

In Jakarta, you definitely sweat. While air-conditioning is present in most modern buildings, even this is not without disadvantages. AC is something you may come to rely on, especially if it's installed in your home, and most definitely if you sleep with it. For these reasons you are unlikely to make much use of the city's *bajaj* (motorized rickshaws) and will most probably go completely *sinting* (bonkers) if the taxi you climb into doesn't have it. And you go even more *sinting* when the one at home breaks down. This is not a good sign. You can only accept the fact that you have become dependent on air-conditioning. You have developed a disorientated concept of the climate, fighting a losing battle against the heat.

At the height of the dry season the air is still — there's no wind. Sometimes the heat is so intense you cannot stand up. All you can do is lie down and try not to move. The heat holds you in its grip. This is called flat-out heat, and unless you stay inside with AC on all day and all your windows closed, sooner or later you are going to experience it. For everyone, things become *"besok aja"* (do it tomorrow). There is no hurry for Indonesia's construction workers, many of whom sleep on site, to finish a building before the season changes and "the nights start drawing in". For people from colder climes it can be hard. One man working in Jakarta found himself cracking up after six months of the heat and had to spend an evening standing in ice water with blocks of ice pressed all over him. This is rather extreme; he could, after all, have just climbed into the *mandi* (water tank) for an hour or so. Yet it is indicative of the discomfort *bule* (white people) may experience in the Jakarta heat.

On a more serious level, there are a number of heat-related illnesses to be struck down by. The most common being heat-cramps, heatstroke, exhaustion and sunburn. Of these the most serious is heatstroke for which immediate medical help must be found. Victims to this horrible condition are unable to sweat, and thus the body temperature is allowed to rise unhindered. Convulsions, coma, permanent brain damage and even death can follow. A less serious form of heatstroke is heat-exhaustion caused through dehydration and salt depletion, coupled with strenuous activity.

Drink a lot of water and don't overheat. With an average humidity of around 90%, you feel continually sticky and damp. You may like to follow the Indonesian example of bathing twice or more a day. Bathing cools you down, cleans off the salt deposits left by your sweat and generally maintains healthier skin. Use a high-factor sunblock; your skin can start to burn in only fifteen minutes in Indonesia.

17

Tempers are tested to the limit in this heat. When things are not working, and you can't seem to get anything done and all the time the heat is screaming down on you, it's all too easy to lose your composure and "flip out". Other than drawing attention to yourself, this will get you nowhere. Indonesians do not readily relate to open displays of frustration. And it's not that they feel any cooler either — they simply have more self-control than you.

The daytime heat in Jakarta is probably no hotter than other cities in Indonesia; it's the combination of pollution, population and frustration which makes it *seem* that much hotter. You become particularly aware of Jakarta's heat if you leave and return to the city. With every kilometre closer comes the realization that you are approaching a cauldron.

The coolest time of the day is between 4 and 6 a.m. when an awful lot of people are already up and about, doing exercises or hanging about. Since the sun hasn't fully risen, it's a relatively pollution-free, quiet, dusky time of the day, not unlike an English summer evening. And then the sun comes up. It shoots up directly to the centre of the sky and sits there for twelve hours, bleaching out all colours, stripping shadow to the bare minimum and being nothing but HOT. By 9 a.m. everything is as hot as the sun. Then later at 6 p.m. the sun, as if under government instruction, suddenly drops from the sky. Yet the heat remains. Big cities like Jakarta are good at trapping heat, so it may feel even hotter after dark.

NATURAL DISASTERS

Perhaps because it is spared many of the disasters possible elsewhere in Indonesia, Jakarta is a relatively safe place to be. Earthquakes and typhoons are common to Southeast Asia but rarely do they afflict regions as far south as Jakarta. Sumatra has had its fair share of disaster, as has Manado, and Flores has been regularly turned upside down by tidal waves. Tremors are theoretically possible in the capital, but you don't need to keep tabs on the latest seismographic readings before going out. For the most part, you need worry more about things like leaking roofs, flooding floors and never-ending traffic jams than being sucked up into a tornado.

The waters around Jakarta Bay are slow and sluggish and, the risk of poisoning aside, nothing to fear. On the south coast of the island upon which Jakarta sits, the story is markedly different. A dynamic undertow and shores that drop like cliffs a few feet into the water make for impressive waves but genuinely dangerous swimming. In January '97, for example, a single monster wave moving east to west claimed the lives of people all across Indonesia. The waters around Pelabuhan Ratu and Parangtritis are infamously perilous and held in great suspicion by locals. A million stories exist of people disappearing into the water upon "hearing" a cry for help or "seeing" a drowning person through the sea-mist.

Being something of a concrete jungle, the risk of death by falling coconut or the spiky monster-fruit *durian* is considerably lower in Jakarta than elsewhere in the country. But it's quite possible to have eaten one too many *durian* which, due to their relatively high alcohol content, may well leave you drunk enough to avoid driving and operating dangerous machinery.

VOLCANOES

If you live in Indonesia, you live near a volcano. The country sits on one gigantic chain of volcanoes, their very presence a welding point for two continental plates. Indonesia has approaching two hundred active ones, in Java alone are some thirty, of which most are quietly active. As a result, the soil in Java is among the world's most fertile, happily supporting some 40,000 species of plant. The tremendously high iron content means it's a deep red colour, and continuous volcanic activity means the land is regularly replenished with a fresh layer of nutrient-rich volcano innards. True, the soil isn't evenly fertile throughout Indonesia but when it is fertile, it's *really* fertile. Have a look in the hole next time you pass some Jakarta roadworks and marvel at the rich, red colour.

Although Jakarta is an area unaffected by volcanoes, there are three nearby: Pangrango, Halimun and Gede. And then there's the most famous of them all, Krakatau. Officially, the casual visitor and bubble-blower is forbidden to land on Krakatau, or rather "Anak" Krakatau ("child" of Krakatau) as it's more accurately known, since the original blew itself up in 1883 and, some forty-four years later, a new one began to emerge. This is excellent advice. On the morning of June 13, 1993, an American woman was killed when the volcano erupted after a climb to the crater. A three-hour drive from Jakarta, it has, due to its relative calm of recent years, once again become a tourist attraction. Best admire it from the Carita Beach Resort, particularly at night when it looks like someone smoking a cigarette in the dark.

HISTORY

Jakarta has passed through much grubbier hands than those it is in today. In the beginning it would have been rainforest and swampland. Today it's more like Pizzaland. One theory about Indonesia's origins is that people started migrating from South China some 3,000 years ago to be met in the middle by Papua Melanesian people coming in the other direction. They would have met on the island of Java and, having liked what they saw, decided to stay. Indian migrants began arriving in numbers in the early days of Christianity, bringing with them influential religion, music and recipes.

But another perfectly plausible theory has it that human life evolved quite independently in Indonesia, and that migrations from mainland Asia weren't half as prevalent as originally assumed. Just a look at the different shades of Indonesian there are will confirm that there is indeed, no "average" Indonesian. It might be tempting to say that the Javanese are the "average" Indonesians, mainly because they are in the middle, but there's more to it than geography. As you might have gathered, in Indonesia, Java wears the trousers. And if Java is a pair of trousers, then Jakarta must be the zip area.

Certain, more remote parts of Indonesia don't necessarily like the idea of a centralized government doing its thing at such a distance like this. Many quiet radicals feel that instead of being colonized by the Dutch, Indonesia is now colonized by the Javanese. But this is a different issue and jumping the gun somewhat.

Evidence of primitive human life exists in the shape of the much-hyped discovery of one very old skull — "Man of Java" — the so-called "missing-link". The skull is reputed to be that of *homo erectus*, a primitive version of the now-standard *homo sapien*. But nothing is ever certain; the skull itself having undergone much speculation of late. Using more advanced dating methods than before, it was discovered that the skull was probably several thousand years younger than originally thought. The implications of this were enormous: that the outmoded *homo erectus* and the superior *homo sapien* had lived side-by-side for a few thousand years; that in far-off places like Java, isolated pockets of *homo erectus* had managed to resist evolutionary substitution? Some people think this explains an awful lot.

But earlier still, some 140 million years ago, there would have been no Java Sea. Borneo, Sumatra and Java were still part of mainland Asia — itself the result of volcanic eruptions when the world began.

It has always been a strategic spot; an ideal shipping lane; a major thoroughfare; a motorway stop-off between India and China. A go-between for the spice islands and the rest of the world. It's a focal point of sorts; surrounded on one side by mainland Asia and on the other side by the best spice islands in the world. Perfect. This would have been an intriguing time to be in Indonesia: no colonial rule, and no Jakarta either. What is now one very large republic would have been a disparate collection of mini-kingdoms. Some say it still is.

Jakarta wasn't anything special at this time, it was just one of many. By the 12th century, Sunda Kelapa — for that's all there was of Jakarta at first — was a reasonably-sized, functioning port governed from the relative distance of the then more important Bogor. Customers to the area at the time included Indians, Arabs, Chinese and Portuguese. The last of these were befriended by the Hindus of Java and persuaded to join forces against the rising number of Muslim states gaining ground in Java. The Muslims, however, were the winners, first taking Banten and then Sunda Kelapa in 1527. They renamed the area "Jayakarta". The history books have the exact date of this "Great Victory" (for that's what "Jayakarta" means) as June 22, 1527 — Jakarta's birthday.

But Sunda Kelapa, or rather Jayakarta, was still nothing special. At best it was a place for the ruler of Banten, one Prince Jayawikarta, to store his stock of pepper reserves. Newer customers to Indonesia's spice trade changed all this. It was the Dutch and the British who were determined to be the sole European distributors of spice. Neither quite managed to monopolize it totally but each was able to set up a trading company. These newcomers were noticeably more violent than previous customers to the area, and from the very start it was obvious they had their sights set on more than just a few cloves here and there.

Everyone knows about the Dutch: they came and stayed for three hundred years and then left for a bit, still calling it their own. When they came back they found nobody wanted them back and trouble ensued. They took away the power of sultanate. They razed the original kraton and mosque that had coexisted in old Batavia. They split the empire of Mataram in two. They wiped out almost the entire population of the Banda islands. And in old "Batavia", as they renamed the city, they held almost everyone as slave.

The Dutch made Indonesia famous to the rest of the world. For the Europeans they popularized the myth of the "mystical east" with their souvenirs; *gamelan* music, rubber and spice. When the trading company ran out of money in 1799, the project was bailed out by the Dutch government, and the real colonization began. They built posh houses in the Menteng area of Jakarta. They made Merdeka square, Lapangan Square, and, when the Suez Canal opened for business, they re-worked Tanjung Priok into the strapping great port it is today. Towards the end of their stay they introduced a few schools (in Dutch) and seemed to be halfway towards encouraging autonomy.

The start of the end came when France went to war with the rest of Europe. The Dutch government, forced to keep a low profile in London, had no one to keep an eye on things down under. Britain sent Stamford Raffles to run the place for five years where, after a shaky start fighting the French who had set up premature shop in the country, he and his crew achieved some positive things for a change. Raffles was embarrassed by slavery and encouraged Indonesian "independence". Nothing much came of it, and even though he left a lot of ideas in the suggestion box, the Dutch were to begin a period of evermore blatant exploitation upon their return.

Unsurprisingly, feelings of unrest grew and grew in the country and just as things were about to boil over, the last ones (and widely considered the worst of all) arrived — the Japanese. It seems Japan had big ideas at the time about being the big fish in Asia, just as Hitler had wanted in Europe. They even scared the Dutch away and initially made themselves out to be a "friend" of Indonesia. But as we know, it wasn't to last, and Japan was left to bow one final bow before going home to concentrate on electronic technology.

When the Dutch came back (again) they found a place which was already calling itself "independent". They didn't like this and did the "logical" thing of putting provocateurs like Sukarno and Hatta in jail. The idea of an independent Indonesia, however, refused to go away and by 1950 the Dutch had to call it a day.

Even under Dutch rule, total administrative control had never been attained. Now things were different. Indonesia was free at last to do what it wanted. Oh dear.

Chapter Two

THE LOOK OF THE PLACE

KAMPUNG

Take the time to wander beyond the confines of the skyscraper and you'll enter the world of the *kampung*. Village life in the middle of a capital city — it's a world away from the shiny office blocks that are meant to be the "real" face of Jakarta. *Kampung* are what make up most of Jakarta. A *kampung* is where most people live — small houses, low-rise, red roofs, thin walls, village dwellings, ramshackle rundown shanty-land. The average Indonesian house.

When moving around the city, Jakarta's *kampung* need not necessarily be that apparent. Hidden behind the bigger, newer buildings and big roads, they are tucked out of sight so they may be partially forgotten about.

Kampung comes in degree — not all are Third World shock-horrors. At the worst extreme, it means a bamboo and cardboard city constructed over an open sewer. Over the years, however, many of the worst slums have mutated into semi-decent (albeit cramped) accommodations, with semi-decent amenities and a price-tag attached. But either way, *kampung* means a lot of people living together in a small area. In Jakarta, money usually only buys two-dimensional space; high-rise housing is still being looked into. The best investment in Jakarta is land. Many areas of *kampung* refuse to disappear simply because they are built on such prime real estate — paying them off would be too expensive.

The origins of Jakarta's *kampung* lie in migrations to the big city at different times from different regions. The first Ambonese immigrants, for example, once they had unpacked their bags and put their feet up with a cup of *teh manis* (sweet tea), would have invited their friends to join them in Jakarta. As would the first Batak settlers, the first Balinese settlers and so on. The evidence is found all over the city in areas with names like *Kampung Melayu* and *Kampung Ambon*. The Javanese and Sundanese, however, were not welcome to set up *kampung* until fairly recently; the Dutch ban on them not relaxed until the end of the 19th century. Any gaps in these original *kampung* are rapidly plugged by the continuing flow of young hopefuls to the capital, not to mention the offspring of the original first-comers.

But the *kampung* of Jakarta continue to irritate the authorities. They think they let the side down rather; that they don't befit what they think the modern face of the city should stand for. They think that everywhere in the city should resemble modern real-estate areas like Bintaro Jaya. Rumours abound of fires being

A kampung is something to belong to, somewhere to come from.

deliberately started in a bid to clear areas of particularly stubborn *kampung,* and thus hasten the transmigration process. And a glance through any daily paper will confirm the deathtrap potential of such confined accommodation.

As for transmigration itself, Jakartans have to be the most reluctant of them all. Even the promise of a free two-roomed house on five acres of land, plus seed, fertilizer, pesticide and tools at the government's expense isn't enough to lure the average Jakartan out of the capital and into the jungle. Because in Jakarta, you see, even if you don't exactly live in luxury, you are at least given a daily glimpse of the type of affluence that just *might* be yours — if only one is patient. And Indonesians are patient people.

You will know when you are in a *kampung*, it feels different — all secular and self-sufficient. Washing stretched between houses and children hurtling everywhere, chickens, *dangdut* music, men in skirts, vests and black hats sitting on rattan-mats — these are the hallmarks of the *kampung*. Religion and unity are well-rehearsed. And so they should be, for these are the defining areas of the city. Everyone comes from a *kampung* somewhere along the line, regardless of where in Indonesia they come from.

KITES

Layang-layang (or kites) are an integral component of the Jakarta sky. Usually handmade in the *kampung* from struts of *bambu* and rice paper, the kites don't stray too far from the standard *intan* (diamond) shape. Tails are optional.

Kites have enjoyed many uses throughout Indonesian history. In long distance sea fishing, shadow-free kites are used to carry hooks and lines out past the breakers. In West Java, bats are caught by kites, while in Bali, humming kites are flown above homes to promote good vibrations. For examples of the more weird and wonderful shaped kites flown around Indonesia and the world, try and catch the annual Pangandaran Kite Festival in West Java.

So what of Jakarta's kites? Stuck in the confines of a city, one way for Jakarta's children to experience a sense of liberation is to fly a kite as high as they can. Since there's little wind in the capital, it takes an effort to get a kite airborne. Some seem to go miles up in the sky before their strings finally break under the pressure. Sometimes things get out of hand between *kampung*, sometimes glass and razors are attached to the strings in order to "down" rival kites. Pedestrians and motorcyclists are known to have been injured by stray kite strings stretched across streets. The wrecks of fallen kites are strewn all over Jakarta.

ARCHITECTURE

Despite guidebook claims about old Batavia (the present day area of Kota) resembling a European city at the turn of the century, people rarely go to Jakarta to admire the architecture. True, the oldest and most historical buildings are found in the north of the city, and the area of Menteng, for example, is a neatly-preserved Dutch suburb; bungalows, gardens and mansions. But there's little confusion whether or not this is Amsterdam when you see the *bajaj*, smell the sewers and get bitten by another mosquito. The tropical heat doesn't lend itself to the European illusion too well either. These days the city is characterized by the kind of high-rise you find in Singapore, but this is only a tiny part of the picture. From the air the city is a mass of red roofs, proof that Jakarta is still mostly residential and low-rise. Even the glossy skyscrapers look odd in Jakarta — all plush, neat and mirrored but only as far as the plot of land stretches. Anything outside this area is characterized by the rubbish piles and general impression that it has yet to be finished.

Architecture is big business in Indonesia and major construction work goes on everywhere. Experts claim Jakarta will look very nice when it's finished. Buildings are knocked up almost overnight here — shopping plazas definitely being among the

Skyscrapers along Jalan Sudirman

most common. Big name outlets and businesses are huge investors in the Indonesian economy, and although the slump of 97/98 saw things slow for a while, Jakarta's frantic construction work continues, even at the expense of safety regulations. Completion work on *Blok M Plaza* was prolonged when the contractors suddenly demanded two extra floors of shop space to make room for a fast food outlet and a cinema, prompting several architects to wash their hands of the project. Jakarta has yet to suffer the disaster of collapsing buildings that Bangkok and Manila have suffered in recent years, but look closely and you will see large cracks running through a lot of the modern buildings.

29

For examples of modern architecture see *Plaza Indonesia*, built in the early '90s, and compare it with the flat, post-colonial building next door that is *Hotel Indonesia* and, at the time (mid-'60s), one of the grandest buildings in Jakarta. The first president, Achmad Sukarno, was an engineering student and keen to re-engineer Jakarta: witness the period-piece sports stadium *Senayan*; an intimidatingly large building reminiscent of the mother-ship at the end of *Close Encounters*, only with fewer light bulbs. Some of the embassies along Jl Rasuna Said and the office blocks that stretch from Jl Sudirman to *Monas* are quite impressive, although very "Singapore" in their layout. The illusion and similarity with Singapore is confined to these few square kilometres, however, for behind almost every mirrored skyscraper is the inevitable sprawling *kampung*. In fact this glaring contrast between rich and poor is partly what gives Jakarta its lopsided charm. Witness the *warung* and *kampung* along the river that runs behind *Plaza Indonesia*. A city in search of an identity? Not necessarily, but perhaps Jakarta should build itself a very tall building like Kuala Lumpur did with its *Petronas* building.

STATUES

Spend any time in Jakarta and you'll come across some distinctive statues. Described by some as "hideous lumps of concrete representing little more than the propaganda of Indonesia's eager first government", and by others as mere "lumps of concrete", there's no denying they are essential features in Jakarta's make-up. While the city's expatriates and visitors know these landmarks under a variety of nicknames, "flaming-pizza man" or "7-up man", they are, to an Indonesian, a concrete reminder of those first flushes of independence. And for a country that was under colonial rule for almost four centuries, independence is something worth celebrating — preferably in concrete.

In Pancoran, where Jl Gatot Subroto passes the residential area of Tebet, stands the tallest of them all: the *Dirgantara* statue. He represents the Hindu monkey-god *Hanuman* and appears to be standing on an enormous number seven. In Kebayoran Baru, on the roundabout at the end of Jl Sudirman, is a statue of similar execution, the *Semangat Pemuda*.

Perhaps the most brutal of all is the *Lapangan Banteng* monument in Banteng square near the Hotel Borobudur. Representing the battle for independence of Irian Jaya against the Dutch in 1963, it appears to have hands twice the size of its head.

In the centre of the city, by the fountains in front of Hotel Indonesia, are "Hansel and Gretel", the official welcome statue of Jakarta. They were erected in lieu of the 1962 Asian Games held in Jakarta, and both characters again possess oversized hands.

Of course not all Jakarta's statues are so tasteless — see the *Arjuna* statue on the edge of Plaza Merdeka or the Henry Moore-ish one in Taman Surapati, Menteng. Not all are made of concrete: see the *Petani* monument by Gambir station — and not all have big hands.

The Lapangan Banteng monument in Banteng square

MOSQUES

With Islam the dominant religion in Indonesia, you find that mosques are not in short supply in the capital city. If you don't see a mosque — or *mesjid* — you are sure to hear one. Size need not be a drawback in the construction of a *mesjid*, since it is popular to equip one with powerful and outstanding loudspeakers to help distinguish it from the neighbouring *kampung*'s.

A small *mesjid* is known as a *musholla*. This could be either part of a larger building, a room set aside in an office, or a building in its own right. Uproar will follow if it becomes known that a newly-constructed building is *musholla*-less. This might be hard for Westerners to get their heads round — people in uproar because there is nowhere to pray. In the West there's significantly less pressure on people to be so outwardly religious. In Indonesia it is in the national constitution.

Every respectable neighbourhood is incomplete without its own *mesjid*. Some areas have more than one; Warung Buncit, Tanah Abang and Mampang are strong Jakarta Muslim stockades where every other building seems to be a *mesjid* or *musholla*. Hundreds are under construction around the city and, with mosque-parts being such big business, Jakarta's equivalent of DIY shops are well-stocked. Indeed, one reason for Jakarta's back street traffic jams would be the *kampung* boys making their roadside collections towards the completion of their particular *mesjid*. Some of these half-baked mosques, many the result of overambitious planners, drag on for years, depending on finances. But no matter, for they can be used as soon as the cement on the floor has set.

The mosque is the centre of the community: a focal point, a common ground — the centre of life for Muslims in Jakarta. You meet your neighbours there, make friends there, spread rumours there, and you can sleep there if you need. Friday prayers between 12 and 2 p.m. are exclusively male and one session which shouldn't be missed if you are a male Muslim. A *musholla* will not suffice on a Friday. Expect to find the streets outside blocked for half an hour or so on these occasions.

In the heart of the *kampung*, away from the big, mad roads, but never too far from the traffic, Islam is practised and practised until it is right. And practise they do. Aside from five daily prayers, and a profusion of Islam-respecting public holidays, are amplified speeches and sermons by "special guests" from the world of Indonesian Islam. Described below is one such sermon:

The men were separated from the women and the Same Old Story began. A large man in a dark suit (very smart he looked) had been hired for the occasion as had someone close-at-hand to adjust the echo-knob on the amplifier at appropriate moments. To look at the speaker, he didn't seem like much fun. His immense importance was clear, however, not only from the dark suit but from the special treatment he was given upon arrival. A glass of hot water and he is off, addressing both quarters separately.

The speaker was using a locally-made amplifier and since the machine wasn't particularly good, paid the price accordingly when it short-circuited, and his ranting was cut short. It was during these moments that a rude joke was thrown in. The speaker was quite expert at combining his message with examples the people could relate to. In using terminology the folk would understand, he was guaranteed a satisfactory exit from his platform and the people promised a safe night's sleep. Pak Batuk (for example) was there with his slow-motion son as if living evidence of why the speaker needed to be invited in the first place.

On such occasions a system of local government was employed with the emphasis solely upon group thinking. Any individual steps forward are made by the speaker on behalf of his audience. That's what he is here for: indeed almost wholly the reason he has been hired to talk this evening and the reason why he isn't from this particular Local Government. "Let an outsider do our dirty work" is what the folk here say ... but not too much of an outsider, it should be stressed, as a great many "in-jokes" are necessary to keep up the flow of his banter. Here the speaker puts a few analogies into play:

He asks the women, "Who washes the clothes in your home?" In unison they reply, "We do!" From their designated quarter, the women enjoy the questioning and the shouting out loud together (which they don't normally do). The speaker asks another about hanging the washing out to dry. Do they? They do. He is just checking of course and leading up to something. The men smoke and listen. They know the speaker is on their side and take delight in the moment. They like to see their women toyed with like this ...

"Should dirty clothes be folded back into the wardrobe?" The men know the answer to this one. The women all answer "no" at the same time. The speaker gets himself worked up. His assistant turns the echo-knob up to full reverb. Pak Batuk joins in. The audience relate to the washing analogy. They sleep soundly later that night. The children, as in all good neighbourhoods, fall asleep on their mothers, not following what this invited guest means about cleansing the Soul and Self through meticulous apology and prayer and its comparison to washing and ironing.

The speaker tries a different approach: simplifying the matter further. Holding up his right hand he elicits a number of possible different uses for the appendage. He finally settles on his point that the left should swing back at the same time the right swings forward. A simple demonstration of what happens when both hands swing forward has everyone laughing. It looks very funny and of course not-right. Walking done like that?

A feeling of calm overcomes the people. The speaker steps down.

The largest mosque in Southeast Asia is in Jakarta. *Mesjid Istiqlal* is found (it can't be missed) in *Lapangan Banteng*. It's an impressive construction, outside and in, yet vaguely reminiscent of a multistorey car park — so rigid is its design. Ask first if you want to enter a mosque, wear trousers and remove your shoes. Don't enter at all if menstruating. Another architecturally appealing mosque is *Mesjid Al Azhar*. Set back from the main road just outside Blok M, it sports an uncharacteristic central calling tower — or *menara* — only slightly less impressive than the tower of the five-tier roofed mosque at Banten. To the expert eye, Indonesian mosques are uniquely different to those in the rest of the world. Invariably tower-less, they depend in the cities on the afore-mentioned speakers to summon the faithful to prayer and, in the remoter parts of the country, on drums. One radical departure from traditional mosque designs is the futuristic *Mesjid Pondok Indah*, just left of the mall. It features a large flat blue-tiled roof over an open-plan bungalow-style building — very effective.

Mesjid Istiqlal is the largest mosque in Southeast Asia.

MONAS

At the very geographical centre of the city stands the national monument, *Monas*. Visible all over Jakarta, *Monas* is a 137-metre high obelisk based (apparently) on those old Javanese symbols of fertility, *linnga* and *yoni*, and built to the measurements of 8, 17 and 45 — the date of Indonesian independence. Its highly phallic design has prompted some to cite *Monas* as Sukarno's last great erection. Although Sukarno (the legendary first president) initiated many of the architectural landmarks that define Jakarta, and instigated construction of *Monumen Nasional* (*Monas*) in 1961, it wasn't until 1975 that it was finished and officially opened by the second president, Suharto.

Suharto (right) prepares to move in on ... Sukarno (left).

Apart from being a great tall block of concrete with a lump of gold on top situated in the middle of a somewhat scraggy park, *Monas* is also the focal point for some of the cheapest dates in Jakarta. *Pembantu* (servants), *sopir* (drivers) and *tukang* (sellers) make up the majority of mooning couples who sit there in the dark. Perhaps it's the overwhelming symbolism of unflagging potency that attracts them there, or merely the fact that you don't have to pay to be there. Such sentiments are expressed in the lyrics of *Ke Monas* by the King of *Dangdut* music, Rhoma Irama: "Where shall we go tonight? What shall we do? Looking for something to do tonight; somewhere not too far — let's just go to Monas." There are a few trees on the west side of the park and these offer a little privacy, particularly for the *pelacur* (prostitutes) and *banci* (transvestites) who work the area at night. "Open daily from 08:00 to 17:00, the monument offers unparalleled views of Jakarta!"

Thirty-five kilogrammes of pure gold are said (in the official tourist brochure for *Visit Indonesia Year '91*) to coat the glittering flame at the top. There is more to *Monas* than meets the eye. The basement is home to a museum offering, apart from the obvious Java Man to Modern Java Man story, a vivid example of historical whitewash. In a series of forty-eight, slightly eerie 3D-displays, the story is told of Indonesia's long struggle for independence. The anti-Dutch uprisings are depicted in garish detail, yet scant attention is paid to the events that led to the attempted coup of 1965 and subsequent inauguration of President Suharto.

President Sukarno had always been something of an eyebrow-raiser, but when the flamboyant leader began flirting with Communist China, while making threats in the direction of Malaysia, many believed he had, politically, lost the plot. And when six of Indonesia's top generals were murdered in what has gone down in official history as an attempt by Communists to seize power, a young General Suharto took his cue to step in and take the reins. Calling his government the "New Order", Suharto condemned Communism outright, sparking a wave of fear and hatred which left thousands of known Communists, suspected Communists and anyone vaguely-Chinese, dead. The spontaneous execution of some half a million people was a shocking chapter in the country's modern history (*Time* magazine reported rivers "clogged with bodies") and, for a new leader keen to make a good impression on foreign investors, best air-brushed from the history books.

With retrospect, it's easy to dismiss such events as mere Asian "madness", but the level of hatred witnessed between 1965 and 1969 was a measure of the growing dissatisfaction in the hearts of the common people. A scapegoat was needed, and a scapegoat was given in the shape of Communism. Deep down, however, everyone knew that the killings were a response to the country's dire state of affairs.

In Indonesia, Communism has become the Big Fear, i.e. to blame every time something "untoward" happens in the country. High-profile rioting in Jakarta then, in July 1996, was a serious jolt to the New Order government, yet it wasn't long before fingers were again pointed at that oldest of scapegoats, Communism. In this case, the violence was attributed to a new and particularly vicious strain which had arrived in the shape of the *Parti Rakyat Demokrasi* (PRD). Its members were immediately arrested and blamed for inciting the riots. That, said the papers, was the end of the matter.

It's the same every time. Following the July riots, anti-Communist rantings were slotted in-between TV ads. Giant posters depicting the "devil of communism" went up around the city, and *Waspada Bahaya Laten Komunis* (Beware The Latent Danger Of Communists) became the slogan of the moment. One TV soap-opera surreptitiously introduced an new character — the neighbourhood Commie. A furtive and *jahat* (evil) individual, he was seen lurking in the sidelines, perverting society and organizing anti-government uprisings within the *kampung*. And by the end of that first anxious week, Communists were being blamed for everything, even for manufacturing the drug Ecstasy — such was the paranoia of post-riot, pre-election Jakarta.

Although the passing of time and blatant rewrites of history, like that witnessed in the basement of *Monas*, do much to blur the events of Suharto's initial presidency, there remains the lingering fear that, at any moment, it could happen all over again. And it did. Three decades later, that same sense of anger returned in an explosion of rioting, looting and mayhem. But for the generations which had been raised and educated under Suharto, the idea that Communism could again be blamed for the country's social and economic problems didn't work. Indeed, it was Suharto himself who was held responsible.

CHAPTER THREE

THE INDONESIAN WAY OF THINGS

RUBBER TIME

You will learn the meaning of *kesabaran* (patience) in Indonesia. You certainly won't last very long if you don't. Indonesians have a view of time and space that is quite different to say, that of the manufacturers of Rolex watches. They call it *jam karet*, or "rubber time". It's a useful concept to learn; it has to do with shrugging off impossible delays, foul-ups and ceaseless corruption; it means never expecting too much. It means giving an extra few days leeway on every appointment made. Business meetings can seem directionless, even futile. The widespread practice of one-to-one dealings, with the all-encompassing method of face-saving etiquette, will test the very limits of those who want their results NOW! Things just don't happen this way — things are never late in Indonesia because everything is always late. Indonesians are people of almost infinite patience. But wear it out and watch out.

FAUX PAS

Indonesians are extremely tolerant people and are happy to forgive almost any blunder on the part of the foreigner. In the most polite circles people strive their utmost to maintain a harmonious atmosphere, whatever calamity may occur. A sign of properly maintained self-control is that an Indonesian is adept at not upsetting others. The greatest importance is placed on preserving a delicate social decorum in which no one is in any way made to feel *malu* (embarrassed), even if this means individual opinions going unsaid.

Contradicting someone, for example, is bad form in Indonesia. When challenged, many people may automatically agree with you when, in truth, they may actually disagree. Confusing? The emphasis is placed on being wary of your own impulses, retaining self-control and doing your best to fit into the "whole" — as opposed to living life as a "loose unit" and actually speaking your mind. Even in the thinking Indonesian's Jakarta, this is still true although less so. Selfish, western-style concerns get more priority these days as the consumer mentality spreads, and age-old traditions of mutual respect are traded for more blunt, outspoken manners.

This said, there are still certain things guaranteed to annoy an Indonesian person. One of them is moaning about Indonesia. They'll wonder why you bothered coming in the first place if all you can do is complain. Why are you here if it's so much better where you come from?

You must be careful what you do with your hands in Indonesia as mistakes are easily made. The left hand is the biggest no-no. Giving and receiving with the left hand makes the average person very uncomfortable, as this particular appendage is reserved predominantly for bum-cleaning after a poo-poo. If you get your lefts and rights mixed up, you should give and receive with both hands to be on the safe side. In rural areas and some of the more humble households in Jakarta, the use of knives and forks has yet to be perfected; direct hand-to-mouth methods are still much in preference, with the right hand of course.

Be prepared to shake hands a lot in Indonesia. When you are first introduced to someone, you might notice them touching their heart after shaking your hand. Arrive at a social affair, and you should shake hands with everyone there, not just the people you know, although exactly where you draw the line is unclear. Go to a wedding if you want to practise hand shaking. Beware, however, of the rude-finger handshake. This mainly occurs upon the introduction of pretty females to excited young males, and involves the shaker's middle finger giving the palm of the other a little tickle.

Putting hands on hips superman-style, which could be considered by some a rather camp pose to strike, is a sure sign that you are *angkuh* (arrogant), if not a bit *marah* (angry). Sticking your thumb out from between you first two fingers is arguably the rudest thing you can do with your hands in Indonesia; as "symbolic" perhaps as the now worldwide misuse of the raised index finger. A fine example of this suggestive fist, for those who want to practise it (or indeed enhance their own fertility, as the superstition has it), is found on the bottom end of a huge bronze cannon, known as *Si Jagur* (which translates as something like "Old Sturdy"), in Taman Fatahillah, north Jakarta.

Pointing is also considered rude, although acceptable if done with the thumb or the whole hand. Beckoning people with a crooked finger or upturned hand is another shock to etiquette. If possible, beckon people, and oncoming traffic, with a downward movement of the hand. Finally, since the head is considered the very "seat of the soul" and therefore special, children-patting is something to be avoided. You get used to it.

One of the problems for an unsuspecting Westerner coming to Indonesia is that such apparently unassuming body language routinely goes unmentioned by those offended. That is to say, Indonesians don't tell you when you make a social error. They probably just smile and say *"tidak apa apa"* (it doesn't matter).

And remember that a smile is not necessarily just a smile in Indonesia. Smiling is used by Indonesians to mask all manner of social embarrassment and confusion. Smiles mean other things. If someone doesn't understand you, they probably just smile. If someone feels uncomfortable with something you are doing or saying, they probably just smile. For the Indonesian, negative and aggressive emotions are dispelled by the wearing of a smile. Inform someone of bad news, or go to a shop to complain and expect the immediate reaction to be a smile. Smiling is a way of softening the blow.

Another way to mask the unpleasant truth is with a highly improbable story or excuse. The reason, for example, why someone lost their job might have been because he didn't eat enough rice — things like that. No one really expects to believe these stories but they do serve their purpose and take the edge off. When an unpleasant truth must be told, it's imparted on a one-to-one basis, preferably behind a closed door.

Perhaps the single most confusing aspect of Indonesian etiquette is the reluctance to say "no". Rather than displease you with what might be the unpleasant truth, Indonesians go to scrupulous lengths to maintain the harmony. If one person is offended, everyone is offended. Instead, people say what they *think* the other person wants to hear, without necessarily being considered a liar. This is a real drawback when asking for directions somewhere. The closest many get to saying no is *"mungkin"* (maybe). The sentiment is sincere enough, but since many Westerners' frustration levels are not equipped for such widespread indirectness, the result can sometimes be nothing less than pure frustration.

In any group, the one person who mustn't be upset is the eldest male present — everything will be done to keep him happy. In *Bahasa Indonesia* there is an expression for it: *"asal bapak senang"* (whatever keeps the boss happy, or something similar). This idea runs the gauntlet of life in Indonesia, from the *kampung* to the skyscraper. For a visiting businessman who just wants to know a company's turnover, it's a real headache. Is this the truth he's hearing or is it what his younger Indonesian partner hopes he would like to hear?

There are a number of things Indonesians do that foreigners might find offensive. Belching after your food, for example, is perfectly okay — proof indeed that you are in healthy, functioning condition. Breaking wind remains, as ever, a universal no-no. Spitting, on the other hand, seems at times to be almost a national pastime. Blowing your nose into a handkerchief is socially offensive, and should be done in private. People will spend the day sniffing if need be rather than blow their nose in public. Regardless of this, it is still alarmingly common to see people clearing their sinuses by putting a finger over a nostril and blowing hard. Nose-picking is generally an accepted habit. People are offended if it's done too vigorously, but the odd nasal-rummage is nothing to be ashamed of. Tongues are not to be shown: when affixing postage stamps to a letter, use glue; most Indonesians would be horrified at having to lick something like that — like a dog.

During a conversation it's okay to ask seemingly personal questions and make apparently personal comments. Asking if you have washed yet is a standard question, as is asking a complete stranger why, for instance, she has only got one child. When you haven't seen someone in a while, it's acceptable to comment on their physical appearance: "you look fat" or "you look old", without being considered especially rude. Amongst themselves, in the safety of the group, Indonesians are free to make cruel and teasing remarks about one another. This isn't meant to upset anyone, but anyone who is weak enough to bite the bait is clearly lacking in self-control.

When engrossed in the conversation of a crowd on the move, a lot of Indonesians seem to not look where they are walking. People are consequently forever bumping into one another, crossing streets without apparent care, and blocking stairs and escalators. To test this theory, stand in the middle of a Jakarta pavement and see how many people shuffle up to you at snail's pace, heads turned to one side, only to jump out of their skin upon impact. And don't get angry when a door gets shut in your face, as holding them open for the person behind you is not standard etiquette either.

When you get invited to someone's home there are all sorts of social blunders to avoid. Ideally, you should remove your shoes upon entering a home, and although many Jakartans are quite prepared to forego this tradition, you should still go through the motions until told otherwise. If you do get to keep your shoes on, try your best not to let anyone see the soles of your shoes. Your host will invariably show you to a room before promptly disappearing for what seems like ages. More than likely you will be given a drink in the interim: hot water, an intensely sweet syrup drink or tea. Indonesians always wait for their host to say *"silakan"* (please, go ahead) before drinking. It's quite acceptable, mind you, to not even touch your drink, whereas finishing it all off in one go indicates a need for more. The compromise is to leave the glass half-full. In polite circles and formal meetings, hot coffee will be served to indicate the conclusion of the meeting. By the time it's cool enough to drink, it's time to go. If you do get to eat, then be sure not to leave your spoon face down on the *piring* (plate), not unless you hope to get some more, for this is what will happen.

To add to the overall awkwardness of being a *bule* (a white person) in Indonesia, you might find people you thought you didn't know very well giving you little gifts for no apparent reason. Presents are not restricted only to birthdays and the like, and are given out with far greater frivolity than you may be used to. Return from a weekend away and be expected to produce an *oleh-oleh* (knick knack) of some sort. Just something small: an extra mango or two, a little snack perhaps. It's all part of Indonesia's complex system of sharing-alike, and it is, after all, the thought that counts. The presents themselves should be opened in private, as it's impolite to expect people to open them in front of you. The Indonesian way is invariably to just smile and nod when they want to say "thank you" for something, so don't think them rude because you blinked and missed it.

Indonesians are polite people — let it be said. Everyone counts, no one is made to feel left out. One expatriate in Jakarta recalls how he'd tried to make a discreet exit from a meeting he'd been invited to. He decided to whisper a fabricated excuse in the secretary's ear about it being his birthday and him having an appointment to keep. The woman passed a note to the chairman of the meeting who, upon reading it, stopped the meeting in mid-flow and made everyone there sing "Happy Birthday" to him three times. After shaking hands with all fifty people, the man was free to leave. And he had only been attending out of politeness.

But it's not all good. Sometimes the "sharing-alike" turns to pure selfishness, such is the Indonesian's expectation that "it's only fair to share". The stories to back this suggestion are limitless. One such story has a semipermanent foreigner in Jakarta expecting a package from home, which was to include a packet of her favourite cigarettes. The package arrived eventually but when she opened it she was surprised to find only three of the original twenty cigarettes had made it through the post. It seems the remaining three had been sent on as a goodwill gesture; the rest meanwhile had been fairly and squarely shared out. In Indonesian society, a single working person living at home is expected to make their bank account details public. Their salary is not necessarily theirs alone to keep. Put a communal dish of food out with the proviso "help yourself" and see everyone's inherent refinement disappear in a flash as they fight to fill their pockets.

The system of titles is an aspect of Indonesian etiquette which foreigners easily get wrong. Depending on who is talking to who, how old the person is and where he or she comes from, different words, titles and expressions must be employed. A younger person forced to cross the path of an elder is supposed to "dip" one shoulder. In Jakarta, only the *pembantu* (servants) do this, the average Jakartan is far too hip for such behaviour.

TITLES OF RESPECT

In Indonesia, age is widely respected. Theoretically, the older a person, the more respect they command. This is revealed in the different forms of address reserved for different folk.

There are, for example, at least three ways of saying "you", depending on whom you are addressing. *Anda* is the most polite form, used between polite strangers as well as in formal writing, advertising, and poetry. *Kamu* is a more casual term, used between familiar friends and family. Then there is *kau*, reserved by parents for *anak-anak* (kiddies) and used between gushing young lovers. In Jakarta they say *loe* (said loo) but only between good *teman-teman* (friends). A middle-aged man you don't know very well should be called *bapak*, or more commonly, *pak*. Mature women are *ibu*, younger ladies *mbak*. Younger men can be referred to as *mas*. These will be the titles that are tagged on the end of every statement, in much the same way that schoolkids tag a "sir" on the end of everything. But don't get muddled: it's respect for age, not authority.

As Jakarta adopts more and more Western attitudes with every passing year, this system of titles is wavering slightly. But still it remains the definite way to address people in Indonesia. It may take some getting used to, but for the sake of gaining the respect of those around you, as well as for your own self-respect, it's an approach worth mastering. In general, Indonesian conversation begins in a highly formal way and gradually becomes more informal as the talk progresses. Nicely nicely, politely does it.

Within the family, *ibu* and *bapak* are how children say "mum" and "dad", but the regional diversity of Jakarta's populace means a million other varieties exist. Modern Jakartan families might just as easily use *mummy* and *daddy*, as opposed to more traditional forms like *mama* and *papa, ayah* and *ibunda* or *mami* and *papi. Betawi* children, however (those native to Jakarta), might say *enyak* and *babe*. And those who want to be really rebellious can use *nyokap* and *bokap*, but such obvious use of slang risks offending people.

In Javanese families, of which an awful lot of Jakartans are somewhere linked to in origin, Grandma is *nenek* and her man *kakek*. Their grandchildren will be *cucu*. Younger brothers and sisters are *adik* while older ones are *kakak*. Their cousins meanwhile, are *sepupu* and their nephews and nieces *keponakan*. The Dutch introduced *om* to the language, it means "uncle" and is widely used by children for all men, family and non-family alike. *Tante* (aunt) is of similar origin.

Another way of maintaining *kehormatan* (respect) is by speaking to people as if they were not there. Speaking in the third person is an affectionately polite, almost cloying, way of talking. It gets confusing: (speaking to you) "Would Derek like a drink?", "Does Derek like rice?" Your immediate reaction is to look about the room to see if there's someone else there called Derek.

But at the end of the day, all white people are known as "mister" — women too.

LANGUAGE

Not everyone in Indonesia speaks *Bahasa Indonesia*: some 20% of the country won't know what you're saying if you use it. To the average person the national language is still a second language, with a regional language taking priority. At best, people learn it alongside their local language. The people in Irian Jaya, for example, are not used to the idea of *Bahasa Indonesia* at all. In their part alone, some 240 local dialects are spoken. (Nor are they exactly overwhelmed with the government's sincere efforts at modernization and schooling: images of foreign-looking Javanese and rice paddies simply too alien for their imagination).

While Jakarta is therefore unique in that it has a certain percentage who speak *Bahasa* and *Bahasa* only, many in the city, mainly those who come to the city from the villages, have to think

47

twice before speaking. Perhaps because the risk of someone not getting your gist first time is quite high, language is kept brief and to the point.

On a basic level *Bahasa Indonesia* may seem unsubtle and blunt; only a couple of words can be used to convey what would be a lengthy sentence in another language. On a higher level it's as complex as any; it is, after all, an entire language. Great works of literature are written in *Bahasa Indonesia* and there's no limit to the range of vocabulary to be learned. Or is there? One word in this language can have several radically different meanings. An obvious example of the language's polysemy is *jalan* which can mean either *road*, the verb *function* or the verb *walk*. Nuances in meaning are achieved more through the *way* people speak, than relying on words alone. So in this way, with meanings more implied than actually voiced, it becomes a test of the listener's interpretation skills that successful dialogues are achieved. Naturally, for the unwarned, things can get very perplexing.

On the other hand, conversations in *Bahasa* are often kept deliberately vague and indirect for fear of upsetting someone and losing face. Speakers often fall over themselves to use the correct title of respect — all this before they have even started saying anything. For many Westerners the indirectness of speech is annoying. For Indonesians it's a sign of great social proficiency that they can interpret the meaning of the most convoluted conversation, and give an equally convoluted response.

Standard *Bahasa Indonesia* is similar in form to the Malay language and littered with Arabic, Dutch and other "loan" words. A lot of vocabulary is spilling over into English, particularly with so-called "new" words and ideas. Words like *protes* (protest) and *krisis* (crisis) have perfectly valid equivalents in *Bahasa Indonesia* (protest = *menyanggah*; crisis = *masa gawat*) yet are consistently used in a pseudo-English way, as if the very concept had been newly-imported with the word.

The overuse of English words has enraged the *Bahasa* purists who have succeeded in "cleansing" Jakarta of many English language names and places. Sometimes, someone in a *batik* shirt in a government office somewhere in Jakarta decides to crack a knuckle, and passes a baffling new law to contra the flow of Western germs. Purists of *Bahasa*, for example, have been lobbying for its sustentation for as long as a couple of generations of Indonesians have had to practise it. In that time, as the city has swelled and consumerism become a virtual way of life, a million shops, businesses and services bearing English names have sprung up. In 1995 this all came to an abrupt end with the passing of the "No More English Names" law. Firms bearing such names were able to get round it by retaining their initials while changing the wording into *Bahasa Indonesia*, albeit with a wonkier meaning.

The purists have a point. To hear *sok tahu* (know-all) pseudo-intellectuals cramming as many English phrases as possible into their press statements is genuinely annoying, especially when there's a perfectly good equivalent in *Bahasa Indonesia*. Football commentaries are the best example. To the unknowing ear it sounds like; *"mumble mumble mumble* goal kick, *mumble mumble* penalty shoot-out, *mumble mumble* blow to the body"*, and so on, proving that football commentaries are boring the world over.

The language is undergoing changes as we speak. The "d" of the old spelling of "Djakarta" for example is rarely seen these days. Likewise the "e" in the old spelling of "Sumatera", and even the ex-President's name: "Soeharto" becoming "Suharto". *Bahasa Indonesia* is very much written as it is pronounced; very much a phonetic language, and these changes therefore can only be good. But real attempts at standardizing *Bahasa* haven't met with complete success. As the dust settles and a couple more genera-tions make it their target language (as opposed to a local one), we should see the definitive *Bahasa* emerge. There are, after all, a million regional influences to contend with, not to mention the

Indonesians' inherent practice of twiddling with their national language as if they were somehow uncomfortable with it. It's almost as if everyone's been told to wear a particularly unflattering set of overalls, and the best they can make of these overalls is to take them in at the sides, roll the sleeves up and sew extra bits on the collars. For Indonesians it seems the temptation is to modify *Bahasa Indonesia*, and make it more comfortable. All signs indicate that this is what is happening. No need to push for its reform, for it is occurring regardless.

Naturally, no one likes a standardized anything. Least of all Jakarta's criminal underground. In the '50s a new variant on *Bahasa* was identified in certain parts of the capital. Known as *Prokem*, it was a cross-mutation of the official *Bahasa*, *Bahasa Sunda* and various *Betawi* dialects. Many of its words were acronyms for longer meanings, while many were completely new words. Some were simply standard *Bahasa Indonesia*, only backwards. It worked well at first, and successfully left the authorities in the dark for a good while, but it wasn't to last long as a secret. The young generations, excited by the idea of a "private language", eventually popularized *Prokem* to the point where today you can buy dictionaries of it and read novels written in it. *Prokem* continues to mutate, continues to be used by the hip young things of Jakarta, but it's hardly a secret anymore.

Bahasa Indonesia was first put forward as the national, all encompassing language in 1922 by the freedom-fighters of the time, and its use was eventually sanctioned by the Japanese in 1945, partly because few people could understand Japanese. *Bahasa* was, and always has been, a user-friendly means of communication. For those prepared to make the effort, it is not necessarily a confusing language.

What follows is a sketch of some of the more common multi-meaning words and their usual applications.

Good examples of the one-word-meaning-a-lot-more are *bisa* (can) and *mau* (want). These are incredibly useful words, and next to *apa* (what), probably the most used words in the language. Consider: ***Bisa*** *datang besok?* (Can you come tomorrow?) and ***Bisa*** *bicara Bahasa Indonesia?* (Can you speak Indonesian?) and the one word answer *Bisa* (Yes I can). Sometimes the question is just one word: *Bisa?* (Can it be done?) and the reply likewise: *Bisa* (It can be done). Look at *Kapan* ***bisa***? (When can it be done?) and *Besok* ***bisa*** (It can be done tomorrow).

As for *mau*, a whole sentence like "Would you like some?" can be expressed with the one word "*Mau?*" ***Mau*** *minum?* (Do you want a drink?) and ***Mau*** *makan?* (Do you want to eat?) and ***Mau*** *muntah?* (Do you want to throw up?) ***Mau*** *pulang?* (Do you want to go home?). *Mau.* (Yes).

We can see from *mau* and *bisa* that the words "yes" and "no" are used differently in Indonesian. "Yes" is usually expressed as part of another word. When you answer "*bisa*" you are saying "yes, I can" and when you answer "*mau*" you are saying "yes, I want … (whatever)".

Tidak is the all round "no" word, likewise the more informal equivalent *nggak*. ***Tidak*** *mau?* (You don't want …?) and ***Tidak*** *bisa?* (You can't do it?) and *Tidak* ***bisa***, *ma'af* (No I can't, sorry). But the answer to a question like *Sudah makan?* (Have you eaten yet?) is *Belum* (Not yet) and not *Tidak* (No), and if someone asks *Kamu orang Perancis?* (Are you French?) you say *Bukan* (I'm not) — unless of course you are. *Bukan* is useful: *Saya* ***bukan*** *orang gila* (I'm not a lunatic) and *Itu* ***bukan*** *mainan* (That's not a toy).

There are four small words to talk about the past: *baru, tadi, kemarin* and *dulu. Tadi* is for things which have happened recently: ***Tadi*** *saya jatuh di pasar swalayan* (I fell over earlier in the

51

supermarket) and *Lagu apa itu*? (What song was that?) *Yang mana*? (Which one?) *Yang tadi* (That one just now) or *Tadi, dia kesini* (He was here earlier). This might be misleading as *dia* can mean "he" or "she" or "it".

For something that happened yesterday or a few days ago, use *kemarin*. For example, *Kenapa hari ini nggak mau*? *Kemarin mau* (Why don't you want to today? You wanted to yesterday).

Dulu is for things that went on a while ago: *Dulu saya merokok tapi sekarang nggak lagi* (I used to smoke, but not anymore). *Dulu ada banyak orang Belanda disini* (There used to be lots of Dutch people here).

Baru has several uses. It can be used for things which have just happened: *Dia baru datang lagi* (He's just come again) or *Dia baru mau kesana* (He was just about to go there). Another use is heard, for example, in a taxi: *Ke sini dulu, baru ke sana* (Go here first, and then go there). The most common use of *baru* is new: *Sepatu baru*? (New shoes?) or *Kamu punya pacar baru*? (Have you got a new boyfriend?) and so on.

For congratulating someone over something, or simply wishing them a good day, use *selamat* something: *Selamat Hari Natal* (Happy Christmas), *Selamat jalan* (Goodbye), *Selamat makan* (Enjoy your meal), *Selamat pagi* (Good morning) and so on.

Dong is a little something many Jakartans tack on the end of a sentence. It's extremely common, although its actual meaning is unclear. It's almost an insult, but not quite. *Hati-hati*, for example, means "be careful", but *hati-hati dong* means something like "be careful even though everyone knows you're the most careless individual there is". It's the closest an Indonesian gets to being sarcastic. Many non-native speakers of *Bahasa Indonesia* use it on the end of every word, as if to make up for a general lack of vocabulary, which of course sounds silly.

LANGUAGE LEARNING

If you want to make the effort (and any effort you make will be warmly greeted) there are a number of ways to go about learning *Bahasa Indonesia*. The local papers often carry advertisements for language courses, and some are available via the major language schools in the city. The British Council in the S. Widjojo Centre, Jl Sudirman, often runs courses, as do many of the expatriate clubs and associations in the city.

For self-study methods of learning, you will need a good book or two. Recommendable is the Periplus Editions publication *Bahasa Indonesia: An Introduction to Indonesian Language and Culture* by Yohanni Johns. Similarly clear and helpful is *Speak Standard Indonesian: A Beginner's Guide* by Dr Liaw Yock Fang and published by Times Editions. It covers the Jakartan dialect well and has a useful breakdown of colloquial terms as well as more formal ways of communicating.

A good dictionary is also quite essential. Widely used is the *Kamus Inggris Indonesia/Kamus Indonesia Inggris* by John Echols and Hassan Shadily. Highly comprehensive, it covers the gauntlet of formal words and terms (with examples to illustrate each) as well as a number of slang words. Perhaps the only criticism would be that it edges too closely towards formal Malay in its examples. While Bahasa Indonesia is of course wholly derived from the Malay language, there are still a number of differences in sentence structure and vocabulary.

Arguably, the best way to pick up Bahasa Indonesia is by exposing yourself to it. For many, simply being in Indonesia means sooner or later acquiring the country's language.

SWEARING

Calling another person an animal is the worst thing you can say to someone in Indonesia. Shouting *babi* (pig) or *monyet* (monkey) and especially *anjing* (dog) will turn heads and leave you with all kinds of explaining to do. The word *brengsek*, common in Jakarta, can be used lightly (as in "damn") or can have a much stronger meaning (like "bastard") — it all depends on how you say it. *Bangsat,* which might translate harmlessly as "bedbug", carries a far stronger meaning, and is almost always an avoidably "bad" word. The same is true for *tai* (shit). The word *kontol*, a particularly vulgar word for male genitalia, is to be used with caution; carrying approximately the same weight that the "F" word does in English.

You find that a number of well-known English swear words are demoralizingly common in Indonesia. This is most probably because TV and cinema are rarely censored when it comes to bad language. Any vague hint at something sexy appearing on the screen, however, is fanatically lopped out of the picture — a kiss between two teenagers on *The Cosby Show* was cut, as was a scene in *Mr Bean* where he drops his trousers — yet bad language and gratuitous violence are left uncensored.

Don't be over-surprised when schoolchildren use bad language on you. Often these are the only words of English they know and they are probably trying to impress you rather than offend you.

HUMOUR

Fear not, Indonesians have an excellent sense of humour. Indeed, to cope with living in a place like Jakarta, they would need to. But what exactly makes them laugh? Bananas? Not particularly. At least not the eternal one about slipping over on the skin of one. People might make jokes about its similarity to a *titit* (willy), so be careful eating one in public. And while an Indonesian man may be easily impressed by a woman's *papaya*, and the *Betawi* are fond of eating a cake they know affectionately as *kue tetek* (tit-cake), food is not generally something to laugh about.

Rude (or *jorok*) jokes are the most popular in Jakarta, the focus of the punchline being usually a not-so-subtle swipe at a man's trouser-facilities or a woman's personal hygiene.

Because sex is something which can't be talked about in an open and frank way, its only outlet is as something to be sniggered about. There is an overall sense of lacking and insecurity running through many of the rude jokes heard around Indonesia. They invariably concern a local woman's "difficulty" at coping sexually with a man of Arabic origin, for example, or of local men being somehow required to get out and compare themselves. Those old chestnuts.

The self-conscious theme of inadequacy is continued in the startling lack of *lelucon bodoh*, or jokes about stupidity. People are all too aware that their country is still somewhat behind in the international stakes. True, not as behind as some countries (and it has certainly done a lot of catching up), yet a sentiment of inadequacy persists which, quite clearly, is no laughing matter. But examples do crop up: a reluctant young woman asks her insistent boyfriend: "Tell me why you think I can't possibly marry you?" "I can't think," says the young man. "That's exactly why," says the girl. Ho ho.

There's limited political humour in Indonesia, hardly any ripping satire and no teasing ridicule of the authorities — not on prime-time TV anyway. But some social comment is tolerated. In the newspaper *Kompas*, is the long-suffering character *Om Pak Si Kom*. A cartoon of the "average" Indonesian, he is uncomplicated and perpetually *bingung* (perplexed) at the rapid changes his country is undergoing. He represents the common man and speaks as only the common man can. In *Om Pak Si Kom* we are given a rare glimpse of the Indonesian sense of irony. But then this is to be probably expected from this most "intellectual" of publications in a country where the average man is still an illiterate rice-farmer. What could be more ironic? More "clever" jokery is seen in the monthly Jakarta publication *Humour* which features an amount of tightly-censored political comment. On a more "custard-pie" level of humour is the daily tabloid *Pos Kota* which is composed almost entirely of cartoon strips, jokes, second-hand car adverts, and sensational news stories.

Indonesians are frankly amazed when they see Westerners taking the mickey so mercilessly out of their leaders and "respected" persons. Yet rarely do they question their own forbidden fruit, that is, the chance to speak their own mind for once. Instead, Indonesians make fun of themselves. They make fun of the regional stereotypes of Indonesia; that *Batak* people always manage to lift your wallet, and that the Javanese can't stop smiling, no matter how depressed they feel. This is depicted in immensely popular TV shows like *Lenong Rumpi*. Entire households gather round the box when these shows are on and roar at the one who bears the closest resemblance to themselves. Everyday Jakartan life is oversimplified to the point of ridicule on these shows. *Tukang parkir* (free-form parking assistants) are the stereotype, slow-smiling Javanese; *"terus, terus, terus"* (straight on) he says ever so slowly as the car backs onto his foot, *"setop, setop, setop"* (stop) is his slow-smiling response. Further laughs are had with the ever-popular TV spoof shows. The joke here is the process of "Indonesianization". Well-known foreign shows are ripped to shreds; a spoof version of *Star Trek*, for example, is full of rice, *bakso* and *warung* one-liners, with its cheap-production costs all part of the gag.

Acronyms are an area where wordplay becomes the joke. For some reason Indonesians love to make shorter versions of their language. Real *singkatan* (acronyms) are a standard part of the language, particularly with official titles and names. *Jabotabek*, for example, is the name given to greater Jakarta, the areas comprising central Jakarta, Bogor, Tanggerang and Bekasi. *Polri* is another "real" acronym, the one for the police force, and taken from the longer title, *Polisi Republik Indonesia*. Sometimes, however, a real word is made into a comedy acronym: *semampai* is a word meaning tall and elegant, but say it like an acronym and it means *semeter nggak sampai* (not even a metre tall). The word for "pretty", *cantik*, becomes *cabo antik* (aging prostitute). Two words for "difficult" are *sukar* which becomes *susu mekar* (big breasts) and *sulit* which becomes *susu alit* (small breasts). *Kondom* becomes *konsultan domestik*, which you'll have to work out for yourselves. The joke may well be on you if an Indonesian asks "*Kamu orang penting?*" (Are you an important person?) They might just be using the comedy acronym of *penting* — *pendek dan keriting* (short and curly). Ha ha.

But it's not like it used to be. Outspoken comedy groups like *Warkop* now refuse to perform like they used to (or were they just requested otherwise?) — such are the limitations the authorities have put on comedy. The authorities it seems don't like the idea of people laughing too much or finding ridicule in what is supposed to be upright and proper in Indonesia. This is why Betawi street-theatre has never been in favour with the big boys — because it takes the mickey so much. Better not laugh too much, better just be quiet, passive and uncomplaining. And that isn't very funny, is it?

GROUP THINKING

"The failure was that we succeeded gloriously to gain freedom for this country, but we have failed to free the Indonesian men and women as individuals."— Mochtar Lubis, writer

Children in Indonesian schools do not ask why. All that's required is the ability to accept everything and question nothing. And anyway, for the average child of a middle-class, outwardly-religious family, there's simply no time to be an individual; their days being swallowed up in a tightly-woven network of social, sports and religious activities. Until recently, this unquestioning mode of acceptance had become a feature of the three decades of relative stability that had defined Suharto's presidency. Certainly one of his greater achievements had been to lower the country's illiteracy rates from almost 50% in the '70s to around the official 15% it is now. Yet while almost all children attend primary school, it remains common knowledge that the more you pay, the more your child will learn, beyond basic "nationalism". Unfortunately for a lot of people, there is little choice. Yet supporters of the New Order government would say that it would be wrong to start complaining so soon into the country's independence, the only real need is to knuckle down and work at making things better. The opposition like to call this wide-scale brainwashing.

Freedom of speech would therefore seem to be an unnecessary and alien concept for a lot of people. Any decisions that need to be made are reached on the basis of mutual consensus, or *gotong-royong*. Rarely do people volunteer an individual opinion, much preferring to go with the flow than redirect it. Being in a group equals safety and freedom, i.e. no one is responsible if everyone is responsible, as any individual actions are dissolved within the group. This includes "bad" behaviour, or what ought to be known as "collective bravado". Under this premise, individuals can do things they wouldn't be bold enough to do on their own: males comment openly on passing females, insults are hurled, political dissent expressed and shopping malls looted.

At a social occasion, nobody wants to be the first to start: "After you. No no, after you." This is island thinking: democratic (in its loosest definition) and collective. For the most part, Indonesians find it easier to share-alike than fight for what they want, or what they think they want.

But just as individual self-sufficiency is alien to the Indonesian, so the notion of collective identity is bizarre to the Westerner. This isn't to say that Indonesia doesn't produce its own thinkers, philosophers and artists — it does: it's just that there are so few who get the chance. Everything is against a person born with free will in Indonesia. The dominant religion in the land teaches that beyond God's, there is no other free will. Schools teach their pupils to accept, be passive and never ask questions, and the government stresses "national identity" and conformity. Coupled with a gargantuan population, little room is left for the individual voice to be heard.

Group thinking might also be the Big Excuse in Indonesia. Just maybe this all-accepting passiveness and seeming lack of self-awareness is all a deliberate put-on. One, somewhat shaky, theory is that people are passively resisting a lot of what is asked of them; passively resisting doing as much as they could do if they really wanted; that their "natural" reticence is nothing more than an excuse for all manner of inadequacy.

Yet still, it's all too easy for someone coming to Indonesia from a "developed" country to use the word "stupid". All too easy and all too wrong. With a population around 200 million, there's bound to be more of everything — and that includes people without necessarily much in the way of formal education. The official line under the all-pervading state ideology, *Pancasila,* is that every God fearing individual has the right to an education. The reality is that most cannot afford to continue studying to any level higher than primary and junior. The only children who are guaranteed the chance of a well-paid career are those of the well off. And since this isn't most people in Indonesia the nation's streets are filling up with scores of semi-educated people — too good for rice-farming but not quite good enough for office work.

Half the problem is that half the people in the country are teenagers, or younger. Funding decent education for all of them is a mammoth task, and for a system that seems intent on keeping voices quiet, probably preferable. While officially, there may well be more Indonesians studying for degrees than ever before, there are still way too many bored young people hanging about on street corners, with no money and no future, hassling passers-by and flirting with crime. In the villages it might be more excusable to sit about on a rattan mat doing nothing all day, but in the big bad city with the high life going on all around, there is more of a temptation for everything — including crime.

In a foreigner's dissatisfaction with life in Jakarta, apparent "incompetence" and lack of "initiative" on behalf of their local counterparts seem to be common factors. On a bad day there'll be no limit to the number of times a seemingly straightforward request will remain unfulfilled with no explanation beyond "*tidak bisa*" (can't) or "*nggak tahu*" (dunno). The brand name technology appears intact: Why won't it work? Why is it gathering dust? Doesn't anyone know how it works? Of course they do, but because so many people have been conditioned from the earliest age to be passive, many are timid about displaying initiative, preferring, as always, someone older and more superior to take the first step. It's no big deal, then, to have a personal lacking in Indonesia because there's always a collective identity to fall back on.

SUPERSTITIONS

It's almost an understatement to say that Indonesians are superstitious. In almost any situation, the immediate reaction is a superstitious one. When Westerners fall ill, they are treated to the logical facts of the matter. When an Indonesian falls prey to bad health, it's a curse; a punishment for something done wrong somewhere along the line. This is why a visit to the doctor is so unsatisfying for many Indonesians, and why, as back up, more traditional forms of diagnosis are preserved. People need to know why they are sick, and what it means. Far greater peace of mind is had by a visit to a *dukun* — the local witch-doctor, clever-feller, and resident medicine man — than is had by a visit to a prescription-happy GP.

No aspect of Indonesian life is untouched by superstition. Even in Jakarta, modern as it is, superstitions prevail. Prayers and sacrifices, for example, are routinely made before any construction work begins on a building site. And in the age of the motor car, only hard mechanical logic would be expected to prevail, yet in Jakarta you can't even get your car fixed without the intervention of the spirit world. The *Bengkel Magic* (Magic Workshop) is a fine example of superstition being taken advantage of commercially. *Bengkel Magic* is a chain of body repair shops whose ethos claims to employ standard methods of repair alongside those of particular spirits. The idea being you bring your damaged car along to the garage, where it remains locked up overnight, once the relevant prayers have been said. By morning, assuming no one has peeked in and broken the spell, the car will have been "cured".

The conflict in the lives of Indonesians is that they *want* to believe that it really is just cold, hard logic that gets the car fixed — they just can't help themselves. Once their superstitions have been aroused, they give in every time. Part of the problem of demanding an overall reformation of the Indonesian system is that politics are so tied up in superstition. The former President, Suharto, was said to have presided over the country like a mystical Javanese king, impervious and imperial and beyond the grasp of ordinary people. To have questioned his position, or his decision-making, was, for most people, too much like tempting fate. That was until a distinctly less superstitious younger generation clubbed together to demand his resignation.

Certain animals are to be avoided by the superstitious of Indonesia. One particularly ominous symbol of impending death is the body of a crow on your doorstep. Such a grim discovery would be ominous anywhere, and in Indonesia it means someone nearby is going to die very soon. If, upon arrival at some long-weekend destination, someone is greeted by a crow's corpse, they are advised to drive home very carefully and go straight back to bed. Hitting and running over a cat is not something to be shrugged off either; the vehicle should be properly washed and blessed before continuing, and the cat's body laid aside. But the vehicle's karma will have been seriously tainted by this catastrophe and people have been known to sell a car purely on these grounds. Fatal mishaps aside, more bad luck (but not that bad) is had when a tormented *cicak* (lizard) jumps at you: all the more reason not to tease them. A single butterfly floating into your house, however, merely signals a guest's imminent arrival. Black cats are symbolic the world over, but here the myth is that a dead person can be brought back to life if jumped over by a black cat.

But don't die on a Monday, you will only be obliged to take someone else down with you. Take extra caution on Thursday nights — the Javanese believe it's the night in the week when all the ghosts are out and about. When sleeping, try not to dream about losing your teeth — it means you are going to lose someone close to you. Upper teeth indicate an older relative, lower — a younger one. If single people dream about snakes, marriage may soon be on the cards. Only bad luck, however, follows the woman who dreams she's wearing her wedding clothes. The apparently unwholesome dream of *e'ek* (poo-poo) is an indication of forthcoming wealth; the more poo-poo, the more *uang* (money). And don't suddenly wake someone from their sleep, give their soul time to return to its body first.

And there's more. When taking a photo, try to avoid framing three subjects in your picture; the middle one is doomed to die soon after. Take precautions if wearing red and green together. Take extra care wearing green in the water, especially along Java's south coast — it is rumoured to bring untold misfortune.

Be careful around the house. Spend too long in your doorway after dark and you'll unwittingly invite the neighbourhood ghouls to come in and mess with your well-being. Houses shouldn't be moved into until someone *yang bisa lihat hantu* (who can "see" ghosts) has first checked the place over for troublemakers. In Bali they wait for the *cicak* (lizards) and other *binatang kecil* (little creatures) to move in before humans take up residence. Once settled, you can take preventative measure against rain by chucking a pair of black trousers up on the roof.

Single women sweeping the floor are advised to make a decent job of it, or else they are destined to end up with a scruffy husband. And the giving of handkerchiefs between lovers is a no-no, spelling a swift end to the relationship.

If you hear dogs or *burung hantu* (owls) after dark, they have probably been startled by something you can't see; something from another world. Perhaps they can see the *kuntilanak*, a grim-looking character in black who snatches new born babies away. Oh, and don't eat a pair of bananas unless you want to have twins.

MARRIAGE

Marriage is still a high-ideal in Indonesia. It used to be that if a woman wasn't married by the time she was thirty, something was assumed to be wrong with her. This sentiment is fading, however, as more Indonesian women become financially independent. However, perhaps because of religious ideals, or perhaps because there are more women than men in Indonesia, there's still con-siderable pressure on single women to get married. And anyway, everyone expects to get married at some point.

In Jakarta you can be invited to weddings from every province in the land. Even if you only mix with a few people and don't stay very long, you are bound to be invited to a wedding sooner or later. There always seems to be one about to happen.

Indonesian weddings are extravagant productions indeed. Even the most humble of families is capable of throwing an outlandish wedding. Low-key weddings don't really happen, not unless the bride is eight months gone.

Depending on the religion and ethnic background of the couple, there will be three or four parts to the ceremony spread, quite feasibly, over two days or even a week, depending on finances. Only close family are invited to the initial ceremony; the reception is where everyone else gathers. The family are an all important part of any wedding. It's said that when you get married in Indonesia, you don't marry an individual — you marry an entire family. The size and splendour of the reception are a direct reflection of the bride's father's intentions. It's a chance for him to impress his long-standing colleagues once and for all, and invite people he would normally be reluctant to approach. The newlyweds themselves are almost dispensable.

The importance of attending weddings in Indonesia is immense. Just as some businessmen establish feelings of mutual trust over a round of golf or a session in the sauna, so relations are improved one hundred percent by attending a wedding, no matter how brief the appearance.

The bride's family is expected to foot the bill. This may involve hiring a *gamelan* orchestra, hiring costumes for several dozen people, hiring a reception hall, transport, a maitre d' to give a running commentary of events, and two large ice-sculptures of the couple's initials which by the end will have melted into one. And of course, tons of food.

If it's a Muslim wedding, the groom should attempt to prove to his bride's family that he can provide financially for his wife-to-be. This he achieves by presenting *emas* (gold), aside from a ring (which is worn on the right hand in Indonesia), and numerous other gifts during the ceremony.

At more or less the appointed hour, the couple walk in, followed by their immediate families. They make their way slowly to the stage, where they will remain for the duration. When the initial entrance procession is complete, a receiving line is formed so guests can begin shaking hands with the couple. Throughout the reception, the bride and groom are on stage, all tucked-in and painted, as the guests file past to *kasih salam* (congratulate) and say either "*selamat menempuh hidup baru*" (all the best for your new life together) or "*selamat bahagia*" (wishing you happiness). Expect lengthy speeches through a PA from numerous family members which may well go on for hours.

As a guest you are expected to give a gift of some sort. The usual clobber a "just married" couple requires is welcomed, although increasingly money is the preferred gift. As an on-the-spot "thank you", guests are given a small souvenir of the wedding; something ceramic like a pair of miniature shoes inscribed with the couple's names.

Don't be too surprised if you wake up on a Monday morning to find the traffic being held up by a wedding procession moving from *mesjid* to reception. Don't be too surprised either to find you can't drive down your street because the neighbours have built a stage in the middle and filled the road with chairs. Quite often a mini-marquee is erected; stretched from one house to another, blocking the street completely. To add to the frenzy, a street-cinema might be set up nearby for the entertainment of the guests. Any open space will do, as long as there's room to hang a sheet up. True to the group-throng mentality so typical of Indonesia, even the smallest *kampung* wedding will have swollen to festival pro-portions by evening. *Sate* sellers and others will have set up shop on the outskirts of the gathering, hovering like expectant fathers-to-be. In this environment new friendships are made, rumours are spread, nervous *cewek-cowok* (girl-boy) glances exchanged, and a ton of *kretek* smoked.

A foreign person walking home through this could not be a more conspicuous sight. Should your Jakarta neighbours happen to be having a wedding reception, and you have no option but to walk through the middle of it, you may as well make the best of it. Get fed, get watered, get introduced, make more friends.

You will know when a wedding is imminent because, to highlight the fact, a number of giant yellow *janur* will have been set up near the reception. *Janur* are decorations. Five metres tall and constructed of *daun kelapa muda* (woven palm-leaf), they bend over at the top like triffids. Whereas *orang Jawa* (the Javanese) in Jakarta erect *janur, orang Betawi* put up *umbul-umbul* which, although of multicoloured bamboo, ultimately serve the same purpose.

The youngest people can get married in Indonesia is nineteen for men and sixteen for women. Written parental consent is required for both parties until the age of twenty-one. Under the

Janur show the way to the wedding reception.

marriage law of 1974, ten working days' notice must be given to the Registrar of Marriages in the district where the marriage is to be performed and two witnesses must be present. If a Muslim women is remarrying, there should be a waiting period of one hundred days before the proposed marriage can be contracted.

SEX

Sex is not a common topic of conversation in Indonesia. Any mention of it is in an embarrassed, jocular form, with a nervous laugh and hand-over-mouth snigger. It's not that people are necessarily repressed, but it's such an unmentionable subject that it remains something to be ashamed of. Basically, it's so unmentionable that everyone is dying to know more. You get the picture.

For the older generation, talking about sex is especially taboo. In Indonesia a fantastic ignorance prevails regarding the mechanics of sexual health and habits. Things are improving slightly; schools have introduced veiled sex education programmes to the curriculum and, *mudah-mudahan* (hopefully), modern Indonesian parents are beginning to feel they can perhaps start to consider thinking about one day getting round to taking tentative steps towards being more frank about the possibility of discussing the subject of sex with their children. Hmm.

Jakarta does have its sex therapists, nonetheless. The most well known being one Dr Naek L. Tobing whose frank methods of explanation and question-answering have made his radio shows immensely popular, while merely inciting outrage among certain quarters.

Other powerful reasons contribute to the apparent closed nature of sexuality. As a way of thinking, Islam has grown steadily disappointed with the West and its ways. The rise in fundamentalism in Jakarta is clearly at great odds with the Western movies, TV shows and attitudes that seemingly promote sexual

67

freedom. This is illustrated by a letter to *Media Indonesia* in February 1995 which read:

> *"I am very concerned to observe the celebration of Valentine's Day in Jakarta. Sadly, a television station aired a Valentine's Day programme which is beyond acceptable values. And this has certainly a strong influence on our young generation. Actually, Valentine's Day is not part of our culture. Moreover, Muslims are now observing Ramadan. To celebrate the day in an excessive way seems to be inappropriate."*

These are the attitudes young people in Jakarta face every day. They are torn between their own natural inclinations, the apparent freedom they see on TV, and the blinkered wisdom of their elders. But other, more deeply-rooted conditions prevail. While the circumcision of boys and girls, as traditionally practised in Islam, has proven throughout history not to hinder male satisfaction in mature relationships, a large question mark continues to hang over the opposite gender's equivalent predicament.

Sex is for sale all over Jakarta. It's not obvious, not like in Bangkok or Amsterdam, but it's not hard to miss either. North Jakarta has the greatest number of organized brothels; the roads off Jl Gajah Mada and Hayam Wuruk are lined with illuminated "massage" services. It's a screaming contradiction that presumptions of Western promiscuity are condemned on one hand while an abundance of brothels are allowed to operate on the other. Is this how real-life goes in Jakarta? The answer is simple — people have to pay the rent somehow. Yet one thing is certain: there wouldn't be any business of this kind at all if there weren't a market for it.

As a negative consequence of Westernization, many Indonesians generally presume that "free-sex" is the norm among Westerners, that AIDS comes from the West, and that Westerners are its chief spreaders. One report claims that AIDS hit Irian Jaya before it did Jakarta, brought in by trespassing Thai fishermen.

Bali, with its well-established tourist and expat scene, was next to have the scaremonger's finger pointed at it.

AIDS awareness campaigns on TV and in the press have been surprisingly blunt in their messages, but there are other obstacles to overcome. Condoms are widely available, but their promotion has been reluctant to say the least, even as a way of checking the spread of AIDS. Religious leaders frown upon the notion of what they consider tantamount to condoning promiscuity. The notion of "safe-sex" is an alien one to the Indonesian way of being, since the only acceptable sex is that within marriage.

The Indonesian Council of Ulama (a Muslim Advisory Council) states that they "neither accept nor reject the use of condoms either in the national family planning programme or in the prevention of AIDS but would support the use in certain cases; i.e. a man infected with HIV would be obliged to wear a condom when having sex with his wife." Official figures said that in August '96, Jakarta had 143 HIV victims, of which half were homosexual. Of the total number, 30% were foreigners and the rest drug addicts and victims of unscreened blood transfusions. In the same month, as a gesture of goodwill, Indonesia donated 1.5 million condoms to AIDS ravaged Cambodia. By law, doctors are obliged to make public the names of those who prove positive to an AIDS test. For a foreigner this invariably means being "requested" to leave the country within three days. Bar girls are routinely tested, say the papers.

There's no sex on television, in the press or at the cinema. All things sexy are censored to an almost ridiculous degree. Buy imported women's magazines and see every bra advert blacked over. There is, surprise surprise, no legal pornography for sale anywhere. On the black market, however, exists a proliferation, much of it unfortunately of Western origin. Unfortunate because it only serves to reinforce preconceived ideas of white people's sex habits. The authorities had closed down most of Jakarta's video rental shops by 1993, in an attempt to stem the distribution

69

of porn, but new technologies like laser-discs, satellite TV and the Internet have defied the tight ban on rude pictures, much to the irritation of the Board of Censors. The Jakarta magazines *Popular* and *Tiras* are styled on men's magazines like *Playboy* but the similarity ends with the front covers, the contents a tame mix of swimwear photos and sensationalist articles. One place where fidgeting couples, young hopefuls, bosses and secretaries drive for some discreet in-car grappling is in the expensive entertainment area of Ancol. Jakarta doesn't have the kind of drive-in "love hotels" that Tokyo does. That would be far too easy.

AILMENTS

Although the city is such a hot, humid and polluted place, it offers fewer everyday health problems than might be expected. Commonly, people in Indonesia seem to suffer from three basic ailments; *sakit flu*, coupled with *masuk angin*, and the inevitable *sakit perut*. What is known as the common cold in the West and rather inaccurately as the *flu* in Indonesia, is a surprisingly common problem. Presumably it's the unhealthy combination of heat, humidity, air-conditioning and electric fans that causes this. For, after standing ten minutes in the midday sun, then jumping into a taxi with an air-conditioning system that is only effective to about three square inches on the side of your neck, before stepping back into the blinding sun, it's easy to see the kind of temperature changes which contribute to cold-germ build up.

For general aches and pains, take the paracetamol-based *Panadol* or the Ibuprofen-based *Ponstan*. You'll find many *apotik* (pharmacy) are very obliging and sell any number of medicines over the counter. It's possible to suffer more serious complaints like dysentery and gastroenteritis, but if you are careful what you drink, you need not be over-concerned.

Officially Indonesia does not have an AIDS problem. While it may be true that there is less of a problem than say, Bangkok, you are advised to take precautions as you would anywhere. Without question.

MASUK ANGIN

If you stand in a draught too long or drive with the window down, you will notice people becoming very agitated. They are worried about getting the most common ailment of all: *masuk angin*. Literally meaning "entered wind", it is not to be taken lightly.

Masuk angin is the reason people take the day off work. It's the oldest one in the book and often dismissed outright by hard-headed Westerners who think it doesn't exist. But it does. *Masuk angin* is an aching, rheumatic-type complaint and readily treated with the wearing of a whopping great "heat-patch" across the forehead. Alternatively you can get *kerokan*. This is a particularly intense form of massage whereby the afflicted individual has balsam rubbed slowly and repeatedly in long lines across the back with the edge of a coin. It's very effective, bringing heat to the surface of the skin and relieving muscular pain, although you do look like a red zebra afterwards. It's quite feasible to have *masuk angin* without having *flu*. Watch out.

FEELING "PUSING"

Listen to loud music for too long or concentrate on one thing for a long time and an individual can complain of feeling *pusing* (dizzy). The first symptom of *pusing* is to be *bingung* or *heran* (confused). If your Indonesian friend comes over all *pusing*, a head massage is the only solution.

SAKIT PERUT

At some inevitable point you are going to get *sakit perut,* a bad stomach. If afflicted, it's best just to drink a lot of water and avoid fruit and fatty foods. Charcoal tablets like *Norit* are good stomach medicines, as is *Entrostop*. The Indonesian equivalent of indigestion, *ðakit ma'ag* is another common complaint, a result perhaps of the tons of *cabe* (chilli) people like to eat. Take *Promag* or the heavier duty *Milanta* if this is the case. Just ask at a *warung* near you.

JAMU

One of the biggest selling domestic products in Indonesia is that of a herbal remedy they call *jamu*. Spend any time in Jakarta and you soon start wondering who the woman in tight *ðarong* and wicker backpack of coloured bottles is. For she is the *tukang jamu;* a travelling medicine show; the local street herbalist. She wanders the streets just in case someone nearby isn't feeling right.

But never ask for a specific combination of *jamu* — describe your general symptoms and the appropriate concoction will be prepared thus. No ailment is beyond the scope of *jamu*. A lot of people still make their own, relying on things nearby as well as a supplement of prepared ingredients to complete the recipe. Indonesians take *jamu* as a back up to conventional medicine. But then in Indonesia, *jamu* is conventional medicine — it's certainly no cheaper.

So what's in it, and does it really work? Well, it sells truck-loads so there must be something in it. Lots of things in fact; mainly extracts of the leaves, roots and herbs which grow all over this fertile land, as well as a ton of other things found only in the rainforest.

But a lot of it is wishful thinking. A lot of the over-the-counter *jamu* (as opposed to that sold in the street) is packaged with pictures of rippling musclemen and sweet-lipped, sultry women on the box. One TV advert showed a woman chatting to a neighbour upon return from the market one morning. Something slips out of her basket. "What's that?" inquires the friend. "That?" says the women, all red-faced and *malu* (bashful), "Oh, that's just a little something I picked up for Bapak." In her hand is a packet of "special" *jamu*, guaranteed to make her husband *kuat* (strong).

Oo-er. Whether or not it does enhance sexuality so vividly remains open to question, but the fact that *jamu* is packaged like Western medicine, i.e., in pills, cream, capsules and powder (and Jakartans are enthusiastic pill-takers) indicates that the *jamu* industry is guaranteed a rosy future.

Jamu has a cure for every ailment.

Take too much of one *jamu*, however, and an Indonesian will get *mabuk*, a term basically describing overall delirium: be it "drunk" or whatever. Indonesian women swear by their *jamu* and are by far its biggest users. Varieties are sold to them along the lines of "essential feminine hygiene". Following childbirth, for example, women are given a variety of heavy *jamu* preparations. A certain external *jamu* is rubbed over the stomach to help remove any stretchmarks, and gallons of internal *jamu* are drunk to help get the woman's insides settled again. She probably took a certain *jamu* to get pregnant in the first place, and another during the course of her pregnancy. Some women change their minds the next day and seek out *jamu* for *terlambat bulan* (late period) — at least that's what it says on the packet.

Chapter Four

PEOPLE TO MEET

BETAWI

As the cockneys are to London, so the *orang Betawi* are to Jakarta. The Betawi are Jakarta's true originals — an authentic concoction of varied cultures and chance encounters. They are fiercely proud of their identity and have an attitude, dialect and culture different from other Indonesians. Perhaps that's why they're so "upfront".

Historically, Jakarta's role as first a minor, and then major centre for business, allowed all manner of influence to creep into old "Batavia", as it was then. Traders from Holland, Arabia and Portugal; slaves from Bali, Sulawesi, Java and China; and mystics from India are just some of the people to have left their fingerprints on the city. Whatever it was that brought them to Batavia, it kept enough of them there long enough to set up their own "camps" in the town. These original settlers to Batavia initially remained loyal to their origins, living in clearly defined *kampung* areas, and trying their best to carry on as normal. By the end of the 19th century, however, their habits, food, music, religions and dress-sense had merged into one. The children born and bred under these conditions were known as the *orang Betawi*.

But with Dutch colonial rule at its fiercest, the Betawi, who were merely considered the offspring of visiting traders to Batavia, were rather lowdown on the honours list. At one point the majority of Betawi were either slaves, servants or labourers. Being born "Betawi" certainly wasn't anything to be proud of in the beginning.

Betawi are not to be confused with *orang Jakarta:* those wide-eyed entrepreneurs who have emerged in massive numbers since Indonesia's independence in 1945. This is a contentious issue. Some of these "Jakartans" want to pretend that they are really something else. In the context of modern-day Indonesia, "Betawi" is a hip thing to identify with. Being Betawi means being the real thing, a part of the picture. You see, in Indonesia, Jakarta is the "happening" place; whenever the latest Great New Thing appears, it's Jakarta that gives it the test run. Things come first to Jakarta, and then to the rest. If it can't make it in Jakarta, then it can't make it anywhere. As the city swells, the emerging numbers of these *orang Jakarta* are set to eclipse the remaining strongholds of actual Betawi — an inevitable shame.

Stereotypically, *orang Betawi* are frank, down-to-earth folk. They are good joke-tellers, good Muslims and good at discussing the current price of land per square metre. They have a unique way of looking at the world. Unlike almost everyone else in Jakarta, who has somewhere else to go to if they need, Betawi don't see themselves in a bigger context. *Orang Betawi* are always at home — the capital city is their *kampung*.

But they do have something of a bad reputation; renowned as the city's hardest workers they are not. The *orang Jakarta*, for example, think the *orang Betawi* are *malas* (lazy). Whereas everyone else has to slave for a living, Betawi work ethics are, by contrast, rumoured to be geared more towards sitting about than say, hawking the street. A typical Betawi way of earning a living is to buy a second-hand car between them and renting it out — anything that lets the business come to them. *Orang Betawi* know they shouldn't have to go anywhere — after all, they come from Jakarta. In truth, though, Betawi have done the real hard work already, historically speaking, when a foreign power ran the city and employed them all as slaves. *Orang Betawi* are therefore *different* to other Indonesians. Nowhere is this more perfectly illustrated than in the food they eat and the music they play.

Tanjidor is one such music and a truly bizarre sound it is too. Imagine a Salvation Army on drugs: a brass band gone wrong. It combines trombones, clarinets and various bits of a *gamelan* set with a hint of *jaipong*. (*Jaipong* is dance-music: just one of the many indigenous sounds of Sunda, West Java). For a challenging listening experience, try listening to any recordings by the mighty *Grup Tanjidor Kembang Ros*. If you feel like dancing to it, do the *yapong*. For other types of Betawi music such as *kroncong*, *dendang* and *gambang kromong* (a Chinese-style of music with Betawi lyrics on top), try dancing the *cokek* or the *ronggeng*. Betawi have a strong tradition of rapping, the most well-known exponent of which was the late great Betawi actor, Benyamin Sueb.

The food Betawi people like to eat, in addition to the obligatory *nasi* (rice) and *cabe* (chilli), is heavy in *kunyit* (turmeric), *lengkuas* (ginger), *kayu manis* (cinnamon) and *pala* (nutmeg). Try ordering a bowl of *nasi uduk, kerak telor, sayur asem*, or *pacri nanas*. But be careful where you order them. Ciputat, Kalibata, Pejaten and Tanah Abang may be some of today's remaining Betawi strongholds, but with each area excelling in a particular variation of the Betawi menu, you may never taste quite the same version of *nasi uduk* twice. Buy a Betawi cookbook to be on the safe side, because even across Jakarta, the Betawi identity is fragmented; each subdistrict offering a subtly different attitude, dialect and food to the next, such is the Betawi allegiance to their square plot.

For entertainment on special occasions, a Betawi household is likely to hire *ondel-ondel* puppets. These two-metre tall characters are wrapped in curtains and have huge papier-mâché heads with multicolored spikes glued all over. Children find them most worrying.

The struggle to keep the Betawi identity alive today is an uphill one. One-time Governor of Jakarta, Ail Sadiron, made repeated attempts during his office to re-establish public interest in Betawi culture. One particular area of interest was *lenong*. A traditional form of Betawi street theatre, *lenong* is brash, comic and improvised. *Lenong* deals with the trials and tribulations of day-to-day living in Jakarta and shows not an ounce of mercy for

Ondel-ondel puppets provide entertainment on special occasions.

authority. *Lenong* has found a new audience of late with the initiation of the *Jaksa Fair*. The fair, held yearly in that central Jakarta strip of fun, Jl Jaksa, is heavy in all things Betawi. Their sense of humour is also seen in the films of the big-lipped comedian, Mandra, and in television shows like *Lenong Rumpi.*

While the bulk of Jakarta's population today probably originates from Sunda or Java, there are sizable representations of every other type of Indonesian to be found in the city, from the *orang China* in the north of the city to the Ambonese stronghold in Kampung Ambon. Things at times seem to have gone full circle: from disparate *kampung* to collective Betawi to disparate *kampung* again, except of course for the addition of the *orang Jakarta* and their mortgages. In the end, the *orang Betawi* are just one of many diversified clans living on top of each other in Jakarta. It's just that they were the first.

CHILDREN

Indonesians revere children. Children are top priority in any situation in Indonesia — always the ones to get that extra scoop of *nasi* (rice). The adoration parents have for their *anak-anak* (kids) is reflected in the names they give: *Dewi* (Goddess), *Intan* (Diamond), *Suci* (Purity), *Ayu* (Beautiful), *Putri* (Princess), *Mentari* (Sun), *Wulan* (Moon), *Ratna* (Diamond), *Dian* (Candlelight), *Kurnia* (Gift of God), and *Mutiara* (Pearl).

During their first year or so in the world, Indonesian babies are in near-permanent physical contact with their mother or *pembantu;* travelling everywhere by means of a *selendang* (sling). Never are they left alone. Traditionally, men are not expected to lend a hand in any way. In Indonesian families, the father is the seat of discipline; the mother is provider of love, as well as resident accountant. The children's obligations, particularly of the first born, are always towards the good of the family. And to support the parents in old age.

Indonesians spoil their children and seemingly let them get away with murder. Discipline does exist, however — in the form of pinching. Whereas spanking would horrify the average Indonesian onlooker, disciplining a child through pinching is perfectly acceptable. Another way to guarantee children's good behaviour is to tell them ghost stories. The heads of Indonesian children are swimming with umpteen variations of child-snatching ghouls, partly the reason Indonesians are such vivaciously superstitious people, and partly why so many of them have to sleep with the light on. One of the worst beings to fear is the *kuntilanak:* the spirit of a Javanese woman who died in childbirth; she appears (to children who don't behave themselves) as a beautiful woman with a gaping hole in her back.

Western children are equally as adored, if not more so. The display of affection for a cute Western baby is, however, sometimes overwhelming. A small crowd of cooing admirers will readily congregate upon the sighting of a white child — stroking hair, pinching cheeks, and loving the kid to death. Obviously, this kind of attention isn't easy for a child to accept, and it's better (if possible) to explain to the child beforehand what to expect and how to react. If being touched does worry a child or parent, then simply say as much. Just say that he or she doesn't like it: *"ma'af, dia tidak suka."* Overall, however, the Indonesian adoration of children makes it a good place to live and travel with them.

For longer-term expatriate children, added difficulties may arise. Since Indonesia is the land of service, with a lot of expatriate family employing several members of household staff, it's all too possible for youngsters to become spoilt. Children who grow up accustomed to Indonesians running errands for them, driving them around, and generally serving their everyday needs, may develop a distorted view of Indonesians. They are certainly in for a shock when they do eventually go home. Other negative effects that living in another country has on children can include a sense of rootlessness, of alienation and of "not fitting in". The child may be confused as to where "home" really is. Having spent a proportion of his or her developing years in a very foreign country, the youngster may have little in common with his or her peers at home — at first, anyway.

Officially, the average family in Indonesia has 2.4 children, which is perhaps a somewhat surprising statistic. The government has been praised for its population control, and in 1983 received a United Nations prize for its "support of family planning". Indonesian women talk unashamedly about their own particular method of contraception. Having grown up with the idea, many are surprisingly un-*malu* (unabashed) about the whole affair.

One TV advert shows a puffball-haired (and somewhat obviously aroused) Jakartan husband giving his wife pleading nods from round the door. She can only look downwards, shake her head and go on playing with their two children. She feels ashamed because there are no contraceptives in the house. Next scene shows the couple sitting before a white-coated specialist. The final scene repeats the eager-husband-round-the-door scenario but this time the response is different and the wife gives a shy smile. Sadly, the advert ends there.

"*Dua anak cukup*" (two children enough) was the well-worn phrase painted on school roofs and other prominent places in the '70s. One of the more conspicuous examples of propaganda is the symbolic two-child "happy family" depicted on the five rupiah coin, the smallest in circulation. Certain religious attitudes also had to be overcome in the implementation of the government's fervent family-planning programme — many Muslims holding the belief that Allah will always provide for them, no matter what difficulties occur; no matter how large a family becomes. The promotion of contraceptives, then, is in stark contrast to Indonesians' inherent desire to surround themselves with offspring. In doing this they assure themselves at least some sort of future insurance. Having children therefore means having a certain security.

On a more sinister level are rumours of a massive sterilization programme in the '70s. One Jakarta woman, then a schoolgirl, remembers how she was given a letter to take home for her parents to sign. She didn't read the letter and her parents never signed it, but she remembers her classmates who did comply, going for a series of injections. She says that to this day, those women remain childless. The subsequent boom ten years later in black market baby-trading may be explained by these unconfirmed allegations.

Giving birth in Jakarta is not a problem, just wait for the contractions to begin and let nature take its course — ho ho. But seriously, there are enough Western-standard hospitals and clinics with enough prenatal and postnatal expertise to make birthing in Jakarta no more of a worry than it need be. Maternity clinics are called *Rumah Sakit Bersalin* in Indonesian. Certain aspects of pregnancy and birth will be strange for foreigners, but as always,

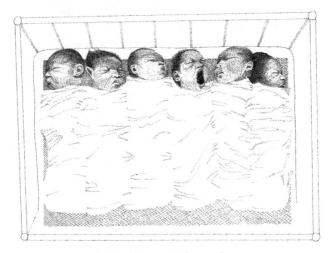

Babies: they come in four-packs too.

perfectly normal for Indonesians. At seven months into her pregnancy, for example, a ceremony is held for the woman to wish her and her child good fortune. During the ceremony, depending on how orthodox the family are, she is bathed in the flower-waters of seven different flowers, changes clothes seven times and eats seven kinds of food. The Javanese especially adhere to this ceremony, believing seven months a critical time in the *kehamilan* (pregnancy). They believe, quite rightly, that the unborn child is fully formed at seven months, and it just needs to "cook" for a while more, it's imperative therefore that a fuss is made. For the mother-to-be, traditions aside, it's a welcome show of emotional support.

When the *bayi* (baby) is actually born, the *ari-ari*, or afterbirth, receives special attention. Again, it's the Javanese (without doubt, the most superstitious people in the land) who know best what to do. An elaborate ceremony is performed whereby the placenta is given a "funeral". The Javanese believe the afterbirth is the "shadow" of the newly-born child, the twin that didn't make it. Throwing it away would therefore be quite wrong. Instead, it's carefully washed and placed in a clay pot along with any gifts the family might want to give. This is a time to make wishes for the newborn baby, a time to influence the *bayi*'s future. If you want it to be rich, put some money in. If you think it will become an artist, put some crayons in, and so on. The whole package is wrapped in white cloth before being buried, and a candle burned for forty days.

In its first few years of life, an Indonesian baby wears various amulets and charms to promote a prosperous future. It may be "tested" in various ways. A pencil, some money, a spanner and other objects will be placed in front of the youngster — the child's future may be determined by whichever one is chosen.

ANTI-HEROES
One of Indonesia's national anti-heroes is a thin little man with a moustache. Born Virgiawan Listanto in 1961, the son of an army general, he is better known to everyone as "Fals" — Iwan Fals. He is Indonesia's Bob Dylan: a protest singer and social commentator; intelligent, ironic and laconic. In straightforward verse, Iwan slams modern Indonesian society, the selfish upper classes and the alarming division between rich and poor. His lyrics represent the unspoken views of thousands of young Indonesians.

At an Iwan Fals concert, young Indonesians are free to make a display of themselves. His shows are a rare outlet for the frustrations of the *kampung* masses. Iwan sings the songs and the audience sing along. They all know the words — words about the appalling state of affairs in Indonesia. Words about ripping it all up and starting again. His 1992 song *Jakarta Sudah Habis* (Jakarta Is Finished) is a startling criticism of the monster that he alleged it had become.

The government has obviously never been too keen on him. One too many of his late '80s concerts ended in violence for them

83

Iwan Fals: he's a poet, and he knows it.

to turn a blind eye. They even banned him from performing under his own name for a long while, and he had to pretend to be in a band called *Swami*. Although far more acceptable than he used to be, his records still represent the massive and rapid social changes that Indonesia is undergoing and the role that the underprivileged play (or don't play) in this change.

His face, with its trademark scraggly long hair and bandanna, is symbolized on buses, T-shirts and in *kampung* everywhere. In 1990, when the tabloid newspaper *Monitor* invited readers to choose who they considered the most popular person in Indonesia, Iwan Fals came in higher than both President Suharto and the prophet Mohammed. The paper, in drawing a neat parallel with John Lennon's famous "more popular than Jesus" racket, was immediately shut down, and the editor jailed.

In early 1993, when the island of Flores was turned upside-down by a tidal wave, Iwan was persuaded out of his semiretirement in Cipanas to play two benefit gigs for the people. The concerts, held at the Lebak Bulus football stadium under the banner: *Musik Kemanusiaan Untuk Flores* (Humanitarian Music for Flores) were a riotous success, attended by 100,000 fans, with only a touch of pre-concert trouble. As a way of pacifying the audience (and proving his religious allegiance), Iwan held the 6 o'clock *maghrib* (prayer) from the stage. He wore a *peci* (little black Muslim hat) throughout. This was an Indonesian rock concert; a concert where the audience pray together beforehand. It did the trick and raised the money, yet it was a long way from his days busking in Blok M.

He has a healthy back catalogue. Recordings to be recommended are many: for starters try *Opiniku*, *Hijau* and *Orang Gila*.

Opini (Opinion) Musica Records

Iwan's second album and the one that catapulted him to fame and fortune in 1985. An entirely acoustic album (it could have been subtitled *Freewheeling*), it finds Iwan full of the joys of fatherhood with the opening track *Galang Rambu Anarki* a perfect example of the wit and wisdom that made him famous. Dedicated to his son (whom he named Anarchy and who, in 1997, died from a suspected drug overdose), *Opini* (Opinion) is an ode to the life and times of modern-day Jakarta: "my dear son, born under the sign of recently-increased petrol prices". Charming, funny and mercurial.

Hijau (Green) Pro Sound

Seven years later and Iwan's Fat Bono period has been and gone. A period in the Hard Rock wasteland sees Iwan's career take increasingly more precarious twists and turns as rioting and violence at his concerts begin to mark him out as a troublemaker. One thing leads to another and he is banned from playing under his own name and forced to mingle "unnoticed" in a band called *Swami*. But with things getting too heavy, Iwan lays low while the fans congregate a permanent presence, many bringing knives in the hope that their hero will leave his mark on them. Iwan resurfaces with this live-in-the-studio album, *Hijau*, a mostly-acoustic affair which slopes off into slow funk in places. Something of a *Blood on the Tracks* for Iwan, his newfound maturity is reflected in *Jakarta Sudah Habis*: "Jakarta is finished," sings Iwan, "don't know if it's because of greed, stupidity or neglect but Jakarta's finished." He's weary but still holding up that little white bouquet.

Orang Gila (Mad Man) Konser Music

Iwan finds his feet again, convincingly mixing programmed drums, acoustic percussion and guitar with the insight and irony that made everyone like him in the first place. Heavier than *Hijau*, *Orang Gila* sees Iwan getting his rocks off on the title track while still being able to say it all with just a guitar (*Satu-Satu*). With a voice that is assured, wistful and seductive, he seems confident to say what he wants without being paranoid, safe perhaps in the belief that things are coming to a head in his huge and confusing country.

In a similar vein to Iwan, though less famous, is Sawung Jabo and the Cirkus Barock. Another artist who likes to go against the grain is the poet-rebel Emha Ainun Najib. All these performers, however, owe it to Gombloh, the Surabaya-based singer-songwriter who died of multiple illness in the late '80s. Although less outwardly political than his modern counterparts, few have been able to match the wit, wisdom and warmth of this very thin performer. Witness the immortal line in his song *Lepen*: *"Kalau cinta melekat, tai kucing rasa coklat"* (when you're in love, even cat shit tastes like chocolate).

Predating everyone by at least a decade, however, is Indonesia's original anti-hero, the Bogor-based poet and playwright W.S. Rendra. Over the years, Rendra's poetry, plays and performances have pushed the edges of Indonesian decency to its limit. Many of his shows have been banned and the man himself,

"Mas Willy" to his friends, has spent time in prison for his art. A controversial character indeed, Iwan Fals reckons Rendra was a far greater influence than Dylan ever was. His work continues to shock and impress. He is an artist of international merit.

Clearly it's hard to speak your mind in Indonesia; hard being clever in a corrupt and overcrowded country; hard being jailed for being creative.

But in May 1998, for one intense moment, everything did come to a dramatic head in Indonesia. With the economy in tatters, the urban poor ransacking shops and stores, and ministers and students calling for the President's resignation, the nation's anti-heroes no longer felt a need to be coy. Almost as if to prove he'd been right all along, Iwan Fals' true popularity was acknowledged in a highly-charged, post-dictatorship concert on August 17, 1998 (Independence Day) to the students of the *Universitas Indonesia*.

And on the day after the infamous Trisakti incident in which four students were murdered by police — a move which culminated nine days later in the resignation of President Suharto, the mighty Rendra gave perhaps his most moving recital of all when he spoke at a memorial service at Trisakti University. "Because we are the current in the river," he read from *Poem of Simmering People*, "and you are a heartless stone; the river shall eventually wear you away."

BEGGARS

Without doubt, you are certain to come across a colourful variety of beggars in and around Jakarta. But nowhere near as many as might be expected for a so-called developing country. Why is this? The reasons are many. They may lie in the regular roundups offered by police, or in the considerable amount of social work done by the *Departemen Sosial*. Or they may lie in the Indonesian's inherent sense of dignity: that they would rather try their utmost to eke out some kind of living, no matter how small the returns.

Jakarta regularly attracts numbers of *orang desa* (country folk) as beggars. They travel from nearby villages and, whether or not they really intended to, end up begging for money in the big city. The busiest times of the year are during redundancies in the rice-growing calendar, and in the month of Ramadan when everyone is obliged to be acting more generously and courteously than usual.

But there are enough beggars and truly appalling sights around Jakarta for the average visitor to be justifiably horrified. Sufferers of leprosy are placed at traffic lights for the day; people with gaping holes for noses grab at your legs as you cross a bridge; immorally young children wander about in traffic banging tambourines. And of course, there's the old "standard" mother-and-child variety; women who are rumoured to hire their babies by the hour as part of their garb. These are, by all accounts, "professional" beggars. Rumours like these persist: that many beggars are simply putting it on.

One such story has a "beggar" grunting and shuffling his way onto a bus with absolute difficulty. The unfortunate man appeared to be lacking in legs and forced therefore to walk everywhere on his hands. Once onboard, the man continued grimacing and making dreadful guttural sounds, and was given as much space as is possible on a packed *metromini*. One passenger, however, became suspicious and decided to follow the beggar to wherever he was going. Sure enough, when the man had made his pained and pathetic exit from the bus, and believed he was comparatively "alone", he quickly unbuckled his legs, leapt up and walked away, small change jangling in his pocket.

But the children are the most worrying aspect. Sleeping street kids are all over daytime Jakarta: stretched out on supermarket steps and huddled in doorways. In 1996, the newspapers reported the bodies of murdered street kids turning up around the city. The grisly discoveries echoed immediately of the similarly rumoured "campaigns" in Brazil to rid its streets of begging children. Are tourists really so fussy?

UMBRELLA BOYS

When it rains, out come the umbrella boys. Demand is high for these young entrepreneurs and in a good hour or so, a pleasing wage is earned. Standard fees for the use of the *payung* (brolly) vary depending how far you need to walk. However, you may be tempted to pay greater sums when you see how utterly soaked and pathetic the children look running along behind you. Some have quite impressive umbrellas; accommodating enough for a couple of people. But this luxury is not afforded to everyone, and most people take refuge under a tree or shop doorway while the *hujan* (rain) lasts. And don't be at all surprised to see street-sellers carrying on apparently unaffected by the rain, albeit with plastic carrier bags on their heads.

AMATEUR POLICE

Jakarta's amateur police are a law unto themselves. The real police who direct traffic on the big roads are either in too short a supply or too chicken to work the back streets, leaving the city's unofficial traffic cops to sort out the mess.

Amateur police are found on every corner of every road where no actual police operate. They call themselves *tukang parkir.* Some have "official" uniforms (green or brown; available at a market near you) but many don't. The best ones blow a whistle nonstop. Many stand vacantly by the roadside, one hand perpetually waving traffic on. From an early age Jakartans know how to direct traffic. It's all some kids seem to know. When parents and elders spend the day hanging about in the traffic, blowing whistles and shouting, some of these ethics are bound to rub off on the small ones. For the kids of Jakarta's *kampung*, the *parkir* is something you want to be when you grow up. And yes, the *parkir* uniform is available in children's sizes.

They do perform some functions on the bigger roads; they find parking spaces for you. They are expert at cramming an almost impossible number of *mobil* into a minute space, and stopping the traffic when you need to back out later. Their directing methods are quite ludicrous; "*kiri* (left), *kiri, kiri, kiri, kiri, terus* (straight on), *terus, terus, terus, terus, kanan* (right), *kanan, kanan, kanan, kiri, kiri, terus, terus*", and so on. Do they really have to do this? Can motorists in Jakarta really not cope with the pressures of unassisted car-parking? Or is it more a case of the common man finding something to do; of finding another way of making a few *rupiah;* of free-enterprise? For sure.

They can turn nasty. They are known to menace drivers and pedestrians into complying with payment. They let the tyres down on a car if it's parked in one space for too long without prior arrangement. Stake your place with a few rupiah. These guys make money as they go and if someone doesn't play the game, then *ma'af* (sorry), a car may well get dented. Think of it as an unconditional road tax. But don't take this apparent vengefulness to heart, they are merely protecting their interests. Although it's never much — *uang merah* (red money) usually — to a *tukang parkir* it's everything.

Why some people won't pay up, however, is clear. Many people see the amateur police as nothing more than an irritation, unbound *preman*, villains, thugs, herberts, urchins, wasters and kackers — the very cause of traffic jams if truth be told. It's unfair to lump the "professional" *tukang parkir* in with the many scally-wags masquerading as Something Useful. While the former are semiofficial, the latter would run a mile at the sight of the real *polisi*. But ultimately, they do a worthwhile job. Imagine you want to go straight over an impossibly *macet* (jammed) crossroads. For a couple of hundred rupiah the amateur police will make a hole in the traffic for you. Off you can go to the next jam.

REAL POLICE

Real *polisi* are plentiful in Jakarta. They wear brown uniforms, brown peaked hats and black leather boots. And on a white belt slung low around the waist, they carry a gun. The extreme tightness of Jakarta policemen's trousers has been the subject of much speculation among the city's populace. What goes on in there? Are they wearing protective underwear? Have they all been routinely "pulled back and tucked in"? The debate rages on. There are some women police in the city, but not in the profusion that the tight-trousered male police are, and are usually limited to a bit of traffic directing and office work here and there, than posturing the day away.

Clearly, since all *polisi* are armed, you don't want to upset one, even if they don't look too threatening riding BMX bicycles. There's a constant police presence in Jakarta and the public at large seem to display a genuine fear of them. *Polisi* have the reputation you see, for stopping people at random and making demands on them. Identification of some sorts is the usual request, and they have very definite ideas about which form of ID they want to see. For an Indonesian, only the KTP *(Kartu Tanda Penduduk)* is accepted. The KTP is an identity card every Indonesian is obliged to carry; it states name, age, address, religion, marital status plus a fingerprint. ID cards are confiscated if the individual isn't carrying enough bribe money. For a foreigner, strictly speaking, it's the passport and KIM/S they want to see. Yet since most people do not perpetually carry their passport, and since the police themselves are not totally sure what ID a foreigner should be carrying, they either dismiss you immediately or dither around for hours debating what to do you for. *Polisi* are known to setup "routine" road blocks, in areas close to the drinking-venues of Jakarta's *bule* (whities). Assuming you have nothing to hide, there's no need to be unduly worried about being stopped. It happens from time to time, that's all.

There's a saying in Jakarta that the laws and regulations here are some of the best in the world, that every sector of society receives its fair and just protection. But with the big boys continuously ignoring these rules, the rest of the country is forced to play the game by example and bend every rule in the book. But then, this free-for-all rule-bending might even be government policy — with so many seemingly contradicting rules to adhere to, it has become impossible for the individual to not be doing something "illegal". Therefore, the state has complete control over everyone and can legally shake down anyone they want at anytime. That at least is how it might be seen.

The corruption of Jakarta's police force is nonetheless infamous. The blame, however, rests on higher shoulders than the average traffic cop who could be said to be merely trying to make ends meet. It's a sad situation indeed, that a police force must unquestioningly follow orders which come "from above" and which are misguided and inconsistent. Newspapers run regular stories about police "arresting the wrong person" or "shooting the wrong person" or "following the wrong procedure". In fact, it's widely assumed that Jakarta's Ecstasy craze is simply the result of police re-circulating the drugs they have confiscated previously.

Police are paid peanuts in Indonesia. It's in their interests then, to supplement their income in order to survive. Bribes are a way of life for traffic police. Minor driving mishaps are quietly and efficiently cleared up with the acquisition of a small, unofficial fee. Basically, the more serious the crime, the bigger the bribe. Corruption has eaten its way through the entire judicial system, from the police on the streets to high court judges. But never assume you can get away with anything; there are just as many judges and police with morals intact, particularly the younger members of the force who, educated and well-aware of their country's reputation for legal jiggery-pokery, are keen to dispel this unsavoury image. Some don't accept bribes; some want promotion and are out to fight crime, nothing more. This is especially true of the plainclothes police who hang around the predominately night-time *bule* areas like Jl Jaksa.

There is the example of one Westerner living in Jakarta who, one evening when drunk, ran down and killed a *sate* seller. Quite rightfully, the victim's family wanted the individual locked up for murder, or at the very least, manslaughter. They were prepared to drop the matter, however, if he could pay a lump sum in compensation. Unwisely, the accused tried to bargain the price down with the family. This merely served to anger the family further who went straight to the high court where the man was given three years.

Another example, although on a lesser scale, concerns another *bule* who, in the early hours, was stopped and questioned as he stood waiting, or rather swaying, for a taxi. When the individual couldn't produce any satisfactory ID, the police (there were two) demanded the man show them where he lived. Very suspicious of this, the man elected to say absolutely nothing and, aware of the reputation the police had, decided under no circumstance to make any payouts. When they arrived at his home, they began to get frustrated that the man still hadn't said anything, nor attempted to give them any money. They questioned the *bule* again; he said nothing. They shouted; still nothing. In the end they looked nonchalantly around the house, and began picking up various things which took their fancy: some tapes, magazines, cutlery. Then they left. So, if you happen to get lost in Jakarta, you know who, or who not to ask for directions.

TATTOOS AND VILLAINS

The American's Women Association's *Jakarta Shopper's Guide* doesn't list an entry for reputable tattooists, and it's probably a good job too. Tattooed people are regarded with great suspicion. It's rare to see a local making an open display of them and everyone else should do likewise. This slightly odd suspicion is a lingering reminder of the frantic cleanup operations conducted by the authorities across Indonesia in the early '80s.

In a bid to lower the city's appalling crime rate at the time, soldiers and military police began rounding up as many hoodlums as possible. (By "hoodlums" they predominantly meant young men, those hanging around on the street all day, with nothing in particular to do — a lot like today in fact). It soon transpired that many of those rounded up had tattoos, and that many of them had matching tattoos. From this point on the emphasis of the operation shifted. The tattoos suggested the authorities had stumbled across an organized world of gangsters — something along the lines of the Chinese triads. "Identifying" tattoos became the main target of suspicion as the operation progressed. This is the sentiment that has lingered — a tattoo equals a criminal. Simple as that.

By all accounts, it was horrifying. Soon after it began, the bodies of underworld criminals started turning up around town. Areas around Petukangan Utara are rumoured to have held host to the "questioning" of a great many of the accused. The average sewer is rumoured to have been their grave.

Reports of similar horror, of bodies in mass graves, began filtering in from other big cities at around the same time. No one wanted to accept responsibility, no one seemed to want to ask any questions, and the matter was hushed up and forgotten. The *orang kaya* (rich people) were certainly not going to complain, they being the criminal's obvious targets. Supposed links between Jakarta's wealthier families and the army put any further investigation completely out the window. It's all rumour and hearsay, but there's no smoke without fire. There was little press coverage of events at the time although rumours since have suggested that many as three thousand people "disappeared".

The old fears returned in a similar cleanup operation in '94, although the emphasis then was on ridding Jakarta of drink and drugs. The police at one point said they would arrest anyone seen hanging about in the streets after midnight without good reason. Almost a curfew but not quite. In the hysteria that followed the July '96 riots in Jakarta, organized criminals, "communists" and people with tattoos were again believed to be to blame, and were consequently the authority's highest priority.

TRANSVESTITES

Transvestites seem to hold a special place in the world of Indonesia. The joke is old but continues to be funny: the man who falls in love one evening with the woman who isn't. Known locally as *banci* or *bencong*, transvestites are the brunt of many a joke in Indonesian comedy. Nearly every TV comedy show has its token *banci* somewhere in the line-up.

The Irianese comedian Ade Juwita has done much of late to reinforce the stereotype of the Indonesian *banci* in Jakarta. He's certainly a sight to behold, with his exaggerated features, and long fuzzy hair pulled back to look like a giant coconut atop his/her shoulders. But constant ridicule is not a good thing. The fact he/she only ever plays low-life characters such as servants and street workers reflects the generally low opinion people have of *banci*. They are tolerated, made fun of, but never totally accepted. Never are they seen in positions of authority. There are no *banci RT* patrolling the streets; no *banci polisi* directing traffic, at least not in Jakarta.

This is in sharp contrast to the time when *banci* were held in higher esteem. In certain parts of Sulawesi, *banci*, or rather *bisus* as they are known in that part of Indonesia, were believed to be something special: a living halfway house between heaven and earth, a communicator between the real and spirit world. Until they were outlawed, that is.

On a day to day level, you are most likely to encounter *banci* at Jakarta's traffic lights where they can be seen "performing" with tambourines. They seem to take particular delight in targeting Westerners, going on to serenade the individual until he or she pays up. It's a very effective method: hardly anyone can ignore a man they have never seen before dressed as a woman singing a *dangdut* song, as you sit in the back of a taxi waiting for the lights to change. Try not to make eye-contact — fatal. *Banci* have no qualms, they will interrupt you in the middle of a meal in order to sing at you if they have to.

The *banci* of Jakarta have their own club going — they are an entire subculture of their own. Jl Kendal, round the corner from the night-time fun area of Belora, is one nocturnal hangout for Jakarta's transvestites, and nothing less than a walk on the wild side. The annual Jakarta Fair often features talent competitions with the city's performing *banci*. They hardly need a platform to perform on, however, their talents being always rather more spontaneously recognized.

PEMBANTU

Pembantu are a plainly unavoidable aspect of Asian life. Love them, hate them, hide from them — there's surely no escaping them. Some might say "servant" or "maid", or even "domestic manager" but these are misleading titles, and serve only to make the speaker sound more important than they probably are. *Pembantu* are literally "helpers". And "help" they do — "help" being the very point of the job. They are there to do things for you — run errands, tidy houses, cook food, pay bills, and countless other little tasks you have forgotten how to do yourself. And all on the promise of an agreed amount of *rupiah*, and possibly board and lodging too.

For Indonesians, *pembantu* are quite normal. For Western people, they take some getting used to. Many first-time visitors are highly uncomfortable at first with the idea of having their underwear scrubbed so cheaply, and so often. For the average *orang asing* (foreigner) it can be a profoundly confusing situation.

To compensate, they might display a reluctance in giving their newly-appointed *pembantu* any task at all. Yet with the gentle coaxing and encouragement of an Indonesian friend, not to mention a little practice, they soon get the hang of telling people what to do. And so it goes from one extreme to another. The foreigner, now confident with the idea of a *pembantu,* begins to apply this same one-way confidence to other situations: in the taxi, at the shops, in restaurants, at work, in the streets, everywhere in Indonesia. The fact that the majority of Indonesians are such apparently uncomplaining folk only encourages some Westerners to treat everyone like a *pembantu.* And this is far more shocking.

Yet there are two sides to every coin. From the *pembantu* point of view, it isn't bad work. There are a lot dirtier jobs to be doing and, besides, everyone has got to do something. As long as you are in work, you are making *uang* (money). And *uang* means security, not only for yourself but for the twenty or so extended tentacles of one's *kampung.* In a country with very little in the way of welfare, people are left to find work in any way they can. And work they do — even the servants have servants.

Get a good *pembantu* and you need never lift a finger again. Complacency comes dangerously easily in Jakarta. Indeed, once used to the idea of *pembantu* it's hard to imagine life without them. They will absolutely run your life for you — if you want. Of course not all are good; certain Jakarta families may change *pembantu* every other day, while others who hit it off with their employers, will stay for years and years.

For the cunning *pembantu*, a foreign person staying in Jakarta makes an attractive employment prospect. Since many Westerners are so bashful about giving someone instructions, the chances of having to do real *kerja keras* (hard work) are considerably less. And even then, the Western employer's guilt invariably pushes them to overpay their *pembantu.* It begins to make you wonder exactly who is being taken advantage of.

Should you ever find yourself in the position of having to hire a *pembantu*, it's worth making it clear exactly what you expect from them. The time they should start cooking, what exactly they should clean, which clothes you want or don't want washed, etc. If you don't, all manner of confusion can arise. They will invariably be living in with you, and expecting a room and *mandi* (bathroom) in with the deal. It's quite possible to have a *pembantu* visit you every day or so but they usually demand higher wages. Painful though it may be, it's better to spell out a future *pembantu's* duties from the word go than have to cope with blushes and sidelong glances later on. Your *pembantu* may simply be too *malu* (shy) to approach you for a job description. Your *pembantu* may be just simple. The best way of locating a reliable *pembantu* is probably by word of mouth. There are agencies which contract them out, yet the price is inevitably higher. Details can be found in the *Jakarta Post* or the Indonesian broadsheet *Kompas*.

Pembantu are actually part of the problem in Indonesia. Every year they take an allotted one month's paid holiday at Ramadan. They turn up at their *kampung* in lipstick and sunglasses, gushing colourful tales from the Mother City. To their *teman-teman* (mates), Jakarta, and the subsequent promise of work, becomes such an appealing idea that half the *kampung* follow her back. Most happily accept any work they can get — good or bad. And if particularly bad, they just don't tell anyone.

The perfect *pembantu* is almost invisible, like air. You might just see her out of the corner of your eye. Dirty plates disappear, books jump back on shelves and guests get refreshed on arrival. The perfect *pembantu* is immaculately clean, an excellent cook, a proficient bargainer, a natural first-aider, a witch-doctor and resident game show host. On the other hand, you might end up thinking they are just a pain in the *pantat*, for after the initial stage of acceptance come feelings of wrath. The unceasing regime of picking everything up after you may quickly drive you nuts. So might their cooking and the way they always buy exactly the same things. And then there are her friends who come to visit and stare. What eats away most at your soul, however, apart from the obvious lack of privacy, is the nagging feeling that somebody you don't really know is living in close quarters with you. You suddenly realise you have been paying someone to do things for you, only they haven't been doing them exactly how you would have done them. And anyway, you wouldn't have minded doing things yourself, you were just being culturally sensitive. This is a bizarre situation. Remember the old one about the king being ruled by his own servants? And the other one about doing things yourself if you want them doing properly?

A *pembantu* might be male or female, young or old, Ambonese or Sundanese. She might be shy or she might be downright *cerewet* (talkative). She might watch telly with you or she might prefer to keep her distance. It would be dangerously unfair to paint a picture of the average *pembantu*, so we best leave it to one of Jakarta's longer-term inmates to describe her experiences with Jakarta's *pembantu* workforce in what is one very typical expatriate household.

Your pembantu *is a she to begin with, twentysomething and either Javanese or Sundanese. She's the first one up every morning. By the time you wake up your house will have been tidied and your yard swept out. This is probably what woke you up — the scraping sound of her broom. Your breakfast will be underway and the subject of any shopping that needs doing that day will have been mentioned. Routines are important to a* pembantu, *to the point in fact of terrifying monotony. Tell her you like* tempe *and you'll get* tempe *every meal.*

The longest-serving pembantu *we ever had was Siam, who was Javanese and short. She was a very hardworking woman, 24 years old, illiterate and apparently, after three years of saying nothing of the sort, married. It seems in order to get out of her marital obligations, she'd left her* kampung *years earlier and joined a* pembantu *agency in Jakarta. She was strong: when the banana trees blew over one night in a storm, Siam was the first one up and* lugging the trunks out front for the rubbish collector. From time to time a gland on the side of her neck would swell up into a worrying half-tennis ball. We gave her the money to seek out the relevant medical advice but she kept quiet about the outcome.

When the family moved to a more strategic, albeit noisier, area of town, Siam lasted a mere three weeks before the firecrackers and passing traffic drove her out. She left suddenly one weekend, appearing in the front room and blocking the TV with her suitcase, asking only that the lady of the house inspect the contents of her luggage to confirm she wasn't lifting anything. She was free to go.

Her departure was a shock and the house was thrown into turmoil. Requests for a replacement were put out and after much fretting, one was eventually promised for the following week. What a long way away that seemed, what a lot of food to be cooked, what a lot of dusting, scrubbing and washing that would mean. Luckily, a relative had a spare pembantu and we were able to borrow her for the duration.

Siam's replacement eventually arrived, a foot taller and called Mita. She was the niece of a friend of the security man at the woman next door's husband's office, and really didn't want to be a pembantu at all. She was a much better cook than Siam (who tended to use the same bottle of cooking oil again and again until it turned black and made all her dishes taste terrible). The new one was also a proficient "dipper". "Dipping" is traditionally what all grovelling servants do when passing in front of their employers — lowering one shoulder. But Mita was very withdrawn and spent her time mostly hiding in her room. To do any work at all she had to first be persuaded out of her room. It couldn't last. The security man who had introduced her to the household was duly summoned and he took her away again, apologizing and saying thank you at the same time.

The house was once again thrown into chaos and smoke signals were again sent out. The result this time was a relative of a friend's pembantu. She was a hard worker admittedly and could cook a fair plate of tempe. Unfortunately, she turned out to be a compulsive liar. From the word go she started stealing small things, keeping the money she was supposed to pay the bills with and boasting of it to outsiders. Her name was Saroh. She would disappear for days on end, only to suddenly reappear at the sink as if nothing had happened. It later transpired that she had become intimately *involved with a nearby (and married)* warung *owner, hence her lengthy excursions to* "cari telor" *(look for eggs). She had to go. Upon return from her latest disappearing act she was confronted by the women of the house. The* pembantu *who had arranged her employment in the first place showed no mercy. Bye bye Saroh. Once she had gone her own love-torn way, little scribbled messages began turning up around the home, mainly childish things like " ho ho", and a few rude words. Odd.*

The final player in this troubled saga was a woman from East Java called Sum, who was a very friendly if not utterly dim woman. At one time in the backyard there stood a fine papaya tree with two almost-ripe fruit on board. One day, some workers in the house next door had leaned over and swiped the two fruit. In her fury at this discovery, she hacked both trees to the ground to make sure no one would ever do it again. Sum had a foot problem and in her idle moments could be seen picking at her feet with a razor blade. Her attempts to treat her foot condition included smearing her room in a horrible yellow jamu preparation which had to be professionally fumigated upon her departure.

Sum meant well, that's for sure, but sometimes her doglike approach to life got the better of her. On the day of her departure I gave her a lift to the bus station. I asked her when and why she'd ever come to Jakarta in the first place. "To make some money," she replied. "Well, have you?" I asked. "No!" she laughed, "but it doesn't matter."

HAVING THINGS DONE

For the *orang kaya* (rich folk), the rising middle classes and those foreigners residing here, Indonesia is the land of service. Try as you might, you can't do things yourself — you have them done for you. Telephones are answered, washing is laundered, bread buttered. Taxis are *dipanggil* (flagged down), rats trapped, visitors dealt with, guests watered and errands run. About the only things you can't have done for you are the basic bodily functions of human existence — everything else you can have done by someone else. A life of doing things by proxy can have its drawbacks, however: the things you have done are rarely done as exactly as they might if you had done them yourself. And when something is being done for you, quite often it wasn't really a job worth doing in the first place, and therefore not often a job done particularly well. *Bingung* (confused)? You should be. Having a *pembantu* (servant) or two around your home simply increases the temptation to send them off doing things, while you sit back and try hard to do nothing. It's not difficult, but highly questionable.

Since there are more *orang kaya* (rich people) in Jakarta than any other place in the archipelago, so there are noticeably more people running errands and living on the edge of other people's lives. The Indonesian wing of the American's Women Association recommends you employ the following staff. First, a *pembantu perempuan* (housemaid). She will do your housework — cleaning, scrubbing, sweeping, rubbing, fetching, receiving, shopping, bill-paying and a million other little things. For heavier household tasks like painting and decorating, minor repairs and general household maintenance, a *pembantu laki-laki* (houseboy) should be employed. A *juru masak* cooks your meals, lays your tables and keeps the kitchen in order. Outside should stand a *penjaga* to guard your house day and night. A *tukang cuci* (laundress) takes care of the household washing and ironing. A *tukang kebun* (gardener) weeds the garden, maintains the pool and keeps the banana trees in shape. If you have children, the services of a *pengasuh anak* (nanny) will be needed and to drive you around, a reliable *sopir* (driver) should be hired.

You might also consider employing, perhaps on a part-time basis, a bartender, a masseur, a nurse, a hairdresser and a personal tailor to make your life as totally passive as possible. In addition to an army of household staff with which to surround yourself, the passing services of Jakarta's million other *tukang jualan* (street sellers) are more than glad to do business and assist in the passive process by parading varieties of everything imaginable past your front door.

A street seller hawks his wares on a shoulder-pole.

When you do do things yourself, people regard you with a hint of suspicion. They might think you are being somewhat *pelit* (tight) with your *duit* (cash). The social pressures to conform to this passive style of existence are therefore enormous. And after all, it's only fair to share — doing something yourself deprives someone somewhere along the line of the prospect of a few extra rupiah. This is how the distribution of wealth works for the urban poor of Indonesia. Riches are filtered off left, right and centre in Indonesia. Some of it goes abroad, some of it is "forgotten about" and never mentioned again, while some of it gets reinvested, and some of it doesn't. A bit, however, trickles its way down into the pockets of the masses. The small change of Indonesia's economy is Joe Public's bread and butter.

103

Chapter Five

SOUNDS OF THE CITY

NOISE

It wouldn't be accurate to describe Jakarta as a quiet place, because it's not. Noise exists at a tremendously high level almost everywhere. Clearly, with so many people living in one place, a certain racket is bound to exist. Houses are usually built with the emphasis on ventilation, as opposed to soundproofing, and it often seems like the street itself is in the room there with you, and vice versa. Walls are thin. For maximum space usage, houses tend to be built to the very edges of their plots. With little left in the way of a garden, you are instead given the chance to hear a variety of *bajaj, bemo, ojek* and other means of Jakartan transport in aural close up.

As well as chickens, dogs and cats, there are lots of children in Jakarta, all of which possess great noise potential. People like to listen to their TVs and stereos at full volume. The obvious compensation for which is that you too are able to enjoy music at full volume. In the *kampung* it's popular to hire a *dangdut* band to play at a wedding party. If you like live *dangdut* music then this will come as a real treat. But if you don't …

In the *kampung*, noise starts early: the tannoy on the mosque is one of the first to get going, once the cockerels have had their say. Jakarta's mosques are a club of their own. By definition, they have to make noise. Apart from five daily prayer calls made through what sounds like a tin bucket, regular sermons are given according to the needs of each *kampung*. There is a wail of feedback as the local boys pass the microphone among each other, do a lot of coughing, "testing, 2, 3" and improvisation on *dangdut* classics. All this before the speaker has even started.

People are up bright and early. Once they have splashed themselves clean in the *mandi*, they start switching things on. Early morning music (which sort depends on individual tastes and the regional bias of the *kampung*) resonates through flimsy connecting walls. Pity the neighbours of a family with massive speakers who turn *jaipong* music up loud at six in the morning. And every *kampung* has such a family. The low ends are the worst offenders, the bass sounds more felt than heard. Even industrial earplugs are rendered obsolete as the sound of a bass instrument vibrates through the ground, and up into the bed.

Outside the window someone dragging their feet is overtaken by a twittering gang of *SMP* (primary) school kids. Passing in the opposite direction is an overexcited clack of chicks led by a neurotic clucking hen. In the distance you hear the *bakso* man coming. You know it's him because his distinctive "jingle" is to whack the side of his kettle with a metal rod. A neighbour puts a *dangdut* tape on. Others start "warming up" their vehicles; revving over and over the engines of a car and a motorbike respectively.

The neighbourhood's *pembantu* are suddenly out in force; sweeping to death front yards and porches. The telephone rings; wrong number. Someone lets off the first firecracker of the morning. More school kids pass. A cat fight breaks out. The fruit, vegetable and meat sellers set up shop outside your window, inviting everyone to come and buy. A motorbike, followed by the first *bajaj* of the day, splutters past. The *bajaj* stops outside your house. Its engine is left running as the driver and your *pembantu* wrestle with a new gas bottle, which is dropped on the floor on the way in. There are no lie-ins in Jakarta.

And in the rest of Jakarta … The traffic makes a racket in a variety of ways; honking horns, silencer-less two-strokes, rumbling buses, and more honking horns. Go shopping and get a headache thrown in for free. Set up at the front of each are more massive and weighty amplifiers playing raucously loud pop music. Glodok,

105

the big electronics market in North Jakarta's "Chinatown" is a wonderful such place in which to go deaf.

SINGING

Indonesia is a nation of natural-born singers. Although few have had formal singing lessons and perhaps few have any real concept of singing in tune, even the shyest, most withdrawn person in Indonesia walks around singing out loud. *Karaoke*-crooning is popular entertainment both in homes and bars so be prepared to have a song to sing when asked. *Lagu cinta* (love songs) always go down a treat, as well as corny middle-of-the-road classics like *Sailing, Wonderful Tonight* and *Take Me Home Country Roads*. Painful, but true.

RADIO

The Jakarta airwaves are packed with a seemingly overlapping abundance of radio stations. On the FM dial it can be hard to tell one pumping station from another. Ever-popular with the hip young crowd, and happily utilizing American jargon, is *Kiss FM*. For the classically-minded listeners there is *Klasik FM* which sponsors a number of events around the town. And for the classically-rock minded there is *M 97 FM* playing nonstop "classic" rock, as well as sponsoring local rock events. Fans of *dangdut* music will need to tune in to *Bandar FM* for the latest sounds. The oldest radio station is of course the national station, *RRI (Radio Republik Indonesia)*, which broadcasts across the entire nation, and which supplies the only official hourly news for every other station in the country.

MUSIC

As each region of Indonesia offers a distinct dialect, dress, food, and attitude, so each region offers its own special way of making music. With so many fiercely-proud people in one place, home-grown music is obliged to sell truckloads in Jakarta. And sell it does. People like their music — it reminds them of home. No need to trek through mangrove swamps with a portable DAT recorder to hear ethnic Indonesian music; just go to a music shop in Jakarta. But catch it while you can; the ruthless advances of technology deem it fit to place Yamaha keyboards alongside the more wholesome and traditional instruments associated with much of Indonesia's music. The clear-cut line between popular and ethnic music is rapidly fading.

Nonetheless, changing times aside, there is some wild, wacky and downright weird music to listen to in Indonesia. Listen to the music of Bali. Listen to a CD recording of the *kecak* and indulge yourself in a sound experience like no other. Listen to the tranquillizing, hammered bamboo music of the *anklung*; or try the fullblown bongo-fury of Balinese bamboo percussion, *Jegog*. Listen to *Rindik*, which is two *anklung* and a flute. Listen to catchy *Tarian* music, the original sound of Minang in West Sumatra. Listen to recordings by *Grup Nelwetties* and try not to be still humming it days later. Listen to the recordings the Fahnestock brothers made around Indonesia in 1941, *Music for the Gods*. Listen to *Iwan Fals*, Indonesia's token protest singer. Listen to *dangdut* music. Listen to all of it.

Shopping for Music

A music fan would therefore be wise to take advantage of Jakarta's tape and CD shops. Tapes are cheap, good quality, with virtually every taste catered for. For more esoteric selections (and imports) you would have better luck in the Chinese-run music shops in Jl Sabang, Central Jakarta, and certain shops in Kuta, Bali and Jl Malioboro, Yogya (where pirate tapes are still for sale), than elsewhere in Jakarta. Otherwise, the larger malls like Pondok Indah Mall have good shops.

107

Until 1989, heavily-pirated Western music tapes made up the bulk of shop stock. Although it was obvious they'd been lifted from LP records, they were excellent value for money and offered superb sound quality. Ludicrous transcriptions of lyrics were supplied, as well as guitar chords. Since the cassettes had to be either 60 minute or 90 minute in length, extra songs were included to fill out the tape. These were usually by the same artist but not always; sometimes an apparently random choice was tacked on the end, either that or the album simply started all over again. For the artists concerned, this wholesale bootlegging was an obvious drawback and in 1990 they disappeared forever, replaced by big name distributors like *P.T. Aquarius Musikindo* who offered the first generic Western-quality cassettes. The only difference nowadays between an Indonesian tape and one bought in a London high street are the words: *"Hanya Untuk Dijual Di Indonesia"* (only for sale in you-know-where) printed somewhere on the front.

When it comes to Indonesian music, there are hundreds of small labels putting out all kinds of local music all the time. By far the biggest and longest running is the *Lokananta* label whose back catalogue is so encompassing it can only deserve to have been digitally preserved before being rotted forever by the humidity. *Mudah-mudahan* (hopefully), since sadly, many of their titles are manufactured in limited quantities on tapes of dubious quality. Indonesian music is still far cheaper to buy than any other, while tapes themselves are still half the price they are in the West. Otherwise, CDs are as expensive as anywhere in the world; namely because all need to be imported (even the pirate copies from China are sold full-price). One advantage of this is that more interesting "bootleg" CDs, which are not normally allowed in reputable stores, are allowed a free reign in Jakarta's where, incidentally, you can test-listen the CDs before you purchase. For LP records and second-hand CDs go to Jl Surabaya.

While there might be a great deal of ethnic Indonesian music available on cassette, the same cannot yet be said for CD. Local pop stars might be well represented but when it comes to digital sound it seems Western music has priority. Japan has always taken a vested interest in Indonesian music and the JVC world sounds series has some excellent recordings from around the archipelago, including some of the best *gamelan*.

Gamelan

The most famous music to come out of Indonesia is *gamelan*, the most celebrated exponents of which have been the Balinese and Javanese. So far, *gamelan* is the only Indonesian music to have gained any sort of worldwide recognition. Over the years, it has been scrutinized, copied and adapted to the point of near confusion, prompting concern from the purists who believe that its cultivation outside Indonesia (in Holland, for example, they'll give you a grant to study it) is somehow missing the point. But foreign interest isn't all bad. Indeed, it was the Dutch who in 1900 came up with *kepatihan:* the written notation of *gamelan.* Yet the purists have a point; for so tied up is *gamelan* with the life-cycle rituals of Indonesian life, that its practice so far from its place of origin is certainly a bit *aneh* (odd).

Gamelan is perhaps the defining sound of Indonesia. For the Javanese it's the music of royalty; for the Balinese it's played for the gods. *Gamelan* is the music Indonesia would send into space if it had a space programme. Yet for many of the younger generation, especially in fashion-conscious Jakarta, *gamelan* simply makes nice background music at a wedding. It's unlikely that young Jakartans are the biggest buyers of *gamelan* records.

The orchestra itself takes on a variety of forms: featuring an array of perhaps eighty different gongs, a few drums and a couple of *saron* (xylophones) to provide melody, all of which are "answered" in turn by optional *suling* (flutes) and vocals. An expanded

109

form of *gamelan* is *legong* which combines dance, singing and drama — rock opera if you like.

The profusion of simultaneous melodies in *gamelan* can play tricks with the hearing. Sometimes it's possible to focus on a single melody but like all good things, as soon as you put your finger on it, it's gone, the floating melody instantly buried in the overall cacophony. At times the sound seems chaotic and random, and just when you want to give in, everything is brought down to earth with a bang on the drum. In *gamelan*, the drummer keeps the show together, controls the tempo, introduces new phrases and melodies.

Gamelan might not be to everyone's taste: the sound is too metallic, too harsh, too alien, the tempo changes too sudden for many Western ears. Scholars of the music argue differently: its shimmering, multilayered, charisma-charged melodies are an acting medium between the human and the spirit world. The average sweating tourist, however, sitting in a hotel lobby watching his complimentary "genuine traditional cultural performance" might not be so aware of the cosmological virtues of *gamelan*. This is part of the problem. The influx of tourism means that many traditional musical forms like *gamelan* get modified, abbreviated and commercialized simply to appease foreign audiences. It shouldn't need to be this way.

But other changes are at play. In the last couple of decades there has been a definite decline in the Javanese cultural chauvinism that has dominated since 1945. No longer is Java the sole heartland of Indonesia. It used to be that Javanese culture would wholly represent the rest of the country, but not now. In striving to emphasize a single Indonesian identity (as opposed to a disparate collection of some three hundred ethnic minorities) the focus on cultural activities has broadened to encompass all of the land's traditions. Today, there is less emphasis placed on *gamelan* as the sole music of Indonesia, and equal importance placed on the entire nation's musical output, at least within the country. Local cassette companies have long realized the need in the market for regional music and nearly every one of the twenty-seven provinces has its allotted space on the shelves of Jakarta's cassette shops.

Degung

Upon the seemingly infinite variations on the theme of *gamelan,* is *degung,* one of the traditional sounds of Sunda (West Java). A truly hypnotic experience, *degung* is like a musical form of valium, and features only the basic selection of *gamelan* instruments with flute and bass drum to the fore to emphasize melody. It's an extremely leisurely-paced affair. If *gamelan* is the multi-tracked studio production, then *degung* is the stripped-down, unplugged, acoustic version. One of the finest exponents of *degung* is the group *Gentra Pasundan*, conducted by the blind flute player and songwriter, Ujang Suryana. Away from its traditional form is a more dynamic pop version of *degung* as practised by the wonderful Nining Meids among others. Nano Suratno is a highly prolific writer and performer of all-things musical in Sunda, including *degung*.

Jaipong

Also to be found in West Java is *jaipong* music. The uninitiated again might think it sounds like more "plinky plonky" *gamelan*-type music, and while it does use some of the gongs and drums of the *gamelan* line-up, *jaipong* is far more humorous and punkier than formal *gamelan*. *Jaipong* isn't just music, it's an attitude. Its lyrics are suggestive; sometimes rude, sometimes not. This difference in music is as obvious as the difference in the people themselves: the overly-polite, formal Javanese and the sassy, nudge-nudge, wink-wink Sundanese. A woman starts the show off: whispering, "oohing" and "aahing" as the rhythm accelerates, slows and speeds

111

up again. Drums are to the fore, and scraping away in between is the *rebab*, a two-stringed bowed instrument producing a distinctly wonky sound. She might have a couple of "friends" there to chant harmonies, ask questions and elicit answers from the singer. When it's going flat out, you start wondering how long they can keep this furious pace going. Then it suddenly stops and everyone starts chatting and joking, until reminded to continue. *Jaipong* is good — listen to any recording by the accomplished *Jugala* group for an introduction to its delights.

Kroncong

Listen also to *kroncong*, one of the original sounds of Jakarta. Strictly speaking, *kroncong* is strings-only music, a reminder of the earliest Portuguese merchants who presumably packed violins, mandolins and guitars on board with them all those years ago. Add further influence from China and Holland, give it to Indonesians to play, dub a *Betawi* dialect on top and you have *kroncong*. These days this music is the mainstay of the middle-aged, or the seriously downhearted. When it's good, *kroncong* is very good; rolling, floating, moving music. Listen to virtually any recording by Hetty Koes Endang, who in the '80s, was responsible for single-handedly reviving the *kroncong* tradition in Indonesia. But sometimes it's dreadful — you are just as likely to find a *kroncong* version of *Tie a Yellow Ribbon Round the Old Oak Tree*, as you are the real thing.

Pop

Pop music is as popular in Indonesia as anywhere else. More esoteric listeners might get in a huff with the predominance of apparent "slush" on the airwaves, but there's really no need. The kind of Western music which is strong on sardonic, thought-provoking lyrics and short on sweet melody is lost on most Indonesians: when they want lyrics to mull over, they listen to Iwan

Fals. But the whingers do have a point. The Indonesian fondness for soppy Western pop music has spawned an entire genre of frankly unlistenable sickly-sweet balladry in Indonesian music. The lyrics to these syrupy recordings often depend solely on the words *cinta* (love) and *hati* (heart) being repeated every other word.

Jazz

Among the upwardly mobile of Jakarta, jazz music is particularly popular, although it is mainly the slick, modern form rather than the traditional. The annual *Jak Jazz* festival is an international affair that attracts a staggeringly diverse variety of performers. In recent years the most warmly welcomed names have been Phil Perry and Lee Ritenour, although the lesser-known sideline performers looking for a break have often been the most interesting. Not always, however — sometimes they turn out to be surprisingly more famous. Spotted playing *Moondance* in the car park section of Senayan was one rather pale-looking Georgie Fame. For the rest of the year, Jakarta's jazz fans have to be content to hang out in jazz clubs like *Jamz*.

Foreign Acts

Big name acts do sometimes play Jakarta, but generally it seems, Jakarta continues to be left off the agenda when plans for a tour of Southeast Asia are drawn up. This is perhaps a historical leftover from the days when pop music was banned outright. Even local acts were punished: the respected rock group *Koes Plus* (one of the country's oldest popular music acts) were hauled in for making *lagu ngak ngik ngok* (Western pop sounds), although the drummer was apparently let off. The first president, Sukarno, was particularly worried about the mayhem which the influence of the Beatles and their ilk might wreak within his newly indoctrinated generation, and so he banned "Western music" altogether. Instead he encouraged Indonesia's musicians to look at their own extensive musical heritage for inspiration. Thus the emergence of *jaipong* and *dangdut*.

Nevertheless, Steve Wonder, Mick Jagger, BB King, Sting, Diana Ross and Deep Purple have all played to great fanfare in Jakarta. But it can get out of hand: Mick's show incited a riot in which a number of people died. As a result, many performers will only play as part of special American Express "clubholder" deals, as opposed to the general public and its associated riffraff. Other fly-by-night teenybopper acts come to Jakarta, but are far too short-lived to merit a mention here. Sometimes posters appear around the town for foreign acts who are totally unknown in the West but who have somehow made it "big in Jakarta" via a fluke of popularity.

Dangdut

Dangdut is *the* music of Jakarta. If you need to know what Jakarta sounds like, listen to *dangdut*. True, it spreads right across Indonesia, but Jakarta and West Java are where this music is made, performed and developed. You hear it playing in every *kampung*, an awful lot of taxis and many non-expat bars — everywhere in fact.

Dangdut first emerged in its most recognizable form in the '60s, and has progressed steadily ever since. Traditionally, the sound is characterized by tabla-type drums (this is where the name *dangdut* originates: the *dang* and the *dut* are sounds produced by beating the drum in a certain way), wailing vocals, flutes, mandolin and fuzz guitar. It has a heavy rhythm section, dominant bass and very "Asian" percussion. *Dangdut* is similar in form to Indian pop music; indeed, early recordings routinely featured a sitar in the line up, and it's still often found alongside Indian pop music in the smaller outlets.

114

Dangdut has grown progressively heavier over the years, mainly through the introduction of electric instruments. The very earliest recordings are essentially acoustic in performance — and quite delightful as a result. These days you are more likely to find *dangdut* in fusion with hip-hop rhythms and rap. Another popular ploy is to *dangdutize* the current hits from around the world. Much as you can buy Smurfs' versions of "Top Hits", so entire albums featuring *dangdut* versions of every song imaginable are available. For the latest mutations of *dangdut,* as well as a regular selection of "golden oldies", tune into *Bandar Dangdut FM*.

Dangdut is basically blues music. It deals with the tribulations of Indonesian life: infidelity, poverty, bad rice harvests and other domestic mishaps, although like blues it just as often deals with lighter subjects. *Dangdut* remains a predominantly working class music. Described as *"kampungan"* (unsophisticated) by some, very few wealthy Jakartans will admit to liking it, although they all seem to know the lyrics.

Dancing to *dangdut* is easy — you simply try not to move. You can put your arms up in the air if you want and sway a bit, but you shouldn't start doing the jitterbug. When *dangdut* is on, couples have to dance (or rather sway) in rows, doing their best not to touch each other.

The Arabic and Malay influences are most strongly felt in the *dangdut* of Rhoma Irama who, through numerous film appearances in the 1980s, helped popularize *dangdut* beyond mere pop music and into a way of life. One of the high points in Rhoma's career came quite recently when he became involved in the 1997 general election. Unfortunately it also quickly became one of his lowest points.

Such is the crowd-pulling potential of *dangdut* that, in order to ensure a good turn out at their campaigns, the three permitted campaigning parties, *Golkar*, *PPP* and *PDI*, began to make increasingly conspicuous use of *dangdut*. But *Golkar*, the ruling party of the past three decades, acquired the prize catch: "*si Raja Dangdut*" (the King of *Dangdut*) — Rhoma Irama no less. *Dangdut* suddenly became a campaign issue with all three parties striving to make maximum use of it. However, not all of Rhoma's fans were impressed, particularly those who remembered his days as a staunch supporter of *PPP*. It seems Rhoma, by agreeing to endorse the politics of *Golkar*, had done a complete political turnaround, turning his back on his previous high-profile association with the Muslim-orientated *PPP*. Many were outraged and instigated an anti-Rhoma campaign. Radio stations could be heard advising the public where to dump their tapes and commit Rhoma's memories to ashes.

But time heals all and Rhoma remains the unrivalled King, despite threats from newcomers like Meggy Z. Perhaps the greatest female singer of *dangdut* is the accomplished Elvi Sukaesih, and more recently Camelia Malik, who has enjoyed some success in Japan. For seminal *dangdut* recordings listen to *Begadang* by Rhoma Irama, *Mandi Madu* by Elvi Sukaesih or *Gubuk Bambu* by Meggy Z, among a million others.

GLOSSARY OF MUSICAL TERMS

While a lot of Indonesian music defies clear definition, and much of it happily bounces around between styles, there are still a great many distinctions to be made ...

From	*Local name*	*Sounds like*
Jakarta	*Ajeng*	Wild gong and "milk bottle" frenzy with "trumpet". Gamelan with attitude.
Jakarta/ Sunda	*Dangdut*	Indian and Arabic pop. Slow or fast. Fat and fun. Woeful. Wistful. Seductive. Sexy. Great.
Sunda (W. Java)	*Degung*	Musical valium. Drum, gong, flute. Introspection.
Jakarta	*Gambang Kromong*	Plinky-plonky, drums, gongs. Wonky.

From	*Local name*	*Sounds like*
Everywhere (mainly Java and Bali)	*Gamelan*	Gongs hit with hammers. Metallic. Hauntingly slow or furiously fast. Ultimately cosmic.
Jakarta	*Iwan Fals*	Protest music. Folk-rock.
Sunda	*Jaipong*	Drums, rebab, attitude. Sassy female vocals. Dance music.
Bali	*Jegog*	Bamboo gamelan.
Bali	*Kecak*	Male vocal gamelan.
Jakarta	*Kroncong*	Stringed instruments. Ballads.
N. Sumatra	*Lagu Batak*	Surprisingly straight folk songs.
Bali	*Legong Bali*	Gamelan as opera. Frighteningly wild vocals.
Sunda	*Pop Degung*	Degung with words. Haunting.
Sunda	*Pop Sunda*	Pop music (would you believe).
Bali	*Rindik*	Bamboo percussion and flute. Tranquillizing.
Jakarta	*Tanjidor*	Brass band gone wrong.
W. Sumatra	*Tarian Minang*	Catchy. Instrumental. Almost Bossa Nova.
Sunda/ Java	*Tembang Sunda/ Jawa*	Zithers, gong, drum, very slow. Vocals. Haunting.
Jakarta	*Topeng Betawi*	Bed springs and Sink plungers. Men at work.

INDONESIAN MUSIC YOU MIGHT FIND OUTSIDE INDONESIA ...

There are a number of recordings available of Indonesian music, the most readily available being variations on gamelan music. But there is more if you look hard ...

Detty Kurnia: *Dari Sunda* Riverboat Records

Detty's second release in the West (she has hundreds out in Indonesia), a Japanese-produced, Jakarta-recorded CD, *Dari Sunda* combines traditional sounds of the *rebab* and the *kendang*

117

with programmed drums and topnotch production. The result is exquisite, only occasionally spilling over into pop-slush and for the most part kept afloat by the sheer veracity of Detty's fantastic voice. "Pop Sunda" they call this: *Dari Sunda* runs the gauntlet of West Javanese pop today, from the traditional sounds of *Mamanis* (the finest recording yet of this particular genre of Indonesian music) to the more up-to-date *dangdut*, rock and pop sounds heard in Indonesia today. The opening track, *Sorban Palid*, should have been a number one.

Various: *JVC Sound Series* JVC

Another Japanese project, the JVC sound series focuses more on the ethnic side of Indonesian music than the popular, from the mighty bongo-fury of *Jegog* to the almost intangible folk-sounds on the Music of Sunda CD. In between are nine CDs featuring the best of Balinese and Javanese *gamelan*. Lengthy pieces (average 20 minutes a track) these CDs are practically everything you need to know about *gamelan* without moving hemisphere. For those who find it too metallic there's an "acoustic" version, *Jegog*. Mammoth lengths of bamboo are whacked, beaten, punched and tickled in an orgy of complex rhythm. The style is that of *gamelan*; the rhythms as intricate and compelling. Two CDs feature the *kecak* dance. Imagine several hundred men shouting, chattering and chanting in unison.

And then there is the *Music of Sunda* CD. A live recording made in Japan, it features an ethereal performance of this most delicate of sounds. The vocals on *Tembang Cianjuran* are like air: blink and you feel you might miss them. You can't quite put your finger on it, but something draws you deeper and deeper into the singer's voice; the sound is both nostalgic and alien; reassuring yet disconcerting. Features tunes and performances by Nano Suratno, one of the greatest songwriters in Sunda today.

Various: *Music of Indonesia* (CDs 1 to 15) Smithsonian/ Folkways

Perhaps the most comprehensive Beginner's Guide to Indonesian Music, this fifteen CD set (there are plans for more) dips a toe into the local music scene in all the right places. Much of this music is utterly unheard of outside Indonesia, and so well-recorded too. From the weird "milk-bottle and dustbin lid" percussion of *Topeng Betawi* (disk 5) to the "bedsprings and sink-plunger" sounds on disc 3. Disk 2 is the pop CD and features essential recordings of *dangdut, kroncong* and *jaipong*, unavailable elsewhere. Discs 3 and 5 concentrate on some of the truly peculiar (and rapidly disappearing) sounds of Jakarta, featuring several tracks in the style of *tanjidor* — arguably the wonkiest music you will ever hear: a Salvation Army on drugs, at least that's what it sounds like. All in all, a superb round up of the Indonesian music scene, but ultimately only the very tip of one enormous iceberg.

Various: *Road to Dangdut* (Vols 1 & 2) Altan

Currently only available on import only from The Far Side in Tokyo (via Riverboat records) this two-part history of *dangdut* music contains some delightful recordings. Mostly acoustic affairs, these tracks mark the progress of this predominantly working class music through the influence of Indian film music, Malaysian folk-pop and Islamic rock. The sound quality might not be the greatest, but the warmth and sincerity of these songs belies any disappointment. Brylcream and *nasi goreng*: this is Jakarta in the '50s and '60s. Great stuff.

Music for the Gods Rykodisc

Even earlier still were the recordings two American boys made around Indonesia in 1941. Lugging huge great 78 disc-cutters everywhere, they recorded an impressively varied amount of music and then apparently forgot about them and left the lot in someone's loft for forty years. They were rediscovered, remastered and put out on CD as *Music for the Gods*. Although the sound quality is what you might expect from half-decayed acetate, these recordings offer a glimpse of a pre-World War II Indonesia long before the tourists had claimed Bali as their own; when it was still under Dutch colonial rule. It makes interesting comparative listening to hear the *gamelan* played by old men of almost sixty years ago to the *gamelan* dished out like smarties to tourists today.

AND SOME YOU MIGHT NOT FIND OUTSIDE JAKARTA ...

Rhoma Irama & Elvi Sukaesih: *20 Top Duet Dangdut* Gema Nada Records

Glitzy, trashy and full of passion, the unrivalled King and Queen of *dangdut* team up for this extravaganza. This is a compilation (one of three) of their collaborations over the years, and is a fine example of what each is good at: Rhoma's *dangdut* is as Arabic as Elvi's is Indian, both are Indonesian and the result is *dangdut* as only Indonesians know how.

Various: *Gubuk Bambu* Gajah Mada Records

Now that's what I call *dangdut*: a highly typical compilation of the current *dangdut* hits collected together on one album. Showcases the breadths and scope of *dangdut* today from its Indian roots (slow tabla and sitar on some tracks) through the Islamic wailing sort and then some. The title track by Meggy Z was an enormous hit and an instant classic.

Nelwetties Group: *Music Tarian Minang* Tanama Records

Sumatran dance music. Light hand percussion throughout with a bass guitar and cheap keyboard on top — irresistible. Among the catchiest music you will hear, the tracks feature a recurring melody that crops up throughout the album, pausing only for some thousand-year-old lamenting and then straight back into the music.

FURTHER STABS AT PURSUING CULTURE

Jakartan radio and TV are, perhaps unsurprisingly, good sources for music and culture. TVRI in particular regularly features a "traditional performance" slot late at night, which might be anything from a *wayang* performance (shadow play) to a display of razorblade-eating black magic. And slotted between episodes of tacky American programmes will be a traditional song or two from a woman in traditional *kebaya* (dress).

For live music (invariably "traditional" or "avant-garde"), as well as exhibitions, talks, poetry readings, "happenings" and other generally "cultured" activities, a trip to the heart of Jakarta's bohemia, *TIM* (*Taman Ismail Marzuki*) on Jl Cikini Raya, no. 73, Menteng, will do the trick. Don't let the grotesque sculptures put you off; inside *TIM* is a quagmire of galleries, theatres and exhibition halls with something going on virtually every night of the week. A planetarium is also housed within, and at the back is the *Institute Kesenian Jakarta*, the city's leading arts training institute. *TIM* produce a monthly programme of events available from the Visitors Information Centre on Jl Thamrin, and you can also find out what's on by checking the local press.

For more refined notions of "culture" — orchestral perform-ances, ballet and theatre — there is the *Gedung Kesenian Jakarta* at Jl Gedung Kesenian, No. 1, Pasar Baru. A beautifully restored colonial building from the nineteenth century, its grandeur seems strangely out of place in Jakarta. On a similarly European theme, although markedly more modern, is *Erasmus Huis* on Jl Rasuna Said Kav S-3. This is the Dutch cultural centre and is attached to the Dutch Embassy. Naturally, it places greater emphasis on

121

non-Indonesian activities than other cultural centres in the city, although it still has a regular itinerary of lectures and shows on Indonesian arts and history. It also boasts some 22,000 books, mostly in Dutch. The major hotels in the city also provide regular performances of arts and crafts. The Hilton, for example, has a resident *gamelan* "orchestra" playing, somewhat half-heartedly admittedly, in the hotel's elaborate foyer.

Many of the city's embassies regularly show films, or give talks (invariably in the language of that embassy). There are a number of "cultural centres" associated with various embassies in Jakarta, and many have their own libraries. *The British Council* in the S. Widjojo Centre, Jl Sudirman, has a good selection of books as well as the latest magazines and papers. Likewise, the *American Cultural Center*, in the Wisma Metropolitan, Jl Sudirman; the *Australian Cultural Center*, Jl Rasuna Said, Kuningan; the *French Cultural Center*, Jl Salemba Raya, Matraman; the *Japan Cultural Center*, in the Summitmas building, Jl Sudirman; and the *Jawaharlal Nehru Cultural Center*, in Jl Iman Bonjol, No. 32, Menteng, specializing in all things Indian. Again, check the local press for details of their current activities, or give them a ring to request a monthly programme.

For a sweatier cultural experience beyond the air-conditioned world of the embassy, various "local" theatres have regular showings of *wayang* and other traditional forms of entertainment, performed invariably in Bahasa Indonesia or Bahasa Jawa. *Teater Popular* on Jl Kebun Pala 1, No. 295 in Tanah Abang, and *Bharata Theatre* on Jl Kalilio, No. 15, Pasar Senen are two such places.

Fine art is big business in Jakarta, and exhibitions and galleries are all over the place. Aside from the aforementioned places, fine art can be viewed and bought in *Pasar Seni;* an outdoor art fair in Taman Impian Jaya Ancol. Artists are generally working "on site" and it's a good chance to see *batik*, *ikat*, *wayang* puppets, and other Indonesian indigenous art-forms in the making. There is also an abundance of private galleries around the city; Kemang is one such area, as is Jl Palatehan, Blok M, which transforms itself by day from the nighttime world of bars and booze into something far more *halus* (refined).

Taman Mini Indonesia Indah is the probably the most comprehensive crash-course to Indonesian culture under one roof — except of course there isn't a roof, only the widest selection of Indonesia's great diversity in one place. Just off the Jagorawi Toll road in the southeast of the city, it was completed in 1975 to accusations that it was nothing more than an extravagant playground for Tien Suharto, the former President's late wife. It has in fact turned out to be Jakarta's most visited attraction, and although it may have been expensive to construct, *Taman Mini* is actually very good. The nation's twenty-seven provinces are represented by twenty-seven full-scale traditional houses, each replete with the handicrafts, clothing and, quite often, "traditional" music of that province. Museums, insect-houses, bird parks, cinemas, lakes, mini Borobudurs and the general feeling of open space are what make this flamboyant project such a success. A cable car ride will give you an impressive aerial view of the spectacle, but be warned: once you have been padlocked into the plastic bubble, there is no going back, and you may well be in for one of the hottest twenty minutes of your life. It's not unlike one of those Japanese "endurance" shows where the contestants have to undergo appalling physical "tests" to win. There are no winners at *Taman Mini*, but all in all — particularly on weekdays — it is a hassle-free and spacious place to stroll about, and well worth the visit.

CHAPTER SIX

PRACTICALLY JAKARTA

HOTELS

Being a foreigner in a city like Jakarta, you find that even if you're not staying in an international hotel, you are at liberty to pop in unquestioned anytime to use the facilities of one. You'll also find that, comparatively, prices for the use of a five-star hotel pool, restaurant and business facility are good. Thus, "breakfast at the Hilton" or "lunch at the Hyatt" are benefits that can accompany "being foreign" in Jakarta and the assumed affluence that this generally entails.

The major international-style hotels are in the city centre, close to the main boulevards: the *Jakarta Hilton International* on Jl. Gatot Subroto is well-established and typically provides the five star, albeit generic, treatment associated with the name "Hilton". Set in 32 acres of garden, the hotel is a fine place to find a bit of anonymity. Not far from the *Hilton* and of similar five-star anonymity are the *Shangri-La*, *Borobudur*, and farther south, *le Meridien*. Newer arrivals to the Jakarta hotel list have been a *Holiday Inn* and an *Omni Batavia*.

The Welcome Statue roundabout on Jl Thamrin is host to a number of hotels and shopping areas, making it an obvious focal point for the first-time visitor. On the east corner of the round-about, opposite the British Embassy, is the *Mandarin Oriental* which has always been popular with business people. The *Grand Hyatt*, which has the backing of Bambang Suharto, the second son of former President Suharto, is built onto the end of Plaza Indonesia on the west of the roundabout. Both are widely considered to be among the city's "poshest". To the south of this is the *Hotel Indonesia*. The original star-rated hotel of Jakarta, it is the place where the city's foreigners took refuge when Sukarno's government fell to pieces in the mid-'60s, and is featured in the movie of that very fraught period — *The Year of Living Dangerously*. Although it seems rather faded and sad these days, there is still certain a sense of history attached to it, and it does have a big pool.

BUSINESS FACILITIES

The major hotels are equipped to handle your fax, telex and telegraph facilities, and they also offer operator assistance for long-distance calling. They may also be sent and received from the Telkom Office in the Jakarta Theatre building just opposite McDonalds on Jl. Thamrin. Faxes are popular in Jakarta and you'll find that virtually all businesses require you to send a fax for every request or meeting you want to arrange, regardless of how necessary you feel this to be. *Wartel* are smaller, privately run telecommunications agencies (they may also be known as *warpostal*) and again can be relied upon for your communication needs.

Office hours vary in Jakarta, but are loosely based around the familiar nine to five model (excepting variations like eight to four). Saturday mornings are a working day for many, and it's altogether possible to do business then. Friday afternoons tend be quiet because of the exodus of male employees to the mosque. Government offices are strict in their observance of these times and Fridays are basically "half-days". Mondays to Thursdays, government offices tend to close by 3 p.m., but are open on Saturdays until 2 p.m.

USEFUL BUSINESS ADDRESSES

Business Advisory Indonesia
Suite 304, Kuningan Plaza
Jl Rasuna Said Kav C.11-14
Tel: 517 696

Jakarta Executive Service Centre
Menara Duta Building
Jl. Rasuna Said
Tel: 516202

Manggala Business Center
Jl Gatot Subroto
Tel: 5700279

Pusat Data Business Indonesia
Jl Kartini 54-1
Tel: 639 1998

World Trade Centre Club
16th Floor Wisma Metropolitan II
Jl Sudirman
Tel: 578 1302

ACCOMMODATION

Like most things in Jakarta, accommodation comes in varying
extremes. Take your pick: some are mammoth and palatial; Dallas-
like homes with swimming pools, umpteen rooms and an army of
staff, while others are more humble *kampung* abodes. Houses in
Jakarta are amazingly varied. Some of the strangest shapes exist
depending on the owner's requirements or whimsy. But roughly
speaking, the cheaper the house, the more connecting walls there
are and thus, the higher the risk of noise pollution. At the cheapest
end, houses have only thin wooden partitions, and a lot of neighbour noise. Yet you may feel more at home like this; you may feel
more "at one" with the people. Maybe. But living too humbly in
Jakarta only serves to arouse the suspicions of your neighbours:
if you can afford to travel away from your country, surely you can
afford to live in a decent house? why choose to live like a poor
person? perhaps you're just *pelit* (mean). If you are prepared to

muck in, contribute to local *kampung* causes, pass the time of day with everyone, and basically not upset anyone by complaining too much or running a brothel, you will be just fine in a *kampung*. If you do get one in a *kampung,* you should consider it an "open house". Neighbours like to drop in, and drop in, and drop in.

For the largest houses, areas like Pondok Indah, Kemang (the original expat zone) and Menteng offer colossal, Spanish-villa style houses where a great many diplomats and the like choose to live. For details of these and other places available, try the classified ads in the English language daily, *Jakarta Post*. These homes come decked out with swimming pools, grounds, AC, jacuzzi, and other modern trappings. Permata Hijau, Simprug (between Pondok Indah and the business district) and the up-and-coming Jl. Casablanca are areas where pricey apartments and houses can also be found.

Night in a middle-class part of Ragunan

Garden is not a commodity in Jakarta, but enough money will buy you some. House prices are still accelerating, but not quite as dramatically as they were in the early '90s. At one point it was almost possible to double your money within a year on a house in the right area. This was made easier in part by the colossal amounts of road work done. New ring-roads were knocked up overnight, previously inaccessible locations were suddenly made accessible to the "big" roads of Thamrin and Sudirman, and the real estate contractors moved in.

For places in the medium price-range, Pejompongan, Bintaro, Cinere and Tebet among others are good places to look. Generally speaking, the south of the city is the favoured half to live. With the north generally taken up with the port goings-on at Tanjuk Priok, copious industrial activity, and the extensive recreational area of Ancol, you are better off looking south of the line that begins with Kebayoran Baru and spreads out towards Bogor. Although this narrows things down a little, there is still the question of which house to settle on and what amenities to surrender. There might be AC in there or a ceiling fan; it might be detached or it might be semi; it might be near a mosque, it might not. Remember, the risk of *gangguan* (disturbances) decreases with every rupiah you pay towards accommodation.

At the bottom end, almost any *kampung* will do, some of the "nicer" ones might be found in areas behind Radio Dalam, Warung Buncit and Cipete. Perhaps the cheapest homes to rent are the ones graffitied over and over with the words *AWAS HANTU!* (Beware of Ghost) — make your own mind up on this. Single rooms are also available to rent, and good value they are too. Known as *kost*, they are a good way for *bule* to become familiarized with the Indonesian way. *Kost* usually have a shared kitchen and bathroom, and are advertised regularly in the paper *Kompas*. Before renting one, however, you should remember that Indonesians are generally very early risers, rendering a "lie-in" a distant memory for many.

One of the major drawbacks with renting any-sized accommodation is the fact that landlords demand two years' rent up front. Sometimes it's only a year, sometimes it's five. You may be able to negotiate a deal where you pay half first, half later but you are still looking at paying a block sum to move in. Certain apartments and luxury-size places are rentable monthly, but the price is not cheap by any means.

When you consider that the rent paid on one of these Jakarta apartments is more than some workers earn in an entire year, it may put things in perspective. Or maybe not; in many respects, Jakarta is as cosmopolitan as any other big city in the world, and subsequently has the prices to prove so. Quality accommodation demands a fair price. Yet even at its most expensive, accommodation is still cheaper than Western rates, and at worst it's the same price as the rest of the world.

When looking for a home you might want to run a checklist of your requirements.

- Check the lower walls for tidemarks and other signs of flooding. Ask the neighbours if this place is *sering kebanjiran* (prone to flooding); you wouldn't want to wake up to a foot of sewage water in your house. Check the ceiling for signs of water damage to see if your potential roof leaks.
- Try and assess the traffic situation when getting to and from the house. Since there isn't any area of the city that doesn't experience a *macet total* (gridlock) during the rush hours, it's an idea to view the house before or after rush hour to see how well the traffic flows the rest of the time.
- Telephone waiting lists are infamously *panjang* (long), so if your landlord insists he can have one installed if only you rent his house, he is not being entirely honest. The waiting list is rumoured to be between four and seven years long, depending who you ask. A house with a phone can easily put an extra million rupiah or two on the rent, such is the demand.

- If you are not Muslim, you probably won't truly appreciate the delights of Islam, so check how close it is to the nearest mosque. You are never going to be far from the sound of one in Jakarta, but if you see a loudspeaker protruding into your potential home, you might think twice before committing yourself. The calls to prayer are made five times daily, at around 4.30 a.m. (*subuh*), 12.00 p.m. (*zhuhur*), 2.30 p.m. (*ashar*), 6 p.m. (*maghrib*), and 7.30 p.m. (*isya*); you might want to view a house at a time that coincides with one of these calls for the most accurate evaluation of the house's noise potential.
- Check to see how many, if any, adjoining walls the house shares. Check for signs of termites by looking for telltale dust-piles. You also should check there's enough electricity coming in to power your household machinery. And check the colour of the water to see if it matches the wallpaper.

One thing that connects all Jakarta houses are the alarming security measures taken to prevent unwelcome visitors. The broken glass, barbed wire and razor-spikes are there to keep people out, not you in. They might look awful and oppressive but such is life in Jakarta. Something else common to all homes is the graffiti, which is scrawled, scribbled and sprayed all over the city.

It must be remembered that in Jakarta everything is built on top of everything else. Every area of real estate has a maze of *kampung* lurking behind. Build yourself a wall high enough, however, and you won't have to see any of the reality of Jakarta. You can then pretend it's actually a nice place.

If you really are unable to sleep without fear of the *orang kampung* coming to get you in your sleep, you might consider living in one of the "mini-America" places in Jakarta. Here life goes on unabashed as it would in any middle-class, American suburban trash-pad; lawns, sidewalks, gigantic satellite dishes, garden sprinklers, committee meetings, coffee mornings, slide shows and optional wife-swapping. All this fake happiness is surrounded by an insurmountable wall and round-the-clock security. Not just anyone can walk in; you have to be invited.

Of course, if you need to go to such extremes for your home comforts, you ought to reconsider, if possible, your decision to live in a place like Jakarta.

FURNITURE AND FLOORS

Given the choice, Indonesians prefer relaxing on the floor rather than in chairs. The furniture in Indonesian homes is mainly reserved as a place for newly-arrived guests to be placed bolt upright in. But there's still a fine variety of furniture with which to fill a house with. Carpets are not normal household necessities in Indonesia, tiled and fake-tiled linoleum are the standard floor coverings, and make for a much cooler and cleaner house. Shoes are out, bare feet are in.

Some of the cheapest and most hardwearing furniture available is that of bamboo. Bamboo comes thick and fast in Indonesia and its natural hollow-block form lends itself perfectly to furniture construction, besides being excellent value for money. The major drawback with bamboo, however, is its noise potential. Bamboo chairs continue to creak and crack disturbingly, hours after the sitter has upped and gone elsewhere. Sex on a bamboo bed is out of the question, unless you feel the need to draw attention to yourself. Being the bottom end of the market, you don't have to look hard to find this kind of furniture, as it's more likely to come to you. Street sellers loaded up high with the stuff make the rounds regularly, keep your *kuping* (ears) open.

Rattan furniture is a common sight in Jakarta homes and can be inexpensively custom-made to your designs. Jl. Duren Tiga in Mampang and Jalan(s) Kemang Raya and Kemang 1 all have reputable *rattan* furniture shops. Ciputat Raya and Jl. Fatmawati are also good places in Jakarta to find furniture. An excellent idea in rattan furniture is The Giant Eggcup Chair. It's a cushion-filled, semicircular dome, some two metres in diameter, which can be swivelled about upon an eggcup-like base. You sit in it.

Yet no matter how posh the furniture, no matter how springy the rattan, chairs and sofas alike in Jakarta are routinely spoiled by the use of protective plastic covers. Presumably in an attempt to maintain the stain-free illusion of the piece being *masih baru* (still new), a plastic cover is stretched over and kept there. Either that or it comes ready-sealed. The cover will remain there through thick and thin; while unwitting foreign guests squeak and squirm on sweating polyurethane, and until what is protected beneath eventually disappears from view in an inevitable haze of wear-and-tear. A similar anomaly also occurs in a great many taxis.

Traditional furniture is harder to find and much of what does exist is heavily Dutch, Chinese and Indian influenced. Indeed, it was the Dutch who introduced teak to Indonesia and were responsible for Java's teak plantations. Yet it doesn't look particularly "foreign", like everything that comes to Indonesia, furniture has had to be distinctly "Indonesianized" before being accepted at large.

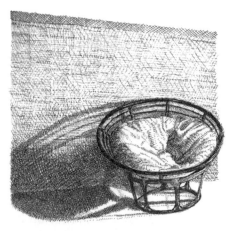

The eggcup chair

Nevertheless, furniture can still be a confusing concept for our country cousins. Have too much furniture and a visiting *orang kampung* (bumpkin) will opt for the floor every time. Put them in a room with two single beds and the next morning find them sleeping on the floor between the two, or even under one. Entire families are accommodated in this way.

When buying a bed, after making sure it's long enough, you need to decide between a standard foam mattress and a more traditional *kapok* (cotton fibre) one. *Kapok* is generally a much harder surface to sleep on, and it needs daily beating to ensure it stays in shape. If not, a trough develops in the mattress after a few nights, and you end up sleeping directly on hardboard.

ELECTRICITY

It runs at 220 V of 50 cycles AC and utilizes round two-pin plugs. If coming from the UK, all you need do is change the plug, and everything electrical you care to bring should function normally (and vice versa). Be warned, however, that wiring is not always adequately earthed, and that in some *kampung,* 110 volts are still used. A great many electronic items in Indonesia are dual voltage; 110/220V. Once settled in your home, have your wires and boxes checked for signs of tampering. It's all too possible to find yourself being poached of electricity by means of a couple of extra wires twisted onto your connection box. You might find to your horror one day that you have been supplying half the neighbourhood with *listrik* (electricity). To clarify matters, turn everything off in your home and see if the discs are still turning.

Ideally your home should have at least a 12,000 volt fuse box, especially if running air-conditioning and other machinery. This will hopefully reduce the number of times your fuses give out on you. Commonly, rooms in Indonesian houses feature only a single electrical outlet, often at light-switch level, so invest in some good quality multi-plugs and extensions. If running sensitive equipment like a computer, you should take precautions against the frequent power surges by employing some form of fuse-based surge protection. Make sure your place is well-grounded against lightning; inadequate grounding will serve the reverse effect and actually attract lightning. In a storm you should switch off all electrical things or risk exploding.

You might also want to invest in a couple of battery-operated fluorescent lamps, the kind that come on automatically when the power outs. You see, if it rains too hard there's a good chance of a power cut, and if it gets too hot there's also a good chance of a power cut. If you're in a hotel or apartment, there's hopefully a generator to keep your light bulbs lit. The blackouts themselves tend to occur in zones; some areas may be without *listrik* for hours while next door seems to be working normally. If it keeps up for more than a day, you can try and call the electric board, PLN, but don't expect any miracles. Keep candles, batteries and torches handy either way.

TV

If you turn on a TV in Jakarta, you should be able to get (at the last count) six channels. The most popular of these appears to be *RCTI (Rajawali Citra Televisi Indonesia)*, a strictly commercial station with adverts every ten minutes. *RCTI* features a mixture of reasonable films, local soap operas, news bulletins, international sport, semi-appalling American shows, truly appalling Filipino/ Latin American "telenovellas", pop videos, government broadcasts and lots and lots of adverts. Many foreign shows are in English with subtitles for you to improve your reading skills of the language. *SCTV (Surya Citra Televisi)*, *AN-TV (Andalas TV)* and *Indosiar* are similar privately-run channels.

TVRI (Televisi Republik Indonesia) is a non-commercial government-run station, broadcast throughout Indonesia, and the oldest in operation. It's a far more sober affair than its counterparts, almost wooden in its presentation, but it does show some good uninterrupted films, as well as *Match of the Day*. One of the best things about *TVRI* is the exposure it gives local music, art and culture: *wayang kulit, jaipong* and *legong* all have regular slots. *TVRI* has a couple of spin-offs: *TVRI 2* and the daytime educational *TPI (Televisi Pendidikan Indonesia)*.

Not to be missed are charmingly regular government propaganda films which national stations (and all cinemas) are obliged to show. With imaginative titles like *Kayu* (Wood), *Minyak Tanah* (Oil), *Kopi* (Coffee) and *Darah* (Blood), these 20-minute features detail the facts and figures of this month's grain exports, and the country's development.

Travel *Bima* class (the so-called "business" class of the railway services) and you can enjoy further televisual delights on a train journey out of the city. The in-flight movie in these *"eksklusif"* carriages regularly consists of a fuzzy and muffled martial arts film made all the more unwatchable by three sets of screen-obscuring subtitles in Mandarin, English and Indonesian.

Domestic satellite dishes are becoming more and more popular in Indonesia, mainly because of the sex which can be seen on them. A dish of at least nine feet in diameter is needed to pick up foreign stations. When it comes to bare flesh, Indonesian domestic TV is heavily censored, even at the expense of the film's plot (*Basic Instinct* lasted a brief half-hour, but was padded out to extra length with commercials). Scenes of violence, on the other hand, are seemingly encouraged on Indonesian TV, perhaps as an angry substitute for the lack of sex. Laser discs, which cannot be censored, are another popular form of entertainment, and rental stores like *Disc Tara* in *Pondok Indah Mall* do a thriving trade at weekends.

Episodes of foreign shows are often repeated at popular request in Jakarta, so don't be surprised to see the same episode you saw last week; *Baywatch* being perhaps the most requested show. Indonesians are avid TV watchers, they seem to watch absolutely everything with the same intensity. Before subtitles were the norm on foreign shows, the announcer would spend ten minutes before the show commenced telling the viewers what to expect in that particular episode of *I Dream of Jeanie*. There is a tax charged on tellies, graded according to the size of your screen. The fee is nominal, and many people ignore it until door-to-door inspectors come calling.

Of course everything on Indonesian TV and radio is at the whim of the government. Shows are regularly put on hold whenever the government decides to publicize its affairs (usually on a national holiday) and dominates all radio and TV stations for the day.

NEWSPAPERS

Within the printed media, the *Jakarta Post* has long held the place as the most "reliable" English language paper. Published daily, it follows a fixed format of local news, followed by national news, followed by world news. What makes it interesting is the fact that, because it is in English (not always perfect but nearly always long-winded), and presumably because this puts its contents one step further from the government regulators (as well as its own contracted method of "self-censorship"), it can be quite candid in its criticism of state affairs, a situation not seen in other Jakartan publications. Thus the *Jakarta Post* is held as a reliable source for the foreign media to base their reports on, and gauge the day-to-day direction of Indonesia. Aside from its political implications, the *Post* is also a good source for the city's entertainment goings-on, as well as giving us probably the most ludicrous letters page in the southern hemisphere.

Other papers in English exist: the *Indonesian Times* has all but disappeared in recent years, but not so the *Indonesian Observer*, owned by magnate Peter Gontha (who also heads *SCTV* and the satellite station *Indovision*), it seems to be more government-friendly and generally more modern-looking than *Jakarta Post,* and has definitely become a close contender to the *Post*. Of the local *Bahasa Indonesia* press, there is *Kompas* which is a well-regarded broadsheet with Christian/Catholic leanings. *Republika* is a similar paper although rather Islamic-oriented. For stories of *pembantu* who murder their employers, who has been seen holding hands with who, and the generally garish sensationalism of the day, the tabloid *Pos Kota* is the one for you. All bright colours and wonky graphics, it seems to be half-composed of cartoon strips. Far more serious is *Gatra,* which is modelled on *Time* or *Newsweek* (widely available in the bookstores and larger supermarkets) and has a similar approach to reporting.

There was, until June 1994, a journal called *Tempo* which was marketed quite openly as being the Indonesian equivalent of *Time* with all the accompanying social comment and criticism. But one day it proved just a little too critical for the government to accept and the following day *Tempo* (and two others, *Editor* and *Detik*) had their licences withdrawn. It was nothing new, however: a similar scenario was witnessed precisely twenty years earlier with *Indonesia Raya* (along with about ten other publications) being found guilty of reporting too heavily on the student riots which Jakarta had experienced that January in '74. The protesters had been complaining about the state of affairs in their country; about the appalling treatment of the poor, and about a government that wouldn't listen to any of it. And of course any newspaper daring to report such a thing was shut down.

TELEPHONES

Telephones in Jakarta are dodgy to say the least; waiting lists are a mile long, lines are constantly engaged, and party lines irritatingly common. The engaged signal is something you will grow to love when phoning around Jakarta. Numbers seem to change constantly as more lines go up and more people subscribe. But don't keep clicking and clicking the clicker; every time you pick up the receiver, you are put in the queue for a free line. Hang on in there; be patient while you can. Rather than snapping the receiver in two with frustration, try again later.

All calls are cheaper by about 25% after 9 p.m. and on weekends. Most international calls still have to be made via the operator but it's possible, if your local connection box can handle it, to get an IDD (International Direct Dialling) line installed. Yet still expect to be cut off several times during your call, throw a few random callers in, and you have a typical Jakarta telephone conversation. Sometimes you can spend the entire conversation with an engaged signal beeping in the background. That's why more and more people are going "private", opting for the mobile phones which guarantee relative ease of communication.

Wrong numbers are a living nuisance in Jakarta, but with numbers mutating so often and codes shrinking and expanding, it's hardly surprising. Some people, however, take unusual advantage of the unwanted invasions. You may begin to wonder why your *pembantu* (housemaid) is taking so long on the phone when you've already heard her say it was a *salah sambung* (wrong number). So who is she babbling to? A typical such conversation might go like this. Here is what they might be saying:

Hello? *Hallo?*
Hello. *Hallo.*
Can I speak to Djody? *Bisa bicara sama Djodi?*
With who? *Sama siapa?*
Djody. *Mas Djody.*
Oh sorry, you've got the wrong number. *Oh, ma'af, salah sambung Pak.*
Oh, what number's this then? *Oh, ini nomor berapa?*
This is 7231187. *Ini nomor 7231187.*
Whose place is this then? *Ini rumah siapa?*

This is Mr Derek's place. *Ini rumah Pak Derek.*

Mr Derek? Where's he from? *Pak Derek? Orang mana sih?*

He's English. *Orang Inggris dia.*

Oh I see. What about you? Where are you from? *Oh begitu, kalau mbak dari mana?*

Me? I'm Javanese. *Saya? Saya orang Jawa Pak.*

So where's this then? *Rumah ini dimana sih?*

Where? This is Ragunan. *Dimana? Ini di Ragunan Pak.*

Blimey, that's a long way isn't? *Kok, jauh sekali sih?*

Where are you then? *Bapak dimana?*

Me? I'm in Pejompongan. *Saya? Saya di Pejompongan.*

Is Djody one of your family? *Mas Djodi saudara Bapak?*

No, he's just a friend. *Bukan, Dia temen aja.*

and so on … *dan lain lain …*

CLOTHES

For visitors from temperate climates, Jakarta's heat and humidity is a test of endurance, so for the most part, light cotton *baju-baju* (clothes) are best. Natural fibres are definitely the ones to wear, the climate leaving little choice as to what can be worn comfortably. If you travel in air-conditioned vehicles and work in an air-conditioned office all day, you have more flexibility in what you wear. Around the house, a *sarong* is certainly the next best thing to being naked, and certainly the coolest. Shorts and T-shirt come a close second. A single jumper is a good idea, for those times you spend in cooler climes like Puncak or Bandung, or if you really do get ill.

Around town, you are expected to dress a touch more formally. While Jakarta (Kuta beach, Bali aside) is the most easy-going place in Indonesia, where the latest fashions are slavishly followed and tailors work overtime to copy ideas from fashion magazines, a woman in a short skirt or a low cut top, for example, is automatically assumed to be of a lower moral standard than her counterparts in fuller, more modest attire. Revealing clothes it seems only turn more heads than are already turned. Modesty is the keyword. This doesn't mean you need to start wearing a *jilbab* (the veiled Muslim headdress) but for a hassle-free passage, wear bikini tops and g-strings on the beach, not while shopping in Pasar Minggu. Indonesians are generally *bingung* (baffled) at the idea of a woman not wearing a bra. You can prove this point by visiting any public swimming pool, and seeing how many female bathers are still wearing their underwear beneath their costumes.

On formal occasions, long sleeved *batik* shirts are the standard garb for men. Woven silk shirts, known as *tenunan sutra Bugis*, are also common, as are some criminally unflattering safari suits, much favoured by civil servants. For the more fashion-conscious these items are not going to be high on the shopping list. The textiles themselves may be impressive enough, with ornate designs of floral *batik* outlined fastidiously in gold, or large geometric zigzags and stripes on the *tenunan*, yet the huge stiff collars and tight underarms of formal *batik* shirts means they are fairly appalling outfits to be seen out in. And they must be worn loose; untucked and tie-less.

Larger-sized clothes are harder to find. If you can't take advantage of Jakarta's many tailors or the fantastic range of ready-to-wear clothes, you should bring clothing with you. The same is true for underwear and footwear, although a great many department stores these days have pricey imported selections. And they need to: the average young Indonesian is a clear foot taller than his or her parents. Clothes for babies and small children are, however, not a problem to find.

T-shirts are big business in Jakarta. So are slogans. The most obscene phrases imaginable jump out at you from young Jakartan chests in every shopping mall in the city. These often sexy or druggy slogans are clearly lost on the wearers — they certainly wouldn't wear them if they knew the actual meanings. But it's in English, so it must be cool. Young Jakartans are fiercely fashion-conscious and those whose parents can afford it, dress to prove so. High-fashion is an obvious outward sign of success in Indonesia. For the vast majority of youngsters, those born into more humble households, bright and colourful clothing is preferred. Perhaps as a way of compensating for their personal lacking, the hardest-up in Jakarta are often the most striking dressers.

When it comes to getting your clothes washed, you might want to avoid giving your *pembantu* the most prized possessions in your wardrobe to wash. The traditional method of *cucian* (washing) is to scrub the item to death on a "skiffle"-board with several kilos of the all-round detergent, *Rinso*. This, coupled with the all-bleaching power of equatorial sunlight soon leaves you with no option other than buying new clothes to wear.

SARONG

Sarong are not skirts, nor are they kilts. *Sarong* are all-purpose lengths of material which every visitor to Asia will end up wearing at some point. Some *sarong*, particularly in Muslim households, are sewn up into cylinder shapes. Many more are the wrappable, cotton-sort which double as slings, curtains, sick-bags, blankets, pillowcases, shawls, tablecloths, laundry-bags, towels and wall-hangings. You don't need to undress to sleep in a *sarong*, just loosen it and pull it up over your head. *Sarong* are worn formally and informally. They are worn formally to the mosque, when visiting the neighbours at *Lebaran*, and at a *pengajian* (Islamic social function). They are worn informally around the house.

There are as many variations on the theme of *sarong* as there are bananas in Indonesia. For a cross-section of *sarong* across the archipelago, visit the textile floor of the *Pasaraya* department store. Here you will see traditional *sarong batik* from Java, heavier *sarong ikat* from Nusa Tenggara and psychedelic ones from Kuta,

Bali. For cheaper ones try Pasar Mayestik or Pasar Tanah Abang. About the only drawback with *sarong* is how plainly ridiculous they look with shoes on.

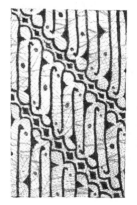 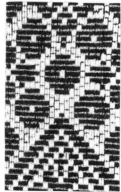 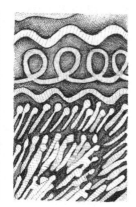

Sarong come in all designs.

SANDALS

Sandals are worn by everyone — rich and poor alike. The sound of dragging flip-flops is a characteristic part of Jakarta's background hum. They cost next-to-nothing to buy and protect your feet from electric shocks, scorpions, the distinct chance of crushing a cockroach underfoot, and slipping over in the *mandi*. But the generally perilous nature of Jakarta's streets means sandals are the wrong things to wear on long walks around town.

Be sure also not to wear your best pair to the mosque, as the risk of getting them nicked is, apparently, high. There's an old joke in Jakarta which asks, "Why don't mosques have organs?" Give in. "Well, if something as *biasa* (normal) as your sandals get nicked, how can anything else survive?"

WATER

Even if you are staying in a hotel or an area of particularly exclusive real estate, your water supply will probably be from a well. Depending on your location, your well will be between 10 and 15 metres deep. If you are lucky, you may hit "clean" water at a lesser depth. Yet if this water hasn't been thoroughly boiled for eight minutes or so, it's best not to risk drinking it. While it's true that the mains supply from the state water company, *Peruahaan Air Minum Jaya* (PAM), is much improved (in the past it was always preferable to use a well), the agony of a *sakit perut* (bad stomach) is simply not worth it. Many households boil up a large pot of water in the evening ready for the next day. Well water, incidentally, is theoretically taxable. And for users of the state water supply, PAM, there is a monthly bill to be paid, payable at the local R.W.'s office.

Jakarta's best water is found in the south of the city. The further towards the coast you get, the more polluted the water becomes. Depending where you are in Jakarta heavily determines the colour of the water. On a good day it's clear and colourless; on a bad day purple, brown, orange or blue. But Jakartans should still count themselves lucky: only 12% of Indonesians have access to "clean" water at all.

Saltwater intrusion is an increasing problem, particularly in North Jakarta. Until recently, most of the city's raw water was taken from the Citarum river in West Java, via the Jatiluhur dam. However, the state water company has had to look further afield for cleaner water, siphoning supplies from rivers in Tangerang, west of Jakarta. But as long as factories and households continue dumping their untreated waste into the rivers and sewers, much of the city's water is going to remain unusable.

There are water purification systems on the market which claim to leave your tap water drinkable; whether they do or not is open to question — boiling is really the only answer. If your water seems to have a high mineral content, and is perhaps a brownish-red colour, it need not necessarily be a health risk, although for your guest's sake you may prefer to filter it to a recognizable colour. The *Departemen Kesehatan* (Health Dept) on Jl Kesehatan, Central Jakarta, will test the quality and contamination level of your water for a reasonable fee. All they need is a couple of litres in a sterile container, and a couple of weeks.

At times during the hot season, the well runs dry. This highlights the importance of getting on well with your neighbours, because it is their supply you will have to borrow while you have your well dug deeper. Either that, or spend a fortune filling your *mandi* with bottled water. Tap water in Jakarta is usually of a painfully low pressure. To combat this, many houses have pressure pumps installed, and elevated water tanks to let gravity lend a hand, and allow at least a little water to be used in the event of a power cut.

These days, of course, every sensible office block and home uses water dispensing machines. These offer both boiling and ice-cold water on tap and, once you have got into the habit, are quite impossible to live without. The most common brands are *Aqua*, *Sosro* and *Oasis*, the bottles of which can be either delivered or bought at a nearby *warung*. It's an idea to clean your dispenser out every now and then; *cicak* and cockroaches are known to find their way through pipes at the back, and up into the bottle with the next "blub, blub, blung" of the machine. You can even keep your machine filled with beer: four to five large bottles of *Bintang* are easily accommodated without going too flat. Drinking water is also sold in bottled form, which is handy for travelling around the city. Some people have been known to carry the same *Sosro* bottle for months, filling it up periodically at every available dispenser. Check for drink seals that might have been tampered with — as the maxim goes, "do not accept if seal is broken". It would be awful to pay for what turns out to be just bottled well water.

Around the house you are going to be using well or mains water for your cleaning and cooking. This is perfectly safe. Well, moderately safe anyway. You can get away with washing fruit in it and it's permissible to brush your teeth with it. You just have to be careful not to swallow any. If you don't like this idea, then use your boiled water or the dispenser.

Either way, with Jakarta's water table being depleted at an ever-decreasing rate, you are advised to try your best to save water. Why then, you ask, do Indonesians so often leave taps running? Simple: the last person to use the bathroom wants everyone to know they are public-spirited enough to care about the next occupant. Of course.

Upon arrival at someone's house, it's more than possible to be given a glass of hot water. This may not seem so appealing, but at least you know it has been boiled. If you want water in a restaurant, ask for *air putih* (white water), *air minum* (drinking water) or *air matang* (cooked water). If you want it cold specify: *yang ∂ingin*. You may wonder when you order a drink with ice, whether the ice has been made from boiled water or not. Good question. This is hard to determine and, although everyone is presumably aware of the dangers of unboiled water, probably irrelevant judging by the way the huge blocks are transported through traffic jams, dragged across streets and dropped on the ground a few times before being put on sale.

MANDI

Get dirty in Indonesia and you'll need the *man∂i*. A home is not a home without one, for this is the bathroom, the water-closet. Basically, it's a water-tank, the size and shape of a large tea-chest, which is built into a corner of the bathroom. The *man∂i* is often a tiled affair, but basic versions are just shaped cement. Indonesian bathrooms always have sloping floors and a hole somewhere for the water to drain. Sitting on the side is the *gayung;* a plastic scoop

The mandi: you'll get used to it.

for pouring water over yourself with. Instructions for use are thus:
1) strip naked 2) fill plastic saucepan with water 3) brace yourself
4) pour all over 5) repeat process to ensure total wetness 6) soap
well all over 7) repeat steps 2 through 4. You get used to it.

Mandi is a verb. It means to shower; to wash; to soap and
scrub. You *mandi* before you *tidur* (sleep); you *mandi* when you
bangun tidur (wake up). If you don't *mandi*, you tend to *bau* (stink).
Mandi is also a noun. You have a quick one. You spend too long in
one. You get stuck in one. You slip over in one. If you go round
someone's house, they ask you if you would like one. An awful lot
of modern houses feature shower units and Western-style baths,
but it's the *mandi* that dominates.

The *mandi* is something worth talking about. A standard
greeting in Indonesia is *"Sudah mandi?"* (Have you bathed yet?)
You have to do it at least twice a day — less just wouldn't be
Indonesian. The water is cold, the country is hot — it feels good
to *mandi*. Exhausted? Hot? Hungover? You'll need a *mandi* to make

you better. In the hot season, for those homes without AC, a *mandi* every ten minutes is the only solution. It's real bathing, after all; it's not showering and it isn't "having a bath". Having a *mandi* is really a continuation of the river washing tradition. They make the most reassuring of sounds, its "splash-splosh" another of the defining characteristics of Jakarta. Hear it early morning and late in the evening; hear it all day.

The unforewarned visitors to Indonesia may be tempted, in their confusion, to climb into the *mandi.* They think: "What do I do? What is this? I'm not sure, maybe I should just climb in. Perhaps the host knew I was coming and filled the bath ready for me, perhaps people in Southeast Asia always have upright bathtubs." Never do this; never climb into the *mandi.* This is very bad form in Indonesia, a social error of massive proportions.

Change the water regularly, otherwise it will quickly become a haven for insect life. Wriggling worm-things and mosquitoes are among the first to set up shop in your *mandi;* their eggs hatching soon after, and you itching not long after that. On the other hand, you might consider keeping a few fish in your *mandi* to eat any passing mosquitoes and eggs. Works a treat but we all know what fish do in water.

TOILETS

There are a distinct lack of public toilets in Jakarta. Using a shop's, restaurant's, hotel's or office's facilities without any other obligation is perfectly acceptable. In many cases be prepared for some appalling lavatorial experiences in Jakarta, particularly in *Padang* restaurants. The toilets at *Soekarno-Hatta* airport are well-maintained, as are ones in star-rated hotels, like the *Hotel Borobudur*, which employ toilet-staff to ensure that the time spent in their *kamar kecil* (small room) is satisfactory. The toilets downstairs at the *Pasaraya* department store in Blok M are less impressive. Although they are staffed and a small fee is charged, which

147

everyone seems to ignore, these *W.C.* (said "way say") feature cubicles with glass doors, particularly off-putting for those hoping for some privacy. Admittedly not plain-clear glass but still, little is left to the imagination.

Do not expect to find paper in Indonesian toilets, as this is still not common practice, although a lot of people are coming round to the idea. No more so than in Jakarta where almost all toilets in bigger buildings are sit-down ones with paper. Traditionally, the left hand is the preferred bottom-wipe in Indonesia: a bucket of water and a left hand is all that's needed. To add to the horror, any toilet paper that does exist is often better binned than flushed, a grim symptom of the dodgy plumbing systems in use throughout much of the city. And in Indonesia, things are flushed up, not down; the standard flush-toilet featuring a pull up handle in the centre of the lid.

Expect some toilets to be "wet" and some to be "dry" — there are no woolly bathmats around Indonesian amenities. True to the bucket-of-water-and-scoop concept of the *mandi*, not to mention the sloping tiled floor, you need to remember to take off your socks before entering. Many offices where Indonesians work alongside foreigners install designated "wet" and "dry" toilets in an attempt to keep both parties happy.

Although the Western style "sit-down" toilet is very popular in Jakarta, the traditional "squatter" is still prevalent. Many Indonesians are *bingung* (perplexed) at the idea of actually sitting down on a toilet. So don't be too surprised to see footprints on the toilet seat. There's nothing essentially wrong with "squatters", but they can be taxing on the calf muscles. And great care must be taken that loose change and wallets don't disappear down the hole — fishing them out is profoundly unrecommendable.

CHAPTER SEVEN

HARSHER REALITIES

Most of Jakarta (and the rest) is constructed around open sewers. Of course, if you're in a hotel or a particular part of a real-estate area like Pondok Indah or Bintaro Jaya, you need not worry too much. For city planners, however, the nature of Jakarta's topography means installing efficient drainage is a nightmare. For most people the *got* (sewers) that do exist, are part of life and, unsurprisingly, a source of mosquitoes, rats and some appalling smells. While it may be true that the general content of a *got* is rain water, *mandi* water and washing-up water (toilet waste is usually fed directly into a septic tank under the house), the combination of humidity and heat results in some memorable *got* smells. And the septic tanks meanwhile, as emptied by official trucks, are routinely dumped unceremoniously and untreated into rivers. Whoops.

Certain times of the year are worse than others. In the wet season, when flooding is common, the sewers overflow, turning streets into rivers. Another potential danger of Jakarta's low-rise nature are wells being dug closer and closer to sewers, increasing the very real risk of health problems.

On a day to day basis, however, you just need to be careful not to fall in the *got* next time you pull up outside your house. It's also very easy to get the wheels of a vehicle stuck down one. And have a look in one next time and be surprised at the little fish apparently enjoying it in there. Worrying.

RUBBISH

Rubbish is a problem in Jakarta: it's more or less everywhere. People chuck it out of car windows, burn it, pile it, sift it, recycle it and deal it. This isn't to say rubbish is lying all around the floors of Indonesian homes — no. But it does seem that any area beyond the confines of one's allotted few square metres is an acceptable place to litter. Outside Jakarta the picture is much the same: rubbish tipped with complete abandon down hillsides and embankments for all to see. Fancy a weekend sailing trip to Jakarta Bay? Think again. Outboard motors face the grave danger of being clogged up with plastic bags — so dense is the pollution. It's no joke, and a condition confined not only to Indonesia: this blatant unawareness of efficient rubbish-control seems to be symptomatic of countries which don't have enough money to go round.

Pemulung — or, in plain English, scavengers — are the characters in the stereotype "Chinaman" hats who poke around in the cement rubbish box outside your house. They make the rounds with large wicker baskets on their backs and picking stick in hand. No one knows who they are, or where they come from, but *pemulung* are Jakarta's unsung recycling heroes. They spend their day sifting through everyone else's domestic waste for metal, plastic, cardboard, paper and glass. (Perfume bottles are a particularly prized find — they can be refilled and resold). *Pemulung* amass huge backlogs of stock at home. This is their capital, after all — someone has got to bring home the bacon.

On a more regular basis is your friendly *tukang sampah*. He is a "professional" rubbish-man, employed on a salary by the local *RT*. He routinely collects the trash from each house and takes it elsewhere. He might refuse, or charge extra, for moving bigger things like tree trunks. Precisely where he takes the garbage is a different matter altogether. In the first instance, it gets piled up in designated piling-up areas before being buried, flattened, bulldozed or burned. Much goes into the sea and stays there. Disposing of what ten million people throw away isn't easy. Space is limited in Jakarta and it has to go somewhere. *Gunung sampah* (rubbish mountains) are constructions to be avoided, especially in areas prone to flooding. Garbage swamps the street and floats off to an unrelated part of town. You wouldn't want to have to push-start a car in two feet of this water.

Methods of giftwrapping are much to blame for the litter crisis. Buy anything, edible or non-edible, and it's wrapped, Sello-taped, pinned, tucked, stapled and wrapped again before you are free to touch it. The raging consumerism that has so mercilessly gripped Jakarta means the packaging industry alone must be worth a fortune. In the past, banana leaves were the all-purpose wrapping paper, but sadly no more. It's those plastic bags with the thousand-year guarantee again.

Some folk complain of a general lack of discipline regarding rubbish. They have a point. The government has attempted to educate the public through TV advertising and campaign slogans like *jangan buang sampah sembarangan* (don't chuck your rubbish everywhere). The long term solution is ultimately the best solution: education. Keep Indonesia tidy.

RATS AND OTHER VERMIN

Unfortunately for its citizens, rats — or *tikus* — are a regrettably common sight in the streets of Jakarta. You'd think that money would guarantee a vermin-free life, but this is not so. Ironically, it seems the richer the area, the bigger the rat. Rich areas may have better draining systems than the average *kampung*, but they also have better quality rubbish outside. And rats love rubbish. The largest may be as big as a foot in length — horrible. In such menacing cases it's not uncommon for cats and other street-dwellers to give way to these giant vermin; to stand to one side while they pass. Not all rats are the giant variety, but there are still enough of them to put you off for life.

You could spend your time preparing traps, laying down *lem tikus* (rat glue) and even shooting them with a pellet gun, but as long as your dwelling is open to the elements at some point (and inevitably it will be) you are going to have your work cut out. The effort might be worthwhile when you assess the damage *tikus* cause: chewed electric cables, food, shoes and furniture. You name it, they sharpen their teeth on it. Just one or two troublesome rats who keep you awake at night playing football in your roof are definitely worth doing something about.

There are rats and there are rats. People have no need, however, to be put off by the tiny, blind voles Indonesians call *cecurut*. They are known as "wall-clingers" (for obvious reasons) and are harmless and vulnerable. Only the most cold-blooded among us could kill a wall-clinger as it squeaks in horror at your presence, and starts running on the spot in its panic to get away. Their panic sometimes gets the better of them, however; shut all the doors and exit points on a panicked *cecurut* and it might well dive down your toilet in desperation. This leaves you with an appalling dilemma: attempt to remove the spinning rodent from your bowl, or simply lift the handle and flush it? Tricky.

CATS

There are also millions of cats throughout the place. Most of them have no tails or at best, only half a tail. There are two conflicting reasons for this. One has it that the cats are simply built this way; i.e., it's genetic. On the other hand, it's rumoured that tails are systematically broken off at birth by whoever is first to come across the litter (a *pembantu* probably). The belief is that, by doing this, there will be more room in the afterlife for human souls, and we could avoid having lots of *kucing* (cats) everywhere, cluttering the place up again. The prophet Mohammed by contrast would not have minded; he was a cat lover and is said to have rather cut a hole out of his prayer mat than disturb his sleeping pussy.

On a more earthly level, you are more likely to be plagued by random litters in your roof, than in the Next World. Stubborn as cats are, your attempts at getting the feline family to "keep moving sir" only results in the cat's reappearance the next day. From here, as the kittens mature and the mother says she can "do no more" for them, only disaster can follow. They crap everywhere, get stuck down drainpipes and worst of all, come crashing through your ceiling when you're lying shut-eyed on the bed. Cats born in the roof do not go away. They hover around your house and live permanently upstairs, flitting from roof to roof and never coming downstairs. But these are the lucky ones; Jakarta's more unfortunate victims are born in the rubbish box outside the house. What a great start in life that must be.

COCKROACHES

As you might expect, Indonesia has more than its fair share of cockroaches. But then, a tropical country is not a tropical country without the sound of cockroaches crunching underfoot. They turn up from nowhere, scuttling silently into your house and up your wall. Big ones get to about two inches in length.

Cockroaches are terrible flyers. When one has been cornered, its only getaway is to take off on a wonky flight across the room, and flop onto the nearest person. A popular place to come face to face with a cockroach is near the drain-hole in the *kamar mandi* (bathroom) where they have probably just spent the last half hour watching you shower. Naked as you are, the feeling of helplessness is overpowering.

Aside from a crunching sound, cockroaches — or *kecoa* — have a distinct smell about them; a kind of rancid, aniseed smell, which only becomes evident once the cockroaches have been and gone. Furniture which has remained unmoved for a while, or piles of untouched laundry in a drawer, for example, are susceptible to this smell. Some say it comes from their urine, others say from decomposition. Either way it's a unique smell which must be experienced to be recognized. Once smelt, never again.

Cockroaches are virtually a way of life in Indonesia. They live behind cupboards, in drains, in the garden, in storage areas, and in cracks and crevices all over the house. With every house open to the elements at some point, there's really no escaping them. Obvious precautions like covers on drains and keeping a clean house will discourage a few cockroaches from entering. While no one loves them, it's better to turn a blind eye to the odd *kecoa* than spend your time chasing every one back outside. If you suffer a plague of them, which can easily occur when a neighbour puts insecticide down their drain and causes the cockroach community to "make a run for it", you are more than justified in enjoying a game of cockroach football.

Other measures can be taken to keep your home relatively *kecoa*-free. The best option being to use one of the many brands of stick-up cockroach killer. These are small, flat plastic things which you stick behind doors, in corners and near drains. Baygon's *Roach Bait Station* is a particularly effective one. The cockroach is attracted to the chemical inside and chooses to go in for a rummage round. The effects of the chemical are not immediate, however, and the cockroach is given time to get home first and have a babble with its friends — so passing the chemical on to the others — before dying.

Whacking them with a shoe may be a satisfying experience but it does leave such a mess across your floor. And it's altogether possible for a lone, twitching leg or other cockroach part to turn up later somewhere on your being: in your pocket, in your shoe or in your hair. Not to mention the appalling gunge which is inside a cockroach, and which is now all over the floor.

Part of the problem is that cockroaches are actually quite big things. It seems so inhumane stamping on them like that. Spraying them with insecticide is also a saddening experience:

the creature squirms and spins around alarmingly on the spot, clearly in great discomfort. A cockroach in the throes of a chemical seizure is even harder to catch as it jerks, stops and jerks like a piston around the room. The chemicals seem to actually speed them up; you can only wait till later to look for the corpse, which will inevitably be on its back somewhere under your bed, legs twitching. Awful.

It has been said that cockroaches would be the only things to survive a nuclear holocaust. The point is certainly proved when you see how resilient they are, how they seem to eat anything — soap, clothes, cement. And of course, when you see how ugly they are.

MOSQUITOES

Mosquitoes (or *nyamuk*) are an everlasting irritation. The only solution, ultimately, is to try your best to ignore them. Good luck. Given the chance, mosquitoes will eat you to death. *Nyamuk* don't care who they bite; where, when or how often. Indonesians, although not totally immune, do seem to possess a certain degree of insusceptibility to the problem. *Nyamuk* seem to take the greatest delight in foreign flesh. The feet are especially prone to bites, but in truth any area of exposed flesh is vulnerable. Particularly vicious are the striped variety, and of these the female is the most feared. In the end, however (when your paranoia has built up), any "small flying thing" becomes a potential danger which must therefore be destroyed.

If you have just been bitten, you need fast relief from the terrifying itch. Rubbing enough *balsam* or mentho-eucalyptus preparation on the area certainly works for most people, and also keeps further *nyamuk* at bay. Certain times of the year are worse than others; in the wet season there are noticeably less *nyamuk* and the ones that do exist are small and ineffectual, their energies being reserved for warmer weather.

Obviously, you should try not to let any still water stay around for long. Change your *mandi* water regularly; this gives them fewer places in which to breed. Avoid having too many clothes lying around: *nyamuk* love clothes. And they love black things. Black cushions will cause them to gather in masses, making the chances of catching several with a single clap of the hand much higher. Preventative measures? Well, there are a number of coils you can burn which are okay if you like a smoke-filled room. The "best" method is to make completely sure that your room has no open windows or holes in the wall. If it has, cover them up. Then bomb your room. Use any number of locally produced sprays. A "good" one being *Baygon* (produced by the German company Bayer, yet curiously banned throughout most of Europe itself). This should be done several hours before you intend to sleep in the room so it doesn't smell and the door should stay shut in the meantime. Too much of these chemicals cause cancer so don't get too trigger happy with a can of fly-spray — it's for killing things after all. Not very eco-friendly but that's the way it goes …

In theory, you should be safe from malaria in Jakarta but it's possible to catch dengue, a similarly soul-destroying, though non-recurring, fever caused by *nyamuk*. You can rub yourself with *obat nyamuk* like *Off* or *Autan*. They are effective but tend to make you feel hotter, not to mention the smell. After a while you may become adept at catching them midair if your reflexes are quick enough. Good luck.

CICAK

Cicak are house lizards that occupy a space in every self-respecting Jakarta home. Bashful creatures they most certainly are, preferring to stick about on walls, behind pictures and in corners. *Cicak* are everywhere — they don't care where they stick. While there might appear to be less *cicak* in a well-off, tightly air-conditioned home than in say, a *Padang* restaurant, all you need do is look behind a

Cicak: they eat mosquitoes.

picture frame and there they all are, hoping for a bite to eat. *Cicak* are wonderful because they eat mosquitoes. *Padang* restaurants are therefore understandably popular with *cicak*.

They are not big; seldom more than four inches, nose to tail. They move in zigzag directions and make clicking sounds to each other. If you startle a *cicak*, they are prone, as a shock tactic, to release their tail, which then wriggles about disturbingly on its own for a while. One of the few drawbacks with these domestic lizards, apart from little birdlike droppings everywhere, is when they die behind a wardrobe without telling you and start making decomposing smells. Not nice.

Less appealing still (and less common) is a gecko known as the *tokek*. It's larger than the *cicak*, light blue-grey in colour with a red back. This particular lizard is heard more than it is seen, and characterized by a distinct call which seems to say *"tokek"* several times, hence the name. Depending on your mood at the time, *tokek* can be heard to say more threatening things. Indeed, the *tokek* plays the same role in Indonesia that the "she loves me, she loves me not" routine does, and can be a deciding factor in any gamble.

In one TV ad for a popular newspaper, a business man was seen making calculated guesses as a *tokek* clacked away in the background; "don't leave it to chance ..." ran the caption.

SMELLS

Jakarta offers the world's nostrils some of the world's richest odours. It would be quite possible to define Jakarta through the diversity of its smells alone. Curiously, since many smells will be unfamiliar to a lot of people's nostrils, first hand experience is really the only way of knowing them.

When things smell good, they are *harum*. When bad, they are *bau*. If you're not sure about something, you should *cium ðulu* (smell first). *Cium* also means "kiss".

Among the good smells floating about the Jakarta air is the smoky, burnt smell of *sate* cooking on charcoal. If you are hungry, it's a genuinely appetizing aroma. If you're not, then it's just the smell of food burning. Passing through one of the fruit markets before midday is a revitalizing experience; smelling every kind of tropical fruit in one go is something worth doing.

Kretek cigarettes are perhaps *the* smell of Indonesia, although some people are understandably nauseated by the strong, sweet smell of burning cloves. The cloves in *kretek* are a smell on their own, although Jakarta is not renowned for the smell of fresh cloves that somewhere like Pelabuhan Ratu is.

Pollution from traffic and industry is a staple smell in Jakarta. Carbon monoxide mixes merrily with the reek of the city's chemical rivers and open sewers. General background smells like these, like the stink of *metromini* and *bajaj*, or the curious fact that certain shopping malls always honk of vomit, are quite forgettable, and after a while, not really a problem.

Another terrible smell Jakarta has to offer is the sickly-sweet smell of dead rats. The smell doesn't become apparent for some time after the animal has died, although those with hypersensitive noses will soon pick up on it. The smell is transitory at first, growing more potent all the time. And just like cockroach urine and deceased *cicak*, it's not necessarily a bad smell at first; only once you have identified the smell for what it actually is, does it become terrible. You may be wondering what "that smell" is for days before the terrible truth dawns, so subtle is the aroma.

Come early evening, and the air fills with the suffocating, acrid smell of burning *sampah* (rubbish). Jakartans seem to have little awareness of the dangers of producing poisonous and potentially carcinogenic smoke, and so everything gets burned with impunity. If your neighbours are filling your house with this evil stench, you have every right to ask them to do it elsewhere. You can try anyway.

The *creme de la creme* of smells in Indonesia is that of the *durian* fruit. The smell of *durian* is phenomenal, it can be smelt on the breath up to eight hours after consumption; even a taxi which has carried someone bearing *durian* will still be smelling days later. The flavour is something different, rather tasty in fact.

DANGER

For a city with such a swollen population, Jakarta is a relatively safe place to be. You are probably safer walking the streets of Jakarta than say, the streets of London or New York. Not that this means you can walk around with a million rupiah in loose change in your top pocket — no. Snatch thieves and pickpockets are genuine threats facing foreigners in Jakarta. If you travel by bus the risk of being robbed is real, particularly of the bag-slashing variety. Gangs are known to operate on buses and it's possible to be confronted, distracted and robbed before you realize what has happened. Rumours of people being hypnotized by thieves have never been taken seriously, but continue to crop up in the press. One woman claims to have been hypnotized by a man on a *metromini*: "Before I knew what was happening," said the woman

"I'd given him all my money and jewellery." Potential scalawags are likely to be bolder in their attempts if they think you have been drinking, so take extra care coming out of discos, bars and the like. Reports of violent crimes against foreigners are, on the whole, comparatively rare, however.

Obvious precautions should be exercised. Lock everything up and keep your eyes peeled. Those who flaunt it are asking for trouble. Vivid displays of gold and glitter only invite attention. When driving around town it pays to get into the habit of locking your door — many taxi drivers habitually do it as soon as you get in. Intersections and markets are crowded areas and it's no surprise to find your vehicle surrounded by hawkers while you wait for the lights to change.

Should you be approached in the street by someone you don't know, you needn't assume they are going to con you out of every last rupiah. Con artists are not common. People are unlikely to try and sell you *Monas*, if they do, tell them you've already got one. Con artists usually take the domestic approach, going from house to house with an envelope and mysterious list of names and donations to the charity of their choice. Quite often, these are genuine appeals for help, making it harder to distinguish when to give and when not. Although confidence tricksters are rare, when they do occur, they like to make up for lost time, as graphically illustrated by the infamous Eddy Tanzil — perhaps Indonesia's most wanted man — who somehow managed to walk off with an alleged 1.3 trillion rupiah. But that's another story.

On a bad day, Jakarta seems to be an accident waiting to happen. The squalid overcrowding in most of the city's deathtrap *kampung* spells Bubonic Plague followed by the Great Fire of Jakarta. Neither have happened yet but they wouldn't be the most surprising events in modern Indonesian history if they did. The Indonesian's own attitudes towards danger can be perplexing to say the least. People have what has been described as a "fatalistic" approach to living, oblivious to all Western notions of lunacy. This is obvious in the way, for example, that uncovered car workshops do heavy-welding on street corners; sparks flying everywhere, children running amok and not a protective-goggle in sight. Electrical appliances, when not regarded with the utmost suspicion, are treated in the same carefree way. The Indonesian death-wish is most apparent in the way they drive. It's incredible there are not more fatalities — perhaps there are. Perhaps the papers have given up reporting traffic accidents.

When tragedy does occur it is accepted with a far more "oh well, that's old whatshisname done with" sort of attitude. The family of a recently deceased individual will invariably treat the circumstance of the death with great superstition. Their way of coping is to view the death of a loved one as if it had been planned this way. Solace can be taken in knowing that there was nothing they could have done to prevent it. It's not that Indonesians are any less emotional, but accidents do happen and life must go on.

Probably the greatest danger in Jakarta is that of traffic. Since pedestrians are given little consideration, you are more likely to be run over by a *metromini* than mugged, raped, attacked, shot, cheated, kidnapped, blackmailed or murdered.

DRUGS

Drugs are illegal in Indonesia. Like much of Southeast Asia, the possession of narcotic drugs is considered a particularly serious offence. Singapore and Malaysia both have the death penalty for drug crimes, and stories of young travellers imprisoned for attempting to bring drugs out of Thailand have been well documented in recent years. The death penalty under Indonesian law is reserved for the carrying, sending, transporting, importing, exporting, selling, buying, delivering and receiving of any derivatives of opium. Specifically, morphine, heroin and any part of the *bunga madat* (poppy plant) which has been cultivated or used in the preparation of an opiate. Personal use of opiates and other "hard" drugs carries a maximum sentence of three years under the Indonesian Drug Law of 1976. Personal use of marijuana carries a penalty of two years, while any form of dealing in the drug carries a maximum sentence of twenty years, plus an unspecified fine. The law also states that foreign citizens will be permanently expelled from Indonesia, once the sentence is served.

There is no open drug use in Jakarta, people are far too wary of the consequences to make a display of it. Persistent rumours that police will reward healthily anyone willing to forward information concerning drugs has led to a state of widespread paranoia, rendering them an unmentionable topic of conversation. Despite all this, drug use is quite rife.

Most of the *ganja* (marijuana) to reach Jakarta is understood to be grown in north Sumatra; regular busts are made on the Sumatran trail, either at source or en route to Jakarta. Other occasional supplies are said to originate from areas surrounding Bandung, Surabaya and Bali. Indonesian marijuana itself is said to consist of an unpredictable mix of leaves, stems, seeds and flowering tops, with everything else thrown in too; chicken feathers, string and even cockroaches. Its distinct "bonfire" smell is instantly recognizable: the occasional whiff surfacing in the air, especially in *kampung* areas, only to be masked at once by the million other smells of Jakarta. There is, however, no smoke without fire. Rumours of police informers are not without a grain of truth; hotel and restaurant owners are required by law to turn in anyone using drugs on their premises.

The most commonly abused substances among the urban poor of Jakarta are pills, mainly uppers and downers, still readily obtainable from the *apotik* (pharmacy) and smaller street-stall outlets. While over-the-counter drugs have long been the mainstay of Jakarta's long-haired community, their grandparents would have chewed betel-nut for kicks. A mildly stimulating effect is had after chewing the right combination of *pinang* nut and *kapor sirih* (powdered lime). Unfortunately it destroys teeth and gums, and turns saliva bright red — not a pretty sight.

In 1993, Ecstasy hit the headlines. It came to public attention via a popular young actress called Ria Irawan, whose Jakarta home was the scene of Indonesia's first Ecstasy-related death. It seems her ex-boyfriend, high on what pathologists later described as "an unidentified amphetamine-like substance", had collapsed and died during a party at her house. Rumours that a "bag of pills" had been promptly disposed of in a nearby river were unconfirmed, and although Ria's career suffered a nose-dive and she never again played the role of celebrity escort to prestigious visitors like Mick Jagger and BB King, the case was never completely solved. Not so Zarima. A less fortunate and lesser known celebrity than Ria, she was jailed in February 1997 for her involvement with Ecstasy. Reports say she went down smiling.

The media was quick to latch onto this new social monster, and Jakarta was gripped in an Ecstasy scare. They claimed the problem was an imported one; that Ecstasy could not be manufactured in Indonesia. A number of bars and discos, particularly those frequented by foreigners like the Hard Rock Cafe and Tanamor were raided, and it was reported that three foreigners, including a Dutchman and a Jamaican, were arrested for dealing the drug. This, coupled with the murder of an important military figure by a gang of street hoodlums, led to a widespread police operation in the early part of 1994. Known literally as *Operasi Bersih* (Operation Clean-up), it was the most thorough purgation of Jakarta in years. Thousands of pills were seized, kilos of *ganja* gathered, hundreds of people arrested, and in a fanatical show of strength, thousands of bottles of beer and spirits, mostly seized from *warung*, were bulldozed live on television.

Ecstasy, however, has not gone away, in fact it has only become more popular. Several more E-related deaths have been reported since the Ria Irawan case, and use of the drug, known locally by Jakarta's sizable percentage of rich-kids as "Satan", is making someone, somewhere very rich. Attempts to curb the illicit trade have been hindered by rumours of police redealing the drug. Threats to close the nightspots where trafficking flourishes have been hesitant, mainly due to the substantial revenue that Jakarta's 3,000 or so nightspots generate. And it's rumoured some of Jakarta's more upwardly mobile names are believed to be responsible for keeping supplies sure and steady. Such is life in modern Jakarta; the higher up you are up the social ladder, the more you get away with. Big time dealers are protected by their status; police busts always focus on the small fry.

Bali, with its large expat community and constant influx of tourists, used to be the place to get drugs. These days it's Jakarta, with its emerging class of demanding super-rich kids, that deals the dope.

WESTERNIZATION

Indonesia shows all the stress of a country trying its best to cope with an assault of Western ideals. Nowhere in the country is this more apparent than in Jakarta. The predominant influence is American as opposed to European; when it's the West that's referred to, it's America that's meant. The relentless influx of American movies and TV shows only reinforces the basic financial gap between not only Indonesia and the West, but between the rich and poor in the republic itself.

From an early age the children of modern-day Jakarta develop a love affair with all-things American. As they get older the love affair becomes less outwardly obvious — though no less intense. With the media relentlessly pushing the all-American image at every opportunity; on every TV channel; in every shopping mall, it seems that only the worst excesses of Western culture are realized. And while it might seem "cool" to the young

Jakartan — that they are somehow a cut above the rest by being "Western" — it is wholly apparent, for the person flying in unannounced, that much of the city's young have ended up looking virtually identical.

When President Bill Clinton came to Jakarta for the 1994 APEC conference, he was driven on a very specific route through the city. Many of the city's eyesores were strategically avoided. Prior to his arrival, *kampung* areas and the like, had been boarded up and the major thoroughfares given a complete whitewash. What the organizers hadn't anticipated was Clinton's unscheduled stop-off at a south Jakarta *kampung* to fulfil his apparent desire to shake hands with the "real" people of Jakarta. What were the organizers trying to hide from the visiting President? Poverty? Beggars? Massage signs? Open sewers? Rubbish mountains? Sweat shops? *Metromini*? *Bajaj*? Jakarta itself?

Driving through the so-called "Golden Triangle" area comprising Jl Thamrin, Jl Gatot Subroto and Jl Rasuna Said, you might be fooled into thinking you were in Singapore. For this is the modern face of Indonesia; the bit they wanted you to see and write home about. The visiting business person who doesn't stray too far outside this "golden triangle" might well believe Jakarta is just another Southeast Asian city "made good" by foreign investment and the plundering of natural resources. This is as modern as it gets. Here, standing tall, are mirrored skyscrapers, five-star international hotels and Singapore-style shopping centres. But lying low behind each office block are the bits you are not supposed to notice: the sprawling *kampung* of Jakarta where traditional Indonesian village life goes on unabashed, and more than likely, where most of the skyscraper's employees live.

In many respects, Jakarta is as modern as it gets. A raging consumer mentality sees the latest fashions religiously followed, the newest American slang words practised, the current pop songs memorized, and the "smartest" drugs abused. But this is only a tiny part of the picture that Jakarta is in real life. When viewed in the entire context of Indonesia, the Golden Triangle and its "important" little people are practically invisible.

There has to be a high degree of conflict in the lives of Indonesians as their country, especially its capital, is flooded with Western influences and ideas. Many Indonesians today walk with one step in the past and the other in the future — one half turned on by the attraction of being up with the times, the other half desperate to stay loyal to the past.

In 1991, McDonalds arrived to great fanfare in Jakarta. It was an immediate success with the young public, but it wasn't to everyone's taste or pocket, with meals costing the proverbial week's wages. During the fasting month of Ramadan, curtains are drawn across the large windows so as to not offend passing Muslims: Ronald McDonald bowing down to Mecca.

Some of that conflict is expressed in the lyrics of Husein Bawafi who, singing in 1955, had this to say about the changing times in Indonesia:

Funny Style

The world spins
The times change
The period now
Is very trendy
With girl's things
And boy's too
And trousers so tight
You can't get your feet in

Hey! Look at that ...
Make no mistake
The one with white foundation
Wearing low cut dresses
Hair in curlers
And all powdered up
She wanders aimlessly around

Girls these days
Really like chatting
Gossiping and arguing
Wearing lipstick
Hair in rollers
They say they're anti-West
But they like rock 'n' roll

The decades since independence have been much like Europe in mediaeval times; witness to the inauguration of a number of rich, powerful families who are destined to be rich and powerful long into the future. Recent years in Jakarta have also seen the emergence of a materialistic "middle-class" which seems prepared to do anything to make its "fortune". The attitudes that accompany such material pursuits are at fantastic odds with the traditions of politeness, self-control and sharing-alike that are so typical of Indonesia, and it might be assumed that this new form of "super-Indo" is all too ready to disregard its heritage for the sake of a pair of designer shoes but, fortunately, this isn't quite the case.

But in truth, who is the loser in this mad game of monopoly? The *kampung* family in central Java, prosperous on the fertile land of their ancestors; safe and secure within their elaborate system of sharing-alike, and free from the unsustainable demands of Western culture? Or the mobile-phone wielding "businessman" in central Jakarta, clueless of his own cultural heritage, illiterate in the language of his origins, and prepared, without apparent hesitation it seems, to sell the land his parents grew up on?

While notions of self-opinion and self-expression are certainly taking root, these influences needn't be considered quite so corruptive. For the most part, Western ideals are absorbed into mainstream ways of thinking. Just as Islam, when it was first brought to Java, underwent a gradual transformation that was distinctly Javanese, so the great majority of Western ideals are woven into the larger Indonesian scheme of things. The traditions of 200 million people are, after all, a lot to compete with.

As the dominant religion in Indonesia, Islam has never been over-impressed with the West and its ways. The rise in fundamentalist thinking in Jakarta has only added to the conflict of Westernization. This uncomfortable way of living, this duality of conflicting attitudes, modern and traditional, came to a head in 1991 during the Gulf War. When Indonesia was called on to show its support, it was reluctant to show allegiance to either the USA or Saddam Hussein. Being an unofficial Islamic country (although it has the world's largest Muslim population, it's categorically *not* an Islamic state), it was expected that Indonesia would show its support for Iraq. (Indeed, Muslim militants planted a bomb, which was later diffused, at the American ambassador's residence). At the same time it had to be remembered that Indonesia depended on America for its foreign aid, which incidentally, was (and still is) an awful lot of money.

The chance to afford quality material items, those advertised on TV every day, is something everyone deserves, yet only the tiniest proportion of the population is, at present, able to do so. But, as ex-President Suharto explained in 1997, imbalances between those who have been able to profit from the country's development drive and those who have been left behind are a fact of life: "Sometimes, some people are able to make the best use of the opportunities earlier than others," he said, "development activities in any country usually open new opportunities which some people can take better advantage of." Yet the fact remains: there are some immorally rich people in Jakarta.

This massive financial imbalance between Indonesia and the West has been highlighted, among others, by American civil rights leader Jesse Jackson who, in July 1996, drew world media attention to the *Reebok* shoe factory in West Java. Clearly bewildered at the way designer sports-shoes were being manufactured in what he accurately described as "sweat shop" conditions, he called for something to be done. How, he argued, could a billion dollar multinational possibly justify selling its products at top price after manufacturing them at such low cost? He described this exploitation of Indonesia's cheap labour as nothing less than immoral; a living outrage. More depraved still is the truth that such misuse of people is merely indicative of all developing countries.

Not all exploitation is bad, however. The land that makes up Indonesia, being so rich in natural resources, has a lot to offer: gold, diamond, silver, mercury, manganese, phosphate, nickel, tin, coal, oil and gas, are all found in fantastic proportions. The problem, however, is getting at them. Cue foreign investors. This is the real reason Indonesia has remained in the West's good books. For despite worldwide coverage of a seemingly never-ending abuse of civil rights, foreign investors just can't wait to get their hands on the wealth that is under the ground. Foreign mining companies supply the required technology, and the deal is a certain split of the winnings. In this way, all sides are kept happy, providing jobs and racking up profit. Western workers, however, command Western salaries, and uncomfortable situations can arise, where Westerners are working alongside locals, doing the same job yet receiving vastly different salaries. Ten times the difference might be a conservative estimate. It can't be good for an Indonesian's self-esteem to get a comparatively lousy salary, after having studied for it. It's genuine cause for concern, particularly when expatriate workers have no formal qualifications. But then, if the work-visa section weren't so ready to accept bribes, perhaps the official line "if it can be done by an Indonesian, then it must be done by one" wouldn't be so openly abused.

Money, as always, is the root of the problem. People see it, hear about it, learn that their country is getting more and more of it, and that they can get a bit of it too if they work at it. The attitude is most prevalent in Jakarta; more people are *gila uang* (money mad) here than anywhere else in Indonesia. And their frustrations

169

just keep mounting. Small change, cheesy-red money does the rounds; getting circulated and recirculated, from the *rumah* to the *warung,* to the bus, to the *ojek,* and back again, it goes round and round. The big money is sent abroad or kept in safer places than the average Indonesian bank. You see, in Jakarta, not even banks are safe. In 1991, one of the biggest private banks, *Bank Suma*, which had hefty investments in and around Jakarta, suddenly collapsed, much to everyone's disappointment. Yet the economic boom of the early '90s was certainly the time to open a new bank, and *Suma* merely reopened under a new name. Six years later, however, overspending and overborrowing had left the economy in ruins. With debts that could not be repaid, the government was forced to follow the advice of the International Monetary Fund, and close down all but the most established banks.

And so the chase for money and the hope of becoming somehow "American" goes on. It must be said, however, that Indonesia is probably far too resilient to be too deeply touched by Western influence. For Western influence is just the latest in a long line of foreign influence. Ultimately, just one of many.

Chapter Eight

BEING FOREIGN

BULE

If you are white and you are in Indonesia, you are a *bule*. A *honky*, a *white-boy*, a *snowflake*, a *gaijin*, a *hindung-ee*, a *gringo*, a *farang*, a *paleface*, a *howie*, a *whitie*, a *big nose*, a *mister*. You are worldly, educated and probably important. You represent a world of wealth, power, peace, free speech, easy living, free sex, drink, drugs, freedom and fun. You also represent some three centuries of colonial rule.

The word *bule* is widely used by Indonesians when referring to Caucasians — *orang bule*. There are alternatives: *orang Barat* (Westerner); *orang asing* (foreigner); *orang Spanyol* (Spaniard). And to some in *Jawa Tengah* (Central Java), Westerners are still *wong Londo* (Dutch) and still smell of cheese and onion. Yet from the *kampung* (village) to the *kantor* (office), *bule* remains the common term for the white-skinned. It shouldn't be misconstrued as a racist term. Rarely is *bule* used in a derogatory way, although in theory that's quite possible, but still it continues to offend the sensibility of Westerners; long-term expats and short-term visitors alike. This one small word highlights the sometimes enormous world of difference in attitude and outlook between life in Indonesia and life in the West.

Bule simply describes something pale. A pair of old jeans could be described as *bule* for example. Many dictionaries define the word as slang for "albino". Besides, in Indonesia and especially Jakarta, people are very aware of their origins and have a strong sense of regional identity. They like to stereotype the people of different regions, perhaps merely to reinforce their own identity. The fact someone is *orang Jawa* (Javanese) or *orang Sunda*

(Sundanese) is a justifiable reason for all kinds of behaviour. The same is true for *bule*.

It seems no one is happy with the way they were born. To be white in Indonesia is considered an asset, to be dark means you have spent too long outside labouring for your living. In short: the darker you are, the poorer you are. Skin-bleaching products are big sellers among the fashion-conscious of Indonesia, as is heavy white foundation. In its most rudimentary form, a whack of talcum powder over the face and shoulders does the trick. Unfortunately, smothering the natural dark of Indonesian skin means it takes on an unglamorous grey complexion. Conversely, many white people's sole priority when visiting a hot country like Indonesia is to get a suntan, go brown and do everything not to look white.

For the most part, life as a foreigner in Jakarta is in your favour, even for the hippiest *bule miskin* (slang: cheapskate, backpacking traveller). For the most part you represent money, and you have a big nose.

MAKING FRIENDS

You won't find it hard to make friends in Indonesia. It's as easy as showing your face; as easy as going out your door. You will find most people are more than happy to make conversation with you. The average person in the street should therefore be considered a friend, not an enemy. They'll look out for you if you look out for them. But being so visibly "different", i.e., taller, whiter, uglier and hairier, you are nothing but a prime target for attention. You might decide that today is not the day for making friends, but no one has told your potential new "friend" this.

Although generally friendships are made in a somewhat instant manner in Indonesia, many Jakartans these days are totally indifferent to the presence of a *bule*. To a degree anyway. The very fact that many trendy young Indonesians choose to ignore foreigners is a reaction in itself. And this is not necessarily a sign of the times: Jakarta has never been easily impressed, having seen it all before.

You might wonder how deep these friendships run; how sincere they really are. Is it simply because you are different? Is that why they are talking to you? Not really. On what is the world's most densely packed island, you don't have much choice in the matter, other than to try and get on with one another. The system is self-supporting; any problems or disputes are settled fairly and squarely through general consensus. It's a case of "the more, the merrier". The more people there are with you, the easier it is to merge into a single collective *orang* (person). Indonesians like to lose themselves in a crowd, it's the finest living example of ego-loss there is. Neighbours look out for one another in Jakarta. *Maling* (burglars) don't stand a chance once someone has alerted the neighbourhood to the fact and hollered "*maling*!" What happens next, however, once the misfit has been confronted, is a lot less friendly.

Jakarta is a good place for paranoids to overcome their fears. With everyone — many of them total strangers you will never, ever see again — looking at you, talking to you and quizzing you about your life so far, almost all the time you are outside your home, you will soon be cured.

As real as friendships are in Indonesia, there may be times when you feel the friendship is going nowhere; that you never seem to talk about anything; that it all seems superficial. It may seem like your friend is pampering to you, or is over-keen to please you. This is just the way of the people; to keep everything smooth and everyone unoffended. Once everyone agrees upon this basic principle, life is a lot smoother and everyone gets to snivel in unashamed veracity.

Whereas the English, whenever stuck in a lift with someone they don't know, talk about the weather, Indonesians try to talk

173

about nothing. They might ask about the other person; whether they have eaten yet, prayed yet or bathed yet. Alternatively, they might talk about traffic jams, or about some good rice that's going around. But, like the rest of the world, they are more than likely these days to talk about what was on television last night.

Indonesians practise what they call *basa-basi* or rather "nothing talk", in which they strive their hardest not to offend anyone by speaking about absolutely nothing. In these conversings special care is taken that no direct reference is made to another person. The subject matter is kept, at best, vague. Very often in Indonesia no one is really sure who is talking to who and what indeed they mean, if anything at all.

HASSLE

A lot of visitors and expatriates complain of hassle in Indonesia. Why is this? Do they mean that everyone stares at you, or at least does a double take? Do they mean that everyone wants to talk to you and ask you the same questions over and over? Do they mean that people are always trying to sell you something and then overcharging you because you are Western and supposedly wealthy? Do they mean that Western women, especially blonde-haired, blue-eyed ones, are in for a hard time? Do they mean that a couple which is one part Western and one part Indonesian is open to an unfair amount of verbal abuse and suspicion? Well, probably.

It's important to consider each of these problems in context, that is, from the Indonesian point of view. From here we may be able to understand better why such complaints arise.

As for the issue of being stared at, it's certainly true that while you are in Indonesia, you are unlikely to be able to move around unnoticed. It's not such a problem in Jakarta, especially in the places where a *bule* is expected to go. That is: the well-to-do residential areas like Pondok Indah and Bintaro Jaya, the offices stretching along Thamrin to Sudirman, major shopping areas like Plaza Indonesia, and Sarinah, the bars and pubs in Jl Faletahan, Blok M and of course, the big hotels. In these places you are guaranteed relative anonymity, especially if walking alone and look as if you know where you are going. However you can still expect a "hello mister" every few minutes.

The "hello mister" factor increases tenfold when you stray from the above places or enter a *kampung*. It increases a hundred-fold when you leave Jakarta. For many Indonesians, "hello" and "mister" are probably the only words of English they know. They are keen to say hello and make a connection with you. They are being bold, nothing more. Take the example of Jakarta's schoolkids who like to hang about in intimidatingly large groups when school lets out. True to the group mentality that is so peculiar to Southeast Asia, Jakarta schoolkids, particularly the teenage boys, love to shout obscenities at a passing Westerner. Hanging out in a group, they are free from all responsibility (and, some would say, a brain) and any individual actions are diffused within the group. In any other situation, and on an individual basis, the story is different.

"Hello mister"

175

Often the only Westerners Indonesian people see are those in trashy American TV shows where everyone shoots each other and women jump into bed with the hero at the end. Pornography is illegal in Indonesia but any that does manage to circulate is invariably of Western origin. This limited media portrayal of *bule* is commonly the only association an Indonesian can make with a white person. Dress modestly and you shouldn't gain so much attention. Revealing dress is just asking for hassle. Let's be honest, being a *bule* means not only being a target but a walking bull's-eye. While *bule* are conspicuous by definition, some Indonesians say that foreigners invite a lot of the attention on themselves — that they dress inappropriately, talk too loudly and too often make an unknowing display of their wealth.

As for staring, Indonesians stare at all sorts of things, all the time. It's quite a normal thing to do, and not considered especially rude. In fact so aware are young Jakartans of this, that they go out on a Saturday simply hoping to be stared at. It's all part of the course; all part of life's great television. A popular pastime in Indonesia is an afternoon spent *cuci mata* — staring.

Bule are generally considered an attractive breed despite certain bad reputations they might have. In a country where almost 200 million people have black hair and few men can grow a decent beard, to see a woman with long blonde hair and a man with a bushy beard is something worth getting an eyeball of, especially when they are a head taller than everyone else around.

As for being talked to by complete strangers, this is certainly true but not something to worry about. Again people are simply being bold. They might want to practise their English, which is why you get asked the same questions again and again: "Where are you going?", "Are you married?", "Where do you come from?", "Which one is better, Indonesia or your home country?" "How many children have you got?", "Do you like rice?" That kind of thing. Even if you can speak *Bahasa Indonesia*, there won't be much variation in the interrogation. Many Indonesians are keen to have a foreign "friend" and, in light of Jakarta's ongoing facelift, hopefully distinguish themselves from the crowd.

At the same time an Indonesian is supposed to know their limits when mixing with Westerners. An Indonesian girl seen accompanying a Western male is open to suspicion: she might be considered a girl of low moral standards. She might well be called *perek*, the acronym for *perempuan eksperimen* ("experimental" woman) — perhaps the worst thing an Indonesian woman can be called. This goes to highlight the negative reputation that *bule* have; that they are promiscuous and unfaithful. The girl might also be considered to be "only in it for the money", that she would do anything for *uang*. The fact that Jakarta has more brothels than the average European capital is apparently not taken into consideration.

Indonesia is a country with limited access to world affairs for the average citizen, not much money per capita, a large and religious population, and where independence from colonial rule is something your grandparents still remember. Try and take these factors into account next time you feel hassled. Rarely are people out to deliberately upset or offend you — rarely.

PRIVACY

Contrary to popular expatriate belief, words for "privacy" do exist in *Bahasa Indonesia*. The words are *kebebasan pribadi*. Admittedly, they aren't the most overused words in the language, the meaning (rather than the spelling) escaping the average citizen. Western notions of "respect my space, please" fly clean out the window in Indonesia, and foreigners need to be aware of this fact — otherwise they are likely to lose their minds. One example might be if, on a rare occasion, you manage to find a relatively empty bus with empty seats. You can guarantee that the next two people on the bus will shoehorn themselves in next to you, even when other

177

seats are available and your seat itself is only a two-seater. Strange for some; normal for others.

Indonesia holds all kinds of world records. It's a country of superlatives: the world's largest Muslim country, the largest archipelago, and Java the most densely populated island on the planet. If everyone in Java stood at an equal distance from each other, each square mile would have a couple of thousand people in it. Privacy is not therefore the most accessible commodity in Java. Walking down a Jakarta side street in the late evening, you may think you are walking alone in the darkness. But let you eyes get accustomed to the dark and you soon become aware of the very many people *lagi jongkok* (crouching) in the dark. Sometimes it's only the glow of their *kretek* cigarette that gives them away. People are everywhere in Jakarta. The only way to guarantee privacy is to close the door behind you. You may never get used to it.

You would assume that home is the one place where you could relax without comparative strangers around you. You would be wrong. More than likely your every step is tracked by a shadowy *pembantu* (housemaid), cleaning up after you, emptying ashtrays after a single cigarette-end, answering the phone before you can get to it and waiting for you to finish in the bathroom so they can mop up after you. Just as you instructed them to do. The irony of the routine that you instigated is that you find yourself avoiding the *pembantu* because you want privacy. You don't want to see anyone. You want to relax at home. You want to put your feet up, sit with your legs apart, pick your nose, leave the toilet door open and do the million other things you can only do with family and close friends, or on your own. It's imperative you make it clear to your *pembantu* when you do, and when you don't want privacy. If you don't like seeing people when you have just woken up, make this clear also. Any kind of rule can be made, there are no fixed job descriptions for the *pembantu*. It's your home, you pay the wages, you make the rules — it's your sanity after all. But then if your sanity is hinged so precariously around maintaining your privacy, you are probably better off having nothing at all to do with the *pembantu* world.

Between people of the same sex, touching is standard practice. When another man rests his hand on your leg during a conversation, the immediate Western response is to recoil in horror. It doesn't seem natural. Conversely, physical contact between men and women is rarely seen in public. This leads to the bizarre situation where two men hold hands on one side of the street, quite obviously good friends, while on the other side, a married couple strive to keep a distance from each other. The space that it seems Westerners need around them to maintain mental stability is virtually nonexistent to an Indonesian. Look at any passing bus, and wonder at the packed conditions inside.

If you are seen doing things alone in Indonesia, people will assume something is wrong with you. People hardly ever do things alone: even on the most mundane task, Indonesians prefer to have a friend come along. Everyone knows everything about everyone else in this country, and no more so than in the *kampung* (itself only a extensive outgrowth of two or three families). Here, even a girl's first *lampu merah* (menstrual period) is celebrated by the preparation and giving out to neighbours of *nasi kuning* (yellow rice) — the all-purpose Indonesian party-stuff. Food appears mysteriously in doorways: the leftovers of a nearby rice-rave. Neighbours know what is in one another's fridges. They know who does what, who works where, who fancies who, what goes on with who, where, what time and how often. Everything.

OTHER WESTERNERS IN JAKARTA

Westerners come to Jakarta for all sorts of reasons. A few opt to live here indefinitely, while some give up after six months. Some come as tourists, almost always passing through Jakarta on their way to better places, and some are "sent", perhaps as part of a multinational "package deal". Other people come looking for work, recommended to the place by a friend. Others decide after a holiday that they like Indonesia and decide to extend their visas. Some return time and again to Jakarta, keeping one foot in the door, as it were. Some come looking for love, or rather the guarantee of cheap sex. Some are tax evaders, some are gay, some die here. Some don't know why they came in the first place, some just can't remember. Some probably don't want to remember. For some it's like dropping out, throwing in the towel, giving up — too sad to face life in their own world. To each his own.

Some have more specific reasons for living in Jakarta: that they want to climb every volcano in the country, or they need a base to collect frogs, lizards and snakes from. The opportunity to spend time exploring the virtually inexhaustible amount of jungle, mountains, coastlines, hot springs and wildlife that make up Indonesia is presented to you on a plate. While travel in Indonesia may not be as hassle-free as it could be, you stand a greater chance of seeing elephants in the wild by being based in Jakarta than you would by living in London.

Jakarta offers the best work opportunities for everyone, be they Javanese, Sundanese, Batak, Betawi, Ambonese, Irianese, Sasak, Diak, Korean, Japanese, Australian, American, Irish or English, all of whom over the years have found a niche in Jakarta and, in their own ways, left their mark. Oil workers comprise a large percentage of Jakarta's expat population, although a great many are in managerial positions, having been transferred to Jakarta by their company. They are invariably male and have wives and children with them. Expat wives in Jakarta have a vibrant social scene going. There's the well established American Women's Association in Cilandak and similar scenes organized by British and Australian women alike. Work as an English language teacher is probably the most viable option for those who come looking for a job on spec.

For people who choose to live and work in Jakarta (as opposed to those who get sent) a variety of lifestyles are embraced. Some live well and spend well, eating in the five-star hotels every night and regularly jetting off to more obvious holiday locations. Some remain exclusively "expat" in their socializing, choosing to mix only with other foreigners, while others marry Indonesians and live a thoroughly Jakartan lifestyle. Some learn fluent *Bahasa Indonesia*, *Bahasa Sunda* and *Jawa* and spend their time discussing the price of rice with the *RT,* while others progress no further than *Bahasa Beer* (*satu lagi* — one more) or *Bahasa Taxi* (*stop disini* — stop here).

The reasons that keep people staying in Jakarta, or returning, are therefore many. The chance of having a comparatively affluent standard of living, the likes of which might not be attainable else-where, is certainly high on everyone's list. Although some things, like cars or glasses of beer, for example, are disproportionately expensive, it can be safely said, despite radically fluctuating inflation rates, that money can still be made to go much further. Take for example Rp 50,000 which, even at its weakest in 1998 when it was worth only about US$5, could still buy you 25 kg of rice, or fifty meals from a street vendor, or hire a maid for a month or a car for a day, or pay for ten haircuts.

Some Westerners let the attention, standard of living and relative prosperity go to their heads. They become "virtually famous". People who are totally anonymous in their own country become celebrated individuals in no time at all in a place like Jakarta. You see, you are always guaranteed a second look in the city. Boys and girls alike are instant superstars: free to re-invent themselves as something far more interesting than they really are. There are make-believe sugar-daddies, would-be white-boy gigolos, pretend gangsters and desperadoes. Some even delude themselves into believing they are Indonesian, speaking a cari-cature of the language with all the well-studied mannerisms of a local. Some surround themselves like they had only dreamed of previously. Some live a life of overindulgence, imagining they are living like a king, surrounded by faithful servants pampering to their every need. Very sad. There's nothing essentially wrong in becoming "famous" in Jakarta, but you may be in for a let down when you move on.

It's important therefore to keep your head in Jakarta. Very generally speaking, Asian people consider the white skin and round eyes of Westerners an attractive way to be built. Likewise, very generally speaking, white people consider the dark Asian beauty a natural asset. These factors, in combination with the fact that much of the country's people are poor, mean that propositions — often outrageous propositions which belie the apparent *kesopanan* (politeness) of the Indonesian character — can come fast and furious. On occasion then, it can be hard to establish whether people are reacting to you as the person you are, with all the character traits you are convinced make you unique from the next person, or simply as a foreigner who represents a distant, strange and unquestionably more affluent world.

The lure of the East-Asian sex scene lingers on in Jakarta and, while it's by no means as obvious as certain parts of Bangkok may be, sex is readily available for those who want to buy it. The bars of Blok M and Belora are populated with all sorts of "nice" girls who wouldn't normally be in a bar, it's just that they arrived in Jakarta to meet their friend who was supposed to be putting them up and it looks like they haven't shown up yet and ... Only an idiot could assume Jakarta was an AIDS-free zone. Take precautions, for everyone's sake.

The common sight in Jakarta of overweight, middle-aged American oil workers with young Indonesian women on their arms has resulted in an unfair reputation that unfortunately accommodates all foreigners. Genuine friendships and relationships happen every day in Jakarta, yet there continues to be an element of suspicion in the minds of a lot of Indonesians when confronted with a mixed couple. You have been warned.

What exactly might a foreigner complain about? Well, they might complain that life is just too "different" for them; that it's so hard to form genuine friendships with Indonesians; that they never have anything in common. For some this is the challenge: to be plunged in the deep-end of a culture so completely *lain* (different) to the West; to attempt to see inside the Indonesian mind with its attitudes to life which, for the foreigner, can be either fascinating or exasperating; to witness a thousand-year culture coping with the increasing intrusion of Western ideals.

They might complain that there's nothing to do in Jakarta. They might complain that the other expats in the city are diabolical. They complain about the heat; that it's too hot to do anything; that the humidity, mosquitoes and racket make life too hard. They might complain that all they get is hassle on the streets. And, rather dramatically, that they want to experience "real" Indonesian life, not merely the trivialities of a small circle of expat misfits. In time, any person choosing to live in Jakarta will find a lifestyle that is *cocok* (suitable) for them. Of course if they really can't get to grips with the Jakartan way of living, then they probably shouldn't prolong the agony.

HIGHLAND GATHERING

The Jakarta Highland Gathering is one of the capital's odder days. It's a well-established part of the expat calendar, and the organizers claim it has become the largest of its kind outside Scotland. It's a chance for The Bule World And His Wife to relax unharassed and be surprised at just how many other Westerners there are in Jakarta.

First held in 1974, the gathering has grown from a small-time act of whimsy into an international extravaganza, capturing the national media's attention every year with its parachute

183

displays, caber tossing competition and bagpipe displays, the likes of which are, unsurprisingly, unrivalled throughout Indonesia. In fact, so thoroughly *bule* is the event, that when you see a queue of Western children waiting their turn on the "knock 'em off the greased pole", it's altogether possible to forget that you are actually in Jakarta. Held for many years in Rasuna Said, it has more recently been hosted in the Senayan complex, opposite the national TV station, *TVRI.*

Indonesia is always well represented at the gathering in terms of traditional dance displays, stone-jumping displays, and rival bagpipe and kilt frenzies from Sumatra. The Indonesian authorities, however, very nearly made the gathering a caber-free event, when, in 1975, the caber was refused permission of entry. The way round this minor detail was to fly the caber back to Britain, and ship it out to Java where it could be unsuspectingly rolled overboard and left to drift ashore in north Jakarta. It has been tossed every year since.

JALAN JAKSA

Jl Jaksa is an admirably self-contained unit in the centre of Jakarta. Around the corner from Jakarta Theatre and Jl Thamrin (and not far from Gambir station), Jl Jaksa is the next road along from the equally self-contained shopping street Jl Sabang (actually Jl Agus Salim, but rarely referred to as such). It's the place where all the backpackers go: Jakarta's equivalent of the Costa del Sol or Torrimolinos and even Kuta beach. There is of course no beach, just the cheapest hotels, guest houses and restaurants in the city, offering "international" cuisine and other trash-travel requirements. It's not the greatest food in the world either but it's excellent value nonetheless; the street *warung* being the cheapest by far. Beer is also sold at a very reasonable rate. An entertaining evening is easily had in Jaksa.

It's a meeting place of sorts; Jaksa's cheap and cheerful approach makes it a stress-free place for everyone to sit about eating, drinking and sweating. Backpackers, other foreigners in the city, local fancy-boys, long-hairs and *cewek* (girls) all like to hang about in Jaksa. As do plainclothes police on the look out for drug dealings. It may even be the plainclothes police doing the offering, so keen are they to nail someone. Noses are best kept clean in Jaksa.

The rather predictable story has it that Jaksa came to be purely by chance. A lone backpacker wandering central Jakarta, searching unsuccessfully for a hostel bed was *kasihan* (pitied upon) by a family at Jl Jaksa 5 — now Wisma Delima — and given a night's accommodation. So impressed was the backpacker that he spread the word, and slowly but surely other backpackers began appearing. The idea caught on and guest houses and hotels sprang up. Jaksa remains the focal point for Jakarta's backpackers and other budget travellers.

Official endorsement of Jaksa came in 1994 (or was it a ploy to make tourists stay longer?) with the first ever Jaksa Fair, a week-long "cultural festival" of food, music and theatre. It's a popular and worthwhile event; a chance to see traditional Betawi street theatre and other performances, the likes of which had almost been forgotten.

The street continues to get bigger. The more people who hear about Jaksa, the more food, beer, accommodation and entertainment that's needed. Many rooms now have AC and prices to match. Which is a bit of a shame.

DISCOS

In 1996, 3,223 nightspots were counted in Jakarta. Exactly who had the job of counting them is uncertain, but they did conclude that many of them were discos. So if it's disco dancing you need, Jakarta offers an excellent, albeit erratic selection, from the tasteful to the outright sleazy. The big hotels always have a disco, and some of them are actually quite good. The *Oriental* in the Hilton, *Checquers* in the Mandarin and the *Pitstop* in Sari Pacific are popular with young rich Jakartans and, although dress restrictions apply — smart, casual dress — and things never seem to really take off, it's still possible to have a good time. More popular with the hip young things of the city would be the *M Club* in Blok M Plaza or *Asmat* in the Patria Jasa Building, Jl Gatot Subroto.

Other, more "earthy" discos and bars can be enjoyed in the streets of Belora just off Jl Thamrin near the Malang river. *Dangdut* music is to the fore and most offer upstairs massage services, as well as the occasional striptease, magic act and live band. Other similarly run outfits operate around the corner from the main drag, and although you can in theory dance, the emphasis is really on other kinds of business. *Lone Star* and *Parayangan* are bars run on similar ethics. Belora, however, is merely a smaller version of a much larger network of discos and bars in the north of the city, in Kota. Here operate a proliferation of every kind of bar and disco. The streets with these bars are so narrow that some establishments have two entrances, one for each side of the street.

The most established disco by far in Jakarta is the *Tanamour* on Jl Tanah Abang Timur. At weekends, it thrives like nowhere else in Jakarta. It's without question the most *rame* (packed) place imaginable; people of every colour, creed and persuasion are free to let it all hang out in the Tanamour. What *nenek* (grandma) would have made of its gyrating, nighttime clientele of girls, gays, rich-kids, *bule,* wide-boys, long-hairs, he/she's and bar-girls is not known, but she wouldn't have been turned away that's for certain. Everyone is welcome at the *Tanamour*.

MEDICAL HELP
Should you find parts of your body are packing in, you are guaranteed "quality" treatment at any number of expensive, Western-

style hospitals. Places like *Rumah Sakit Pondok Indah* on Jl Metro Duta Kav UE (tel: 750-0157), *Rumah Sakit Pertamina*, in Mayestik on Jl Kyai Maja 29 (tel: 720-0290), and the *Medical Scheme* in the Setiabudi Building on Jl Rasuna Said, Kuningan (tel: 525-5367/ 520-1034) are well-established "posh" sick-houses (as *rumah sakit* so delightfully translates). They offer English-speaking doctors and even ambulances, so don't fret (at least not until it's two hours late due to traffic). Always popular with expatriates is the *AEA International Clinic/SOS Medika* on Jl Puri Sakti 10, Cipete (tel: 750-5980/750-6001: emergency). A visit to the *Medistra* hospital on Jl Gatot Subroto is more like a weekend away at a five-star hotel and its prices are graded accordingly. It is a lovely place to get sick, however.

For lesser ailments simply head for the nearest *Doktor Umum* (general practitioner). For teeth trouble you need a *Doktor Gigi* (dentist). Always have enough money with you, as you are unlikely to get credit — it's awfully disappointing being turned away from a hospital. The above named "posh" places take credit cards but in any other place, like the government hospital *R.S. Cipto Mangun-kusumo* in Salemba or *R.S Jakarta* on Sudirman, where medical students get to practise, cash is required. In some of the less modern hospitals, the family of the patient will be expected to provide food, medicine and even special equipment if necessary. The doctor will of course advise them which ones to get, but don't assume all hospitals are well-equipped.

There are a great many well-trained medical professionals dotted all over Jakarta, operating under private practice as *Doktor Umum*. Their hours of practice vary and no guarantees can be made about the quality of service. When in the doctor's room, don't be surprised at the way the nurse defers so haplessly to the doctor. Until given the nod by the doctor the nurse is obliged to remain impassive and motionless, even if one of the waiting patients has gone purple.

STRESS RELIEF

Methods of stress relief vary from person to person. Some start eating. Some start drinking. Some have to lie down with the curtains drawn and all the taps running. You don't want to go to prison by doing something outrageous so it's best to try and contain any wilder inclinations. Although Westerners are reputed to make well-respected cellmates in Indonesian prisons, invariably ending up teaching the entire prison to speak English, it's probably not the best way to gain experience in the field of applied linguistics.

So where do you go when it's all too much? What do you do when you can't take any more? What outlets are there for your frustrations in this blighted and hostile city? For if you are in a bad mood in Jakarta, you are in the worst place in the world. You will wonder what made you ever come in the first place. The heat will make it difficult to breathe. Your head will get hot. You feel sweat running down your legs. No taxis stop for you, except one who kicks you out halfway. A busload of people stare at you. Appalling things go on all around, and no one seems to mind. Everybody starts to look ugly. The Goat's Foot Soup you had earlier starts repeating on you. Someone with a cheese-grater for a voice starts a conversation: "Why aren't you married?" they ask. "Do you get paid in rupiah or dollars?" Another door is shut in your face. Another person asks you where you are going. Another shop overcharges you. Another group of children start laughing and pointing. You realize the hairdresser you visited earlier has made a hilarious wedge (a la *kampung*) of your hair. You start wishing you were in prison.

When this is your frame of mind, you will need to have some pre-planned remedy at hand. It's up to you in the end. Just don't blame your *pembantu*.

— Chapter Nine —

EATING AND DRINKING

EATING IN

If eating at home in Jakarta, you have a fantastic choice of meals to have your *pembantu* (housemaid) cook you. Yes, more than likely it's the servant of the house (or of the month) who prepares the food you eat at home. It's no great sin in Indonesia to be clueless about cooking: the men of the house are never expected to lend a hand in the kitchen, and women are under little pressure either, most having grown up with servants around. So let's assume your food is being cooked for you. Since the "average" *pembantu* in Jakarta is from either Sunda or Java, there's more likely to be a profusion of Sundanese and Javanese dishes appearing magically on the table, as opposed to such Batak specialities as dog-meat, which a servant from that particular region might be tempted to dish up. Fortunately for dog lovers, there are very few *pembantu Batak* around, in Jakarta at least.

Indonesian dishes are rice-based, with a side vegetable, meat and chillies. Pork is not generally popular, since most Indonesians are Muslim, but it does crop up in Chinese dishes. Vegetarians are shown little sympathy in Indonesia. The very concept of "no meat for me, thanks" is something quite alien to the average cook, and even so-called vegetarian dishes probably have some diced chicken thrown in somewhere. To an outsider perhaps, Indonesian food is pretty much the same: rice, something *pedas* (hot), and covered in *kecap* (soy sauce). Of course, when you look at cooking in closer detail, you become more aware of subtle differences in method and flavour. Only time will tell. Best keep eating.

189

You could be served up any one of a million of dishes. Here are some of the more common ones: *nasi goreng* (fried rice), *cap cai* (a Chinese-style mix of veg and bits), *bakmi goreng* (fried noodles and things), *nasi rawon* (plain rice, black spicy veg and beef soup), *nasi rames* (plain rice, veg, eggs, meat, coconut), *lontong* (banana leaf-wrapped rice "sausages"), *gado-gado* (steamed and raw bean-sprouts, veg, hot peanut sauce), *gulai ayam* (yellow, curried-chicken broth), *gulai kambing* (same but with goat meat), *pisang goreng* (fried banana), *tempe* (fried fermented soya cake), *tahu goreng* (fried tofu), *bistik* (fried beef with gravy: sounds like "beefsteak" — get it?), *ikan pindang* (yellow curried fish), *telur pindang* (same but with egg instead of fish), *fu yung hai* (sweet and sour omelette), *kari ayam* (curried chicken), *kari ikan* (curried fish), *sop ayam* (chicken soup), *sop apa saja* (any soup you want), *sayur bayam* (spinach soup), *sayur asem* (sour vegetables), *lalapan sayur sama ikan goreng* (fried fish, fresh veg and chilli sauce), *sayur lodeh* (veg and coconut soup), *oseng-oseng* (fried veg and optional *tahu* bits). Lack of food is definitely not one of Jakarta's shortcomings.

EATING OUT

Eating out is better than eating in because you don't have to feel guilty about having someone cook your food. And you don't have to look hard to find it; Jakarta's food invariably comes looking for you. Little wraps of food are paraded past you all day long, pushed through car windows at every set of traffic lights in the city. But beware of some of these snacks; don't be surprised to find a sausage running through your cup cake, or some other weird combination like cheese and chocolate.

People eat like it's going out of fashion. The Indonesian style of eating is "little and often" with emphasis on "helping yourself". Invite people round to eat and they won't be expecting to sit up at the table with a plate of hot food. Rather than a weighty block of one meat or one veg, people prefer a selection of smaller dishes to choose from. A ton of rice is cooked up early in the morning and, along with other things, stored below a plastic cover to keep flies off. The best example is in a *Padang* restaurant where, the instant you sit down, a thousand multicoloured dishes are presented to you, leaving you to pick, consume and pay for what you eat.

There's such a wide variety of food for sale in Jakarta, it's difficult to know where to start. Italian, Indian, Chinese, French, Dutch, Japanese, Korean, and Mexican cuisine aside, Indonesian food alone has enough varieties to keep the most dedicated eater busy for years. Food from the 27 provinces is fully represented. It's on sale everywhere: from the *kaki lima* (mobile vendors) and *warung* (street stalls), and an amazing assortment of restaurants; some cheap and basic, others posh and expensive. There can be no excuse for going hungry.

The distinct regional varieties of food on sale in Jakarta speaks volumes about the actual size of Indonesia. For, after eating one's way around the archipelago, you become aware that "Indonesia" is just a name; a bold circle drawn in black marker-pen around a group of islands with a land surface area of over 2 million sq km. With so many different places accounted for under the name "Indonesia" come regional differences in the people themselves. Just as Padang food, with its blend of dry and fresh spices, is hot and fiery, so is the reputation of *orang Padang*, who are considered just as fiery and outspoken. And just as *orang Jawa* are considered the most subtle, sweet and innocuous people of Indonesia, so is their food, which uses fresh spices with sugar to take the edge off. They are what they eat, it seems.

Yet this association of food with personality is more deeply-rooted than mere regional differences. It's taken for granted that different kinds of food can directly influence an individual. Eating "hot" food, for example, really does heat a person up, both physically and mentally. Eat too much food of a slippery consistency, and expect to come over all slug-like. This association is most obviously practised in the use of the traditional medicine *jamu* in which texture, strength, degree of sweetness and colour are given a free reign to influence an individual's psyche.

If you need, and an awful lot of people do, you can fill your belly on a fantastically low budget. Or you can choose to spend a near fortune on cooked food; Jakarta has it all. The cheapest, and arguably the most authentic Indonesian food, is that sold by the *kaki lima*. These are five-legged, two-wheeler, mobile restaurants which hawk the streets day and night. Fast food is not an American concept; it never has been. In Indonesia, food is brought to you, ready-prepared and on a plate — what could be faster? But like American food, most of the *kaki lima* serve fried food.

Commonly offered dishes from *kaki lima* include *sate, rujak* (fruit salad), *bakso* (meat ball soup), *soto ayam* (chicken soup with noodles and veg), *bubur ayam* (chicken and rice porridge), *mie pangsit* (a ravioli-style dish), *nasi goreng* (fried rice), *mie rebus* (boiled noodles), *mie goreng* (fried noodles), *kotoprak* (cooked and chopped noodles, beansprouts, tofu, peanut sauce and more), *gado gado* (mixed fresh and boiled vegetables, also with a peanut sauce), *hotdog* and *hamburger*. Unfortunately, quality is not guaranteed with *kaki lima* — you just have to take your chances.

Washing up facilities are never very advanced on a *kaki lima*, limited usually to a bucket and any running water there happens to be nearby. Supplying your own plate, and seeing the food cooked with your own eyes should dispel any major fears you may have about hygiene. Qualities in *sate*, for example, vary enormously. Depending how economical the *tukang sate* (sate man) is feeling, that is, how much actual meat rather than skin, fat and gristle he uses, and how many peanuts he puts into the sauce, inevitably decides the quality of the *sate*. If you're happy with the results, make a mental note of the seller for future reference.

There exists in Jakarta a recurring social myth that cats, rats and dogs are used in *sate*. This might well be "just one of those stories", but then again, might well be true. A trip to one of the city's established *sate* houses is probably the safest bet: *Sate House Senayan* on Jl Kebon Sirih, Kebayoran Baru or *Sate Pancoran* on Jl Raya Pasar Minggu are two such places well known for their excellent *sate*.

Horror hygiene is here though, from the flies that collect all over the food displays in Padang restaurants (not to mention the pavement descaling of fresh fish) to the pizza you order, which has had to travel through several tons of raging traffic-pollution to reach you. And without wishing to put you further off your food than you already are, be warned that alarming quantities of the carcinogenic flavour enhancer, monosodium glutamate (MSG) are still widely used in Indonesian street food.

When eating out, the next step up from the *kaki lima* is the *warung*. These offer the above same dishes and a whole lot more. The emphasis at a *warung* is on home-cooking. Seafood and fish dishes like *ikan pecelele* are rarely sold by *kaki lima*, but readily available at a *warung*. The same is true for *nasi uduk*, *Padang* food, *Indomie* (boiled "pot" noodles), *tempe*, *martabak* (a rather weighty pancake: sweet or savoury), *tahu*, *sayur asem*, *burung goreng* (fried pigeon), and umpteen varieties of *rendang* (a hunk of meat in a thick, hot, red sauce).

At the most rudimentary level, *warung* are simply *kaki lima* that have come to a standstill, while at the most sophisticated level they offer steak and Italian. Some *warung* have chairs and tables, some just a plank of wood to seat everyone, although many people are happy to simply *jongkok* (crouch down) to eat. You may even find yourself sitting on various car-body parts and tyre-piles; many *warung* are makeshift affairs converted by night from garage workshops. Depending on your upbringing, however, you may find the entire experience less than appetizing as you settle down to eat next to an open sewer with rats. Maybe. But this is Jakarta street food — what do you expect?

The warung offers home-cooking at down-to-earth prices.

Indonesians will eat parts of animals that Westerners would not normally consider. Ask for some fried chicken and you can expect the entire fried animal, head and all. Offal is popular stuff to eat; brains, lungs and intestines being essential ingredients in many Indonesian dishes. Fried, dried chicken-blood is a good appetizer, as is goat's head soup. You might follow this with a dog or catfish sandwich, or maybe some penis soup. Okay, so these aren't the average *warung* dishes, but then again, not entirely out of the question.

At *rumah makan* (restaurants), the most complete choice of food is on sale. Every area of Jakarta has a selection of Padang, Batak, Sundanese and Chinese restaurants, to name but a few. Many have impossibly long menus which, dish by dish, would take years to get through. The point being that they could, if they wanted, cook up these dishes; that they are within the chef's capabilities, that's all.

194

Rumah Makan Sunda (Sundanese restaurants) are good. The food is fresh; you choose a fish from the tank on your way in. *Ikan gurame* is a particularly tasty Sundanese dish: a deep-fried, fresh carp straight from the tank. That's it: just a great big, deep-fried goldfish. Former keepers of goldfish will get to see their pets in a new light; they will be able to eat them. Hygiene need not be so much of a worry in these restaurants. Sinks, or wash basins, are dotted strategically around every restaurant.

The fruit juices served in a good Sundanese restaurant are impeccable. While Padang restaurants have the monopoly on good *juice alpulkat* (liquidized avocado, vanilla and sugar), the rest belongs to Sundanese restaurants. If you're lucky, you will eat your food to the accompaniment of Sundanese *degung* music to help with the digestion. The choice of music can sometimes make or break the meal in a restaurant. Particularly if you're in a *warung* in Blok M and a man in lipstick is serenading you.

PLACES TO EAT

Naturally, restaurants do come and go in Jakarta and even seemingly popular ones can disappear overnight. At one point it was possible to sample the delights of food from every province in Indonesia simply by walking down Jl Asia Afrika (opposite the Senayan sports complex). Perhaps because it was considered too rough-and-ready for the forthcoming *Visit Indonesia Year* promotion, the whole *warung* collection was moved to a location which was hard to access (it was next to a dual-carriageway) and slowly but surely the lot of them disappeared. It is still possible to experience the nation's food under one roof by a visit to the basement of the *Pasaraya* department store in Blok M. The major hotels frequently feature buffets centred around the theme of Indonesian food.

For food in the top range of restaurants, you are fairly guaranteed a "safe" (if not somewhat generic-style) meal at most of the major hotels in the city. Otherwise, you might like to book a table in the revolving restaurant that is the *Empire Grill* atop the Menara Imperium building on Jl Rasuna Said, Kuningan. Similarly *mewah dan mahal* (posh and expensive) is the Italian restaurant *Ambiente* within the Hotel Aryaduta on Jl Prapatan, Menteng. If you want to spend a fortune on the type of food you could have cooked at home for about 1% of the price, visit the *Oasis* restaurant in Cikini: serving "classic" Indonesian dishes, the place is popular with a small up-market crowd.

Indonesian food is obviously not hard to find. Some of the better, mid-range Indonesian restaurants to be recommended are: the Sundanese *Raden Kuring* restaurant on Jl Raden Saleh, Cikini. Good Padang food can be had at *Nasi Kapau* on Jl Melawai, Blok M. Also famous for a couple of good padang eateries is Jl Sabang (round the corner from the backpacker's hangout of Jalan Jaksa) in the centre of the city.

Chinese food is quite abundant too in Jakarta, particularly in the famous "Chinatown" area of Kota in the north. Found all over the city is the popular *Bakmi Gajah Mada*, a fast-food style noodle house. Elsewhere there is *Dragon City* on Jl Sudirman which serves excellent food, although at a price. For perhaps a livelier atmosphere and more authentic Chinese food, there is *Nelayan* which has various outlets including Pondok Indah Mall and Gedung Manggala Wana Bakti, Jl Gatot Subroto.

Some excellent Indian food is also to be found. Notably, there is the popular *Shah Jahan* restaurant in the Sahid Jaya Hotel on Jl Sudirman, and the *Hazara* restaurant on Jl Wahid Hasyim 112, Kebon Sirih, which serves distinctly north Indian cuisine and is popular with a young mixed crowd. *Akbar's Palace* in the Wijaya Grand Centre is a well-established Indian restaurant serving very reasonably-priced cuisine.

And then there are those bastions of the American "empire", the fast-food chains. *McDonald's, Burger King, Kentucky Fried Chicken* and *Dunkin' Donuts*: they are all here, in every shopping mall, and always fabulously popular. For other American "food" and accompanying entertainment, there is *Planet Hollywood* on Jl Gatot Subroto (which upstairs also offers probably the best cinema in town); *Hard Rock Cafe* operates on similarly predictable lines; *Thank God It's Friday* is another one which has become increasingly popular, with various outlets around the city including Taman Ria.

The economic crisis that gripped Indonesia in 1998 witnessed a new form of eatery emerge. Touted as "street cafes", they are basically up-market versions of the *warung* which have existed happily all over Asia for centuries. Somewhere between a restaurant and a *warung*, the emphasis at a street cafe is on quality food at a competitive price — with the added bonus of bumping into a celebrity while there. As a way of boosting their flagging incomes, not to mention meeting the demands of a public which still wants to eat out but can no longer afford restaurants, a number of minor celebrities have opened cafes in their name — the pop singer Desi Ratnasari, for example, has one named after her hit song: *Tenda Biru*. Traffic pollution is not a problem with these cafes either; being restricted to certain compounds around areas like Monas, Mesjid Al Azar and Menteng.

RICE

Rice is currency in Indonesia. You don't talk about the weather in Indonesia, you talk about rice. You talk about the quality of it, the size of the grain, the taste. It comes in several colours including *beras merah* (red) and *beras hitam* (black), but the most recognizable form of rice is the generic *nasi putih* (white).

There are lots of words in *Bahasa Indonesia* to describe different states of rice. *Gabah* is the real, just-picked thing. *Beras* is the dehusked item. Cook it, and you have *nasi*. Cook it incorrectly and you might have a sticky matter known as *ketan*. Don't cook it long enough and you will have an unappetizing bowl of *biji limau*.

Cook it perfectly and it's *nasi pulan*. Get served a ration of rice in prison and it's known as a *pelabur* or *ramsum*. Fry it; you have *nasi goreng*; cook it with coconut, it's *nasi uduk*. Sticks of squeezed, wrapped rice-sausages are called *lontong*. Rice porridge is *lecek* or *bubur*. Cook it for a banquet and it's *nasi angkatan*. The equivalent proverb to the one about crying over spilt-milk is *nasi sudah jadi bubur* (the rice has already turned to porridge).

If your poster of the President falls down, glue it back up with a dab of *nasi lem* (rice glue). If things are getting you down, why not turn to *sake*? This pleasant and potent rice-drink works wonders for your outlook.

Civil servants and the like are given a sack as part of their salary which, in their bids to find the purest rice, is subsequently hawked around the neighbourhood like dope. The best rice in the land is a particularly refined strain known as *Beras Cianjur*.

Rice is truly a political issue in Indonesia — the basis upon which governments may rise and fall. Indeed, it was after a 1973 shortage that former President Suharto pledged national self-sufficiency in rice — a move which, perhaps being so intimately linked with the Indonesian psyche, overshadowed his other, more questionable policies. The administrative body behind this im-mense task was the State Logistics Board — or *Bulog* — which, through supplement and subsidization, managed to stabilize rice prices, achieve self-sufficiency and reduce poverty.

In hindsight, however, this achievement led to a degree of political complacency which, when the economy collapsed in 1998 causing rice prices to rocket, culminated in some of the worst social unrest in decades — and the ultimate demise of Suharto's government.

The contested issue of rice continued in the wake of Suharto's resignation when, after months of crippling economic crisis and the drought-induced failure of crops that year, it was revealed that *Dolog Jaya* (the Jakarta Logistics Agency) was siphoning off over half Jakarta's 5,000 ton daily requirements. The arrest of the agency's former head, Ahmad Zawawi, centred on allegations that subsidized rice was being sold for personal gain — a crime of corruption which carried the death sentence. And with half the population officially below the poverty line at this time, the news that donations and subsidies from Japan, Pakistan and other countries were being resold at profit, brought further social uproar.

But with the big boys seemingly protected in a web of legal wranglings, it was the ethnic Chinese of Indonesia who again became the focus of resentment for the poor and hungry. Although they represent only 4% of the population, the ethnic Chinese are known to dominate the economy in significant ways — including the private rice trade. Since the crisis first arose, it has been the Chinese shopkeepers and mill-owners who have been targets of repeated attack. In the eyes of the hungry, this may alleviate the situation temporarily, but with Chinese-Indonesians too afraid to do business and countries like Taiwan reconsidering rice-aid in light of these sentiments this can prove only detrimental.

FRUIT

As long as you are in this country, you must take full advantage of the fantastic range of fruit available. Fruit keeps you healthy. Fruit keeps you working. What better way to line your stomach in the morning than by drinking an entire liquidized mango?

Clearly, since the climate is tropical, the emphasis is on soft, juicy, exotic fruit as opposed to unexciting second-leaguers like apples, oranges and grapes. There are rumoured to be twenty-four varieties of banana alone in Indonesia: red ones, long thin ones and strange, small, three-sided ones. Not all are edible, mind you. The best ones to eat are the short and sweet *pisang emas* and the larger classic, *pisang Ambon*. Indonesia is in fact the world's top grower of bananas, producing in 1996 some 4.8 million tons which were exported to the US, the United Arab Emirates, Singapore and Europe. Unfortunately it is not the most reliable which accounts for its meagre 2% share of the world market.

Check out the *manga* (mango), best eaten from June onwards, and the unbelievably sweet and juicy *nanas* (pineapple). Indonesian *nanas* is often eaten with salt to take the edge off, while avoided altogether by a lot of women, believing the *nanas* makes them *gatal* (itchy). Cutting a pineapple is nothing less than an acquired art-form; ask someone to show you how it's done. Pineapple bought from a vendor, however, will have been pre-peeled, sliced and bagged, so no need to carry a *golok* (machete) around with you. If you like to grow your own, few things are easier than pineapples: simply plug one in the ground and wait.

Belimbing (starfruit) is a cool, refreshing, earth-watery flavoured fruit. Cut a slice to see its five-pointed star shape. *Jambu air* are crunchy, pinky, bell-shaped numbers, full of water (hence the name, *air*) and commonly eaten as *rujak* with a chilli, peanut and palm-sugar sauce. Fruits like *jambu air* grow in Indonesia with the same free abandon that conkers do in England. They grow like weeds, the season starting around September. If there is a tree near you, fill carrier bags with it and make yourself popular by giving them out.

Manggis is the love-fruit of Indonesia. Available between November and February, *manggis* is the most sensual, the most erotic of all fruit. Purple-brown in colour, the outer shell cracks open to reveal a thick, rich mauve, almost marzipan-like, flesh beneath. Finger your way through this, and you reach the edible part; an exquisitely flavoured tight, white cluster of dribbling segments. *Manggis* is a notoriously difficult fruit, its ripeness easily misjudged. Often only half its inner charms are edible; the other half having already over-ripened into darker bits.

Duku are edible marbles. In Jakarta they are piled up for sale by the roadside: *Duku Palembang — yang paling manis*. A thin pale skin peels back to reveal a sweet, segmented flesh with a stone in the middle. Eat too many and you urinate a lot.

Jeruk Bali has been described as the fruit you are given when you wake up for breakfast on your first morning in Heaven. It's like a user-friendly grapefruit: sweet, segmented, self-contained.

Rambutan are the bright-red, softly-spiked numbers which appear in the wet season; they are not dissimilar in taste to *leci* (lychee). *Alpukat* (avocado) are another good thing. For a truly fulfilling *minuman* (drink), liquidize an *alpukat*, add palm-sugar, a squirt of chocolate or vanilla and you have *juice alpukat*. Fantastic.

Salak (or snake-fruit) are distinctive for the perfect snakeskin that covers them. Peel carefully and it comes off whole to reveal a nutty, crunchy, dry flesh of three or four stoned segments. The sweetest ones are *salak Bali* and *salak Pondoh*. Each fruit featuring three segments: two large and one small. Two sweet, one not so.

Beware of a large spiky fruit known as *durian*. Or rather beware of its smell, which is like some terrible foot condition and subsequently banned on most airlines.

But don't bother with Indonesian oranges.

COFFEE

For drinkers of coffee, Indonesia offers arguably the best in the world, once you are used to it. While European approaches to coffee are either in the style of the mini expresso or the particularly tasteless "instant" variety favoured in England, the Indonesian approach is neither. Order *kopi* in a *warung* and expect a large glass of watery-sweet brown stuff. If they know you are not stopping or if they have simply run out of glasses, you'll get it in a plastic bag with a straw in the top. Because the coffee is unfiltered, the drinker is left prone to regular mouthfuls of grit. Spoons are conveniently left in glasses so more stirring can be done. Once drunk, an inch thick block of sediment is left at the bottom. This of course sounds appalling and indeed, if you don't like your coffee this way, it is. However, take the coffee and apply a different approach, i.e. filtration, and you are left with something to behold in drinkability terms. The coffee itself is best made with water that has just boiled, as hot as it gets. A percolator is good but not essential — you might want it more "instant". Leave it to brew for a minute or so before filtering. Expect some sediment towards the end but nothing compared to a *warung* coffee.

There are a wide variety of coffees on the market and a surefire winner is the *Kapal Api* brand. They package coffee from a number of provinces, each with a subtly different taste. You could do worse than buy a packet of *Kapal Api Special* by way of introduction to the delights of Indonesian coffee. *Bali Dancer* is a recommendable Balinese coffee. For those still hankering an instant coffee powder, you need to buy *Indocafe*.

Possibly the finest coffee in the land is that from Toraja, Sulawesi; one of the finest available brand names being *Arabica Kalosi*. For a truly fantastic pot of this check out the Toraja coffee drinking section at the *Pasaraya* department store. Expect to pay fairly shocking prices for the privilege, but for anyone who claims to be into coffee, spoiling yourself at least once in your life with this particular *kopi* is a necessity.

DRINKING

Despite the overwhelming presence of Islam, alcohol is freely available in Indonesia. It's advertised on TV and on almost every menu in the land. Although you might be frowned upon seen buying several crates of beer at once, a lot of *orang-orang* (people) these days admit to enjoying a drink. In fact, Westerners are almost expected to drink, even encouraged. But it isn't always happy-hour in Jakarta. If the *Nahdatul Ulama* (NU), or "Revival of Religious Scholars", a highly influential, Jakarta-based council has its way, alcohol will be banned altogether. Their proposals stem from an apparent indignation that the government is profiting from apparently "undesirable sources" by taxing and controlling alcohol so heavily.

Buying beer from a *warung* remains the easiest option. *Bir Bintang* and *Bir Anker* are reasonable tasting locally-produced lagers. Debate continues to rage as to whether Indonesian beer is "cut" with formaldehyde-type chemicals in order to give it a longer shelf life in the tropical heat. Surely not. Beware of cans and bottles that look like they might have been on the shelf too long or in direct sunlight. Or ones that have gone rusty.

Ask for a beer in a hotel or restaurant and you find that the price shoots up. A single glass of hotel beer costs twice the price a large bottle of *warung* beer does. You are free to drink with abandon in Jl Peletahan in Blok M, and around Jl Gajah Mada in Kota, to name but two. It might be useful to remember that all bars and restaurants are subject to closure on Indonesia's many national holidays, whereas hotels remain open. The big supermarkets, *Metro, Hero, Pasaraya, Kemchicks, Sogo, Golden Truly* all have good selections of beverages and imported spirits. It helps if you have a card, or a friend with a card, for the *Duty Free* shop in Kemang.

WATERING HOLES

There are a proliferation of bars, ranging from the near-respectable to the plain seedy — to be experienced in many areas of the city. The major hotels offer stress-free drinking; usually to the accompaniment of some form of entertainment. Some like the Grand Hyatt and the Hyatt Aryaduta even feature attempts at "pubs" such as the obligatory kit-form Irish pub, *O'Reilly's* and the *Tavern* respectively. Filipinos are well-known for their cabaret-style performances, and the upwardly mobile of Jakarta can often be found frequenting venues such as the *Fountain Lounge* in the Grand Hyatt hotel, and *B.A.T.S.* (stands for "Bar At The Shangri-La") which offer good food, music and enough pomp to keep the business-minded crowd happy. Up-to-date details of these venues and the entertainment they offer can be found on the "Where to go in Jakarta" page in the *Jakarta Post* and the "Where to Unwind" section of the *Indonesian Observer*.

Popular with the Chinese-descended of Jakarta are the seemingly endless choice of bars and discos in the area known as Kota in the north of the city which comprises the main arterial road of Jl Gajah Mada and Hayam Wuruk. While many are quite obviously massage parlours and little else, "proper" bars are available if you look hard enough.

For the hardened Jakartan expat it is common knowledge that Jl Paletehan in Blok M offers itself (at nighttime at least) as pretty much an expat-only zone. The most well-established bar and restaurant by far is *The Sportsman*, which is well-known for its quality food and "respectable", relaxed atmosphere. Featuring two floors; the upstairs offers snooker and pool facilities. Coming close behind in the Jl Peletehan popularity stakes are bars like *Top Gun*, *Pentagon* and *Oscar's* which, although obviously less "respectable" than *The Sportsman*, can still offer a relatively anonymous break from the outside world.

For the trendier Jakartan and younger-minded expat an evening spent in the *Jimbani* bar in Kemang might be a lot like anywhere else in the western world: pumping music, video screens, lasers and all the hip attitude necessary. Similar pretensions can be experienced in the *Cafe Batavia* on Taman Fatahillah, Kota. Open 24 hours, it is a tasteful affair featuring a rather genteel restaurant above a more raucous bar area. Another nice but pricey joint for the well-off is *Jalan Jalan* atop the Menara Imperium in Jl Rasuna Said, Kuningan. The generic American-style *Hard Rock Cafe* is also a popular place for the city's pretty young things to be seen, as are local spin-offs like the *Fashion Cafe* (on the ground floor of the BNI building, Jl Sudirman) and the *Elvis Cafe* (in the Arthaloka building, also Jl Sudirman).

But wherever you end up drinking, you do not want, if possible, to be forced into buying the *Mansion House* range of spirits. These moderately inexpensive drinks are rumoured to be little more than water and alcohol, plus the relevant flavouring. Hangovers are supposed to be worse in this hot climate, but no one is completely certain. If you're really not sure then drink a fair amount of water before you call it a day. Or just don't drink.

SMOKING

In contrast to their hyper-moral Singapore neighbours, Indonesians, particularly the men, seem to smoke heavily. Is this because cigarettes are so much cheaper, or because cigarettes are such a large generator of revenue? Smoking might even be encouraged. The street kids all do it and no one says a thing.

You can smoke local versions of most American brands and an assortment of imported brands. Pipes are not common, neither are hand-rolled cigarettes, although some imported rolling tobacco is sold in the big department stores, along with *Rizla* (local papers are gumless). Some superbly mild rolling tobacco is sold in the markets of central Java.

For a smoker, Indonesia offers few restrictions. The freedom to light up is granted almost everywhere in Jakarta. And while it's true that in recent years people have become more aware of the dangers of both active and passive smoking (mandatory health warnings on packets were introduced in 1992), don't be surprised to see people blatantly ignoring no-smoking signs. If this is a problem for you, there's little you can do about it. You are more likely to cause offence and outrage than see the aberrant cigarette stubbed out, and therefore best advised to just leave the offending environment.

The preferred smoke in Indonesia is the aromatic *kretek* (clove) cigarette. *Kretek* smoke is one of the defining smells of

Jakarta. Expect to be asked to "leave the premises" if you light one up in your home country. There are a number of varieties on the market; the most popular being *Gudang Garam* and *Djarum*. *Kretek* are filtered cigarettes, mixed with tobacco, and have either a sweet flavour, as with *Djarum*, or salty, as with *Garam*. If you are bold enough, try *Dji Sam Soe*, the king of the *kretek*. These mammoth, conical, hand-rolled numbers take an estimated 20 minutes to smoke. Ironically, since cloves have anaesthetic properties, smoking them effectively numbs the lungs to any damage done.

Chapter Ten

WAYS OF SPENDING MONEY

MONEY

There isn't enough — or is there? Whilst Indonesia may have experienced record-breaking growth rates, and presumably been able to put some away "for a rainy day", the average person is quite definitely not rich. And yet if the amazing growth rates of the last ten years kept up, experts reckon Indonesia would be a world super power in no time. Or would it? Hard to imagine really.

Indonesia's wealth is mostly underground. Getting it out is costly and for the time being, heavily dependent on foreign companies who inevitably demand half the winnings. And as for the half that's left; so far it has been up to a select few *Bapak* (literally "father", but encompassing "boss") to keep most of this new-found wealth. Unlike the "new money" of some Arabic countries, which has transformed their modest populations in only a couple of generations, Indonesia simply has too many people to make an even stab at dishing it out fairly and squarely.

Obviously, money is a touchy subject in Jakarta, both for those who have too much of it and those who spend each day carrying out an impossible human task because of it. In Jakarta, a middle class has emerged for the first time in Indonesian history. They live in slap-up real estate areas like Bintaro Jaya, have two-point-four-children, drive hire-purchased cars, shop in shiny malls, and pay life-threatening mortgages. Many are Chinese in background. But they mustn't be confused with Jakarta's *super*-rich who live in areas like Menteng and Kemang—those are above the law and nothing more. They are the untouchables of Indonesia.

For the great many, the only money they get to handle is *uang merah* (red money). It's not a pretty sight: great, tattered handfuls of cheesy-red 100 rupiah banknotes do the rounds over and over again in Jakarta, and are in particular favour with bus conductors who can count them in the most extreme conditions. They say some people are *gila-uang* (money mad) — that they can think about nothing else. And this is the attitude that prevails in Jakarta, that everyone can get a bit if they have a go. Money is there for the making. This is why everyone comes to Jakarta. Trouble is, it's nowhere near as simple as that.

It used to be that a single rupiah was divided into ten, each one a *sen*. This would have been an infeasibly low currency, and until recently was one of the world's lowest known currencies. It was so low in fact that it had to be withdrawn from use and substituted with boiled sweets. Manufacturers and supermarkets alike continue to enjoy putting prices on their products which are outside the 5 rupiah range. Since the lowest coin in circulation is the 5 rupiah, and just supposing you are owed 3 rupiah as change, what should you expect? Naturally, boiled sweets. This is of course a transparent outrage — madness itself — yet ultimately just one of millions of apparently insubstantial rip-offs in practice all over Jakarta (and the rest). Put a lot of insubstantial little things together, however, and suddenly you have enough money to open your own bank and start lending it out.

People are very fussy about their money, the state of it that is. A slight tear on a single note is enough to render any business transaction redundant. At the same time, as is so typically true of the living contradiction that is Jakarta, you will be handed an appallingly sordid piece of money that you can only assume must have been at one time a banknote; ripped, shredded and the front and back sides sellotaped the wrong way round. Ugly money.

It's quite possible to declare yourself "coinfree" in Jakarta — that you only deal in notes. It's true: with the 500 rupiah note (green and small) serving the very bottom end of one's daily needs, even the tightest among us are encouraged to beseech "keep the change" and attempt to feel generous without feeling guilty about being "rich" in a "poor" country.

One result of having so many people reliant on small change is when the time comes for a company's staff to get their salaries. Enormous wads are counted off on automated wad-counting machines, piled up in plastic carrier bags and given to the office boy, who has been sent to collect. A hundred Pound Sterling in usable, day to day notage is physically enormity in Indonesian rupiah. For safety's sake, a complimentary envelope and rubber band are supplied.

The largest banknote, which was introduced in 1994 as the Rp 50,000 note, continues be treated with suspicion. Big shops with money in their tills accept it, but for the average man, the average *warung*, the average *bajaj* and *ojek,* it's simply impractical. The 50,000 is for the new middle-class to carry when shopping and going out at night. And when drunk, to happily give to a taxi driver in the belief that it is only a Rp 5,000 note.

Gambling is officially illegal in Indonesia but practised on every street corner in the land. One form of organized gambling is the *arisan*. Groups of like-minded people contribute a fixed amount of money to the event. Names are pulled at random from a hat and the winner, apart from getting to keep all the money, is obliged to host the next meeting. If you're the first one to be selected, consider it an advance. If last, it's like a savings account. It's a "safe bet" indeed because, one by one, everybody wins. *Arisan* are basically a good excuse for a chin-wag, and very popular among housewives.

Westerners are assumed to be rich — always. They are assumed to carry large amounts of "dollar" on their very being; stuffed into every pocket; stray banknotes floating behind them; four-poster beds constructed out of sovereigns. Westerners are therefore under a certain pressure to "dish it out" — a bit at least. Expect to be considered *pelit* (miserly) if you don't leave a tip, or spend too long counting your cheesy-red money in public. And it's only fair; anyone who complains about the cost of living in Indonesia deserves to be taken to one side and questioned.

There are six state owned banks, each focusing on a different aspect of the economy. *Bank Indonesia* is the issuer of currency. *Bank BNI* is geared towards the industry. *Bank Dagang Negara* is behind mining. *Bank Rakyat Indonesia* is the poor people's bank, its concerns are smallholdings and farming; *Bank Bumi Daya* does forestry and big time farming, and *Bank Eksim* takes care of import and export dealings.

ATMs are useful and on the increase; many banks have them already and there are sure to be more in the future. Foreign banks are also well-represented in Jakarta, and European currencies are slowly gaining more recognition. But will people get richer? Maybe. It may take a hundred years, it might not. In the meantime, the masses are free to walk in gleaming shopping malls and imagine they are rich.

SHOPPING

They say you can get anything in Jakarta — anything at all. Shopping is what Jakarta is all about. It's the process of buying and selling, offering and accepting, that keeps the rupiah moving. Obviously to get anything at all, you'll need money, as nothing comes free in Jakarta. You might not necessarily need unending wads of it, however. If you really want, you can easily spend a few million rupiah; alternatively you can go shopping on the smallest amount. Every level of society has its market so to speak. Even when people don't have any money to spend, they still go window shopping. It's a popular way to spend an afternoon — watching other people go shopping and imagining what you would buy if you had their money.

Foreigners who come to Jakarta are invariably not "poor" by any comparative stretch of the Indonesian imagination. Even the "poorest" visitor would still need to drop several thousand rungs down the Jakartan social ladder before arriving at the bottom rung which is a way of life for many folk. Many foreigners in Indonesia, particularly those working there on company orders, are afflicted with a most frightening condition: that of too much disposable income. With food, labour and everyday living coming so cheaply, the rich-white-man-abroad is morally obliged to reinvest at least some of his earnings. So he goes shopping.

For the expatriate housewife with a spending fixation, it must be heaven cruising Jakarta's shopping malls, "high" streets and street markets with a carrier bag of their husband's cash. And this blind materialism is not confined only to expats — no. There are just as many painted, middle-aged Indonesian wives of Jakarta rich men doing the same. They are seen glittering their way 'round town, instructing people left, right and centre, busy on the spend. Actions like these stem from a crass desire to keep up with the latest Western trash in the full knowledge that theirs is still quite a poor country. It must be highly uncomfortable for them. It must be highly uncomfortable for everyone; for the local super-rich; for the foreigners. And especially for the shop assistants who spend the day giftwrapping products with price tags bigger than their own monthly salary.

Probably the best shop in Jakarta is the *Pasaraya* department store. If you have only got time to visit one shop in Jakarta, visit *Pasaraya*. It's the Harrods of Jakarta and definitely not the worst place to kill a few hours. Within the store itself you are free to spend as much money as you can. It even has its own in-store radio show. Get sprayed, rubbed and painted on your way in by the ever-present promotion girls, and enjoy the air-conditioning. There are several in the city — each with a distinguishing catch-phrase. In Blok M there's Pasaraya *Big and Beautiful*. Further north on Jl Thamrin there is *Young and Trendy* and in the east there is *Fine and Golden*.

In the basement of the *Pasaraya* store in Blok M (arguably the best of the lot) is an overwhelming array of cheap to moderate eating places. They offer the best and the rest of Indonesian dishes. It's a popular place to find Jakarta's young hopefuls hanging out and staring at one another. Built onto the side of *Pasaraya* is the *Seibu* supermarket, which was built to replace the supermarket formerly housed in *Pasaraya's* basement. Featuring an excellent fruit selection, quality meats, dairy produce and a ton of imported products, it is everything the foreigner desperate for neon-lit shopping requires. The neon near-perfection is somewhat spoiled by the so-called "fresh fish" often on sale. Being still alive, the fish is certainly "fresh" yet living in water so murky that they are probably best kept as pets rather than fry-ups. Outside by the store's entrance is the sort-of-trendy *Croissants de France* cafe. For many years a gay hang-out, it has always served decent cakes, pastries and bread. Nice.

The other six floors of *Pasaraya* are crammed with things from all over Indonesia. Every kind of *batik, ikat* and textile is on sale, as well as all the latest imported clobber. The occasional fire in the Electrical and Sports department has had cynics mumbling about insurance scams but nothing is ever proven. In July '96, particular criticism was made of the Thamrin store when management decided to ignore a bomb threat made against the store. They claimed it would have been futile trying to get everyone out in time, so they chose to keep quiet about the incident and hope the caller had been bluffing. Fortunately he was and no harm was done. But all in all, *Pasaraya* is a perfectly self-contained place in which to go shopping. And not overpriced really.

There are other good supermarkets in Jakarta and other good department stores. The *Hero* chain is a reasonably reliable supermarket with outlets around the city, the most comprehensive being that in Pondok Indah Mall. Another well-established super-market is *Golden Truly*; a touch more downmarket than *Hero*, it can be found on Jl Thamrin, and numerous other locations. Electronics at often good prices is catered for in Glodok Plaza in North Jakarta. For strictly imported goods (and selected local produce with appropriate price-labels) is the expat-wife's favourite: *Kemchicks* found in Kemang, South Jakarta.

Dotted at regular intervals in Jakarta are mammoth, air-brushed promises of malls-to-come. There might not even be any houses there yet, it might still be an area of relative jungle, yet already its future will have been determined by a contractor's billboard. Singapore-style shopping malls are the future of Jakarta. Plans are under way to cover Jakarta in these pleasure-domes. For besides offering a multitude of shining shops, they also accom-modate restaurants and cinemas. Guests staying in the Grand Hyatt Hotel who don't wish to breathe unadulterated Jakarta air have nothing to fear. The hotel is built into the side of the mammoth wonder-mall, Plaza Indonesia, and so there's no need to go outside at all. The Plaza Indonesia and Pondok Indah Mall complexes are definitely among the "happening" places for Jakarta's weekend rich-kids. Their *kampung* cousins, by way of contrast, are the ones running around in the traffic outside the mall; flagging down taxis and lugging other people's shopping for a small fee. Other important malls in the city include the Blok M Plaza Mall, and the new and enormous Taman Aggrek Mall, off the Tomang Toll, via Jl Gatot Subroto.

The real bargains are had in the street markets. Three of the best (and there are many) are *Pasar Mayestic* in Kebayoran Baru, *Pasar Tanah Abang*, northeast of Plaza Indonesia, and the area of *Mangga Dua* in the North. They offer probably everything that the air-conditioned *Pasaraya* does — you just have to know where to look. Produce in Jakarta's street markets are rarely laid out in alphabetical order — the only thing to do is ask. And bargain. Good

213

prices can be had on everything from real gold to fake Gucci watches, if only you know how to bargain correctly. The point when bargaining is to come to a compromise about being interested in something while trying to look as if you really couldn't care less. Even if you don't feel confident bargaining, you should always ask for a discount on what you are buying. You nearly always get one.

When you walk into a shop in Jakarta, it might look as if the place is deserted. Don't be fooled; a quick glance over the shop counter should end any doubts you have. For down there on the floor, hiding from the general public, will be several noodle-eating shop assistants. On other occasions you get swamped by a thousand uniformed shop assistants with nothing to do. Many shops in Jakarta are ridiculously overstaffed, and there are consequently an awful lot of bored shop-staff dying for a customer to attend to.

If you need a pet or fancy an unusual filling in your sandwich, visit one of Jakarta's animal markets. The bird market off Jl Pramuka in the centre of town is a malodorous complex of birds, cages and droppings. Ask around and any number of endangered species will be offered your way. For flowers, fish and aquariums try Pasar Barito in South Jakarta.

Very often in Jakarta, you will simply end up shopping by accident. The shopping comes to you. The widest variety of produce imaginable is paraded past your front door on a daily basis by the city's million *kaki lima* and "shoulder-pole" sellers. These characters are out there, plying their trade in all weathers. An underground economy, they probably make up about a quarter of Jakarta's workforce. This is self-employment at the most minimum extreme. Still, it pays better than the average factory worker.

And should you be in transit, then what better place to purchase a blowpipe, than at every set of traffic lights in the city? But at closing time, when all is sold and bought, it must be

Jakarta's main bird market on Jalan Pramuka

remembered that in Indonesia, the government, their family and cronies remain the nation's shopkeepers. The rest of us are mere customers.

215

WARUNG

Jakarta wouldn't be the same without its *warung*, nor would much of Asia in fact. Every street corner needs a *warung* for people to pop to. Where would people meet if it wasn't for the local *warung*? Where are the people who do nothing all day going to do nothing all day, if not at the *warung*? It's a worrying thought. If the government of Indonesia suddenly banned *warung* tomorrow, the whole archipelago would have to go to supermarkets to buy their daily consumables, they would have to join singles agencies and take up patchwork at night school in order to make friends and keep up with the gossip. They would have to start eating at home and cooking for themselves — it would be a nightmare. Fortunately, not even Jakarta has sunk to such depths and *warung* exist happily in all shapes and forms, all over the place. Remember this: there's always a *warung* open somewhere near you. It doesn't matter what time you need something from one: painkiller for a toothache, more beer and cigarettes, more fly-spray, an egg, whatever, there will always be one to help you out of your crisis.

Some might want to split hairs and say that, strictly speaking, a *warung* is actually only a tent-affair. But in Jakarta the term is used loosely to encompass corner shops, cafes and restaurants alike. Some start out small and expand over the years into something far sturdier and concrete than their humble bamboo and plastic origins. Some are large, tile-roofed numbers which are clearly fixed buildings. They probably would have started out as simple *warung* and slowly taken root. Open air restaurants are *warung*; an area of tarpaulin or plastic somehow held up and over the goings-on. That's all really, there's actually nothing much to simple *warung*. No glamour, no refineries — nothing. Something to keep the rain off and that's it.

Some are so small there's barely room among the stock to seat a human being, let alone stand up. Yet these mini, lockup *warung* are more often than not lived in by the owner and family.

And a *warung* can be passed on down the family. They are a good investment. To own a *warung* is to be self-sufficient; to have dropped out of the rat race; to be pampering to no-one's needs. It simply means being there and staying there and letting everyone come to you, which they always do. Great.

TAILORS

Tailors are cheap and abundant in Jakarta. People use them in a very casual way, like going to the newsagent, or popping out to buy an egg. Many stores employ resident tailors: buy something "off-the-rack" and have it cut, altered and sewn before the garment even leaves the premises. Buy some cloth from the Indian run shop, *La Mode* in Pasar Mayestik, or from the second floor of Melawai Plaza in Blok M and have yourself measured up. Take in your favourite bits to be copied; add an inch here or there, and you will soon be looking a treat.

Some of the cheaper ones operate in sweat shop conditions. Operating in the particularly sweaty indoor market that is Pasar Blok M (next to the *Matahari* department store), is the self-styled *Mr Wonderful*. A talented and reasonably-priced tailor, he enjoys minor celebrity status with his customers. When interviewed by the *Jakarta Post* about his popularity, he claimed it was because he fashioned "artdresses" for his clientele, as opposed to simply sewing bits of cloth together in a certain way for money. Also in Pasar Blok M are various *toko kancing* (button shops) selling a bewildering selection of buttons. A good mid-priced tailor is *Melawai Tailor* on the corner of Jl Melawai IV in Blok M. All in all, a decent shirt and trousers would cost you the same as a meal in a big hotel. Cheap.

Of course the price depends on the cloth you go for and where you choose to be measured up. And there are a million tailors to choose from in Jakarta.

HAIRDRESSERS

There are also a million hairdressers to choose from. The cheapest is a roadside barber who will give an excellent trim for an absolute pittance. Barbers like these are invariably situated below trees to allow for at least some shade, as well as a place to hang the mirror. A newspaper with a hole cut out for your head to collect the clippings is all part of the service. It's best to go before or after the rush hours to avoid the full force of the traffic pollution.

There are some excellent hairdressers in some of the markets. Simply take along a photo you have cut out of a magazine of a haircut you have seen on someone. Or leaf through the shop's own collection of cutouts and the hairdresser will endeavour to copy it. At the same time, there are some terrible things that can happen to your hair in the hands of an enthusiastic hairdresser keen to experiment with your *bule* (whitie) hair. For expensive and fashionable haircuts, try the hairdressers in any large mall.

A good head of hair can actually be an investment for some. It is not uncommon for some people to save their hair clippings and brush-deposits in the hope of selling them for use in a wig. There are well-established traditions of wig use among Indonesian women and many are still quite unashamed about wearing one. Naturally, the longer the hair, the greater the value of the potential hairpiece. Many, however, are kept in the family: a young girl with long hair might, for example, be persuaded by her elders into cutting off her flowing locks in order to make a nice wig for *nenek* (grandma).

Generally speaking, Indonesian men have little in the way of facial hair. Pencil-thin moustaches are common and all other facial hair, even that from a mole, is grown as long as possible in the attempt to affirm masculinity. On the feminine side, many Indonesian women are lucky enough to be free of unwanted body hair on legs and armpits. For the most part, Indonesians have very thick heads of hair, which lends itself perfectly to almost any haircut. Men with long hair look particularly cool. But sometimes the individual strands are so wide that no amount of hairdressing can help, and all it can do is stand on end. To promote a good head of hair, baby's heads are routinely shaved at three months of age. It tends to only come in one colour, however, and although *hitam* (black) is the predominant shade, it's surprising how common dyeing to jet-black is. Sometimes when the light catches it, natural Indonesian hair shows off tinges of red and amber.

COPYRIGHT

Copyright laws are relaxed to say the least in Jakarta. Have entire books copied at a fraction of the shop price with a colour reproduction of the cover too. Photocopy shops exist all over Jakarta and every office worth its salt employs people specifically to do photocopying. The same lax laws apply to video cassettes and computer software but not audio cassettes. Video rental stores were common until about 1991 but tighter legislation led to their replacement by harder-to-bootleg laserdiscs. Until 1989 pirate music cassettes were the norm but this all stopped when the big companies moved in.

Basically it's a free for all. *Jurassic Park* was available on bootleg video mere days after its official release in Jakarta. It seems someone had smuggled a handy-cam into the cinema and thus earned a small, quick fortune. Slapdash unauthorized translations of popular books are hastily assembled and put on bookshop shelves. The popular British soap-opera, *Eastenders*, had its theme tune stolen to be used in TV advertising, and the children's programme *Teletubbies* underwent a similar corruption. Wholesale rip-offs of *Disney* merchandise become cheap and cheerful children's books. *Asterix*, *Tin Tin* and *Garfield* are kidnapped in the same way. It's a shame: Indonesia has a limitless wealth of legends, folk-tales and storytelling — it does not need to copy so many other countries' ideas.

PHOTOGRAPHY

Photographers will have a whale of a time in Indonesia, and ordinary people are able to indulge themselves too. Film (said *filum*) is cheaper, as is *cuci cecak* (processing and printing). Photo shops are busy places: Jakartans, like the Japanese, love taking photos of one another standing in front of something. Be it the "Time We Went To McDonalds", or "A Man We Met At The Mall", or "Our Neighbour's Circumcision", it gets its photo taken.

The dominant photo shop in Jakarta is the green *Fuji Film* shop. Using fast, automated printing machines (for all C41 films), they claim to be able to print films in a record twenty-two minutes, although the average wait is rarely less than an hour. Their cheap and cheerful approach is not without its drawbacks, staff often having little idea about such basics of film-handling as not treading on negatives. Fuji staff also have the infuriating habit of only printing the pictures which they think we would like. Pictures that look a touch "arty" or blurred, or several frames of a similar picture get ignored, so ask them to *"tolong, cetak semua"* (please print the lot). Should your package reveal pale-looking photos or pictures with one colour bias, assume the chemicals in their machine need topping up. And ask them to do it again. Blok M has lots of good photo shops, and quite a few bad ones too.

For decent enlargements, an excellent choice of films, new and used camera parts and repairs you can do worse than to visit *Jakarta Foto* on Jl Sabang. Kodachrome slide film is sold at *Jakarta Foto* but be warned: to be processed it must be sent out of the country. The professional photographer working in Indonesia should look to Singapore for the most reliable processing. For the unfussy snapper, Jakarta is just fine.

In terms of taking pictures you have an endless choice of subject matter to photograph, both day and night. The sunlight bleaches out a lot of colour from photographs. Because it sits so high in the sky, the sun robs your pictures of nearly all the shadow.

A polarizing filter will bring back some of the shadow and darken skies. A fill-in flash is a good idea on these occasions to avoid too much contrast. And you have about an hour in the evening before it's dark when shadows get long.

Jakarta looks particularly photogenic at night. Drive up Jl Ciledug Raya towards Pasar Kebayoran Lama at night and see the night market in progress. Streets are lit entirely by gas lamps — an excellent light source — and which, in combination with a high-speed black and white film, make for very effective pictures. If you put a tripod up, some weird and wonderful colours are had after a few minutes on *film berwarna* (colour film), particularly low ASA films, with the B shutter.

People in Indonesia are generally very receptive to being photographed but it's only polite to check first. In tourist areas you may be asked to pay before you shoot. Some Javanese are superstitious about being photographed in groups of three, believing it tremendous bad luck and that one of them will soon come a cropper. A lot of Indonesians don't smile in photographs, perhaps because smiling is associated with a lack of self-control, perhaps because they have bad teeth.

Chapter Eleven

WAYS OF GETTING ABOUT

TRAFFIC

It's not good. It takes longer to get from one side of Jakarta to the other, than it does getting to Bogor from Jakarta. At first glance, short distance travel in Jakarta is a nightmare scenario. A faster option is to take an *ojek* (motorbike) with which you can weave in and out of traffic and overtake the worst jams, but entirely at your own risk. *Ojek* may be the fastest, but they are quite definitely not the safest. Keep your legs flush to the bike, or risk having one wrenched off by a bus.

Being the smallest vehicles on the streets, *ojek* have no option other than obeying the pecking order of Jakarta's traffic. Smaller vehicles can only give way to bigger ones. In theory, a person must give way to an *ojek*, which in turn must give way to a *bajaj* (motorized rickshaw), which has to give way to a car, which in turn submits to a *kijang* (van) or *mikrolet* (minivan), which has to make way for a *metromini* (mad orange bus). The problems start when you have, for example, two *metromini* heading towards one another. Which one is supposed to give way? Tricky. One of them certainly should, and at the last millisecond one of them nearly always does. People with pacemakers are warned.

This seems to be the prevailing logic of Jakarta's traffic. While it appears nothing short of bedlam to the casual observer, it should be pointed out just how few major accidents do actually occur. You might expect to be involved in a minor car crash on a daily basis when you first experience Jakarta's traffic, but this is not the case. True, there are an awful lot of dented vehicles to be seen in the city, but nowhere near as many as might be expected. Serious accidents between large vehicles, particularly intercity buses, are rumoured to be far more frequent than the papers actually let on, the rumour being that traffic accidents are in fact so commonplace that the media has given up reporting them.

Aim for the middle of the road and swerve only when absolutely necessary. Keep your eyes open at all times. One-way signs, white divider lines, no-entry signs, and other road regulations are often meaningless to drivers in Indonesia. And police. Jakarta is one of few places in the world where you can be stopped for driving carefully.

Never assume you have the right of way in Jakarta, there is always someone, somewhere taking a "short cut" the wrong way down a one-way street. Keep your eyes peeled too for the many makeshift "roundabouts" intended to slow traffic at crossroads. Basically unlit oildrums, they make a horrible sound upon collision. Be wary also of Jakarta's alarmingly high curbs. Certain roads like Jl Buncit Raya are "dual carriageways" and have certain sections of lane separated by foot-high dividers. Driving over one in the dark, which unknowing drivers are prone to, completely wrecks the undercarriage. Also in place are a billion *polisi tidur* ("sleeping police" speed humps), there solely to wreck a car's suspension. They were certainly not intended for slowing the traffic, as this is the last thing drivers do when approaching them. One of the few things that will slow traffic down is the colour yellow. It symbolizes death and is a sure sign that a funeral procession is imminent. The traffic slows for a hearse, but not an ambulance.

It's said that driving unleashes the evil in everyone, and Indonesians are no exception; normally placid individuals are transformed into raging dictators once behind the wheel. Fortunately, there are more passengers than drivers in Jakarta. Drivers honk their horns constantly, especially when approaching corners.

Use of the horn means only "I am hurtling towards you, watch out because I might run you over." When drivers leave one indicator flashing continuously, or flash their headlights, they want you to give way. This is particularly alarming in the case of vehicles which are moving rapidly towards you. A constantly flashing indicator means they have no intention of giving way. You move.

Jakarta's traffic jams are phenomenal. Engines are turned off, windows unwound and all hope lost. Even the city's many toll roads are jammed to the back teeth. Giving drivers the option of buying a few hundred metres of "freeway" simply doesn't work. The root of the trouble lies in the fact Jakarta is based around a single main arterial road, running north to south. Jakarta's concentric "design" means that the centres of public activity are bang in the middle of the city. There isn't necessarily a lack of roads, it's just that everybody wants to get to more or less the same place at the same time. Jakarta's administration has it seems, given the public a city which simply invites traffic jams.

The situation is exasperated further by the seemingly random way traffic regulations are chopped and changed. It's quite possible to drive down a road one day, only to find it running in the opposite direction the following day. This was very true of Jl Melawai Raya in Blok M which, during the construction of the bus terminal, was changed overnight from a two-way street into a one-way street. To confuse things, the following week it became one-way in the other direction and a week later, a single bus lane running in the opposite direction to the one-way traffic was introduced. The constant construction work being done in Jakarta is another disruption to the traffic flow. To add to the confusion, it's common for one length of road to go through several name changes before it comes to an end. No one is sure which road ends where and which starts where — best of luck.

Clearly, the safety of the pedestrian in Jakarta is of little importance, and you really do need to look both ways before crossing. Having said this you may be surprised by the way many Indonesians, particularly in crowded areas, cross the street seemingly oblivious to the traffic, leaving drivers to swerve around them. It has been suggested that the reasoning behind this lies in the potential trouble that would befall anyone unfortunate enough to run down a pedestrian. The ever-present threat of a lynch-mob emerging from nowhere in a matter of seconds is, apparently, sufficient reason to walk across the road with your eyes closed. And it has to be understood that for Jakarta's citizens, streets are multipurpose extensions of the *kampung* — a place to hang out, play badminton, football. Traffic is almost peripheral.

Attempts by the government to stem the terrible traffic jams have included the introduction in 1992 of a "three-in-one" system. This meant that any vehicle wishing to travel on the main roads of Sudirman, Thamrin, Rasuna Said and Gatot Subroto had to have at least three passengers inside. The irony is that drivers had to resort to hiring extra "passengers" to fulfil the quota; drive down any of the roads approaching the main thoroughfares before 10 a.m. and see hundreds of potential "jockeys" waiting to be hired. Invariably children, they charge a minimal amount depending how far you are going. Yet the clamour among the kids to land themselves a vehicle is so fervent that fights regularly break out, whilst drivers who refuse the "service" often have their vehicles banged. In 1998 this project was scrapped and replaced with a system of stickers. Vehicles wishing to enter the same "restricted" area had to display one of three prepaid stickers: a single entry sticker, a one day unlimited entry sticker or a one month unlimited entry sticker. Other attempts to lessen the traffic jams have included the long-running (and, at present, totally impractical) idea of building a subway below Jakarta, and the idea of forcing drivers to pay a road tax to drive down a certain street at a certain time.

But no matter. Because all in all, being given a licence to drive like a nutter on a regular basis is surely nothing less than liberating. Jakarta is a good place to learn to drive. If you can drive unscathed in Jakarta, you can drive anywhere. Guaranteed.

BUSES

On the face of it, Jakarta's bus system appears nothing less than absolute mayhem, and to an extent it is. But behind the apparent chaos, a certain structure prevails. If you don't mind the packed conditions, the interrogation, the heat, the risk of being robbed, the pollution and the generally painful progress from A to B, then buses are a good way to move around town.

The three main services operating in Jakarta are the orange *Metromini*, the double-deckered *Bis Tingkat*, and the modern *Patas*. A ride on a *Metromini* incurs a fixed fee *dekat jauh* (near or far) — highly economical. The drawbacks, however, with *Metromini* travel are many. The discomfort is exceptional, even if you do manage to get a seat.

Soon after you get on, someone behind you invariably throws up. You ask if they're okay and they say *"tidak apa apa"* (it doesn't matter) as it flows the length of the bus. After a few minutes, when it's clearly hot enough to fry rice, you start wondering why no one has opened a window, only to be reminded how very fearful Indonesians are of anything remotely draughty. The belief is that any lengthy exposure to wind results in untold health problems known primarily as *masuk angin* (entered wind).

Indonesians are notoriously bad travellers, which is surprising since they do an awful lot of it. It's not such a problem for the youngsters but many of the older generation are fearful of riding even an escalator, let alone an intercity bus. Getting robbed isn't hard either. Pickpockets and bag-slashers operate happily on these buses, sometimes hijacking an entire vehicle in order to give each passenger a thorough going-over.

The number of people that can be crammed into a single *metromini* is beyond belief. People are stuffed in to the point where the bus leans over so much, it practically moves forward on two wheels. And still people continue to pile in, many of them transporting enormous chest-high parcels, sacks and boxes of bed stuffing and prawn crackers. Passengers end up hanging out of the door and holding their breath inside. And still a couple of buskers manage to squeeze on and start jamming. Indonesians are extremely resilient it seems; old people, heavily pregnant women and knee-high schoolkids alike are thrown around the bus with the same blank abandon. *Metromini* always go as fast as possible, they make no concession.

Metromini operate on a commission-only basis. The driver and conductor hire the buses themselves and take their wages in cash from fares collected. They are understandably keen to pick up as many passengers as possible, no matter how close the destination. Buses must therefore travel as fast as possible in order to complete the route and start again. *Metromini* drivers are infamously bad. If one is heading towards you, give way. They overtake on hills, on corners, and when it's three or four cars deep. Any driving tactic that is remotely dangerous is practised by the *metromini* drivers of Jakarta.

It's no joke. In 1994, a *metromini* travelling at idiotic speed came off a bridge and plunged into the Ciliwung river, killing everyone aboard except the driver. Relatives of the dead later set the bus depot on fire, while the driver, after being tracked to an address in West Java, was thrown in *penjara* (jail). Similar horror was played out on an intercity Jakarta-Bandung bus in March '96, in which all 31 passengers were incinerated inside the bus. It crashed because the driver had nodded off after taking two barbiturate pills. But *metromini* drivers never learn: two years later near Jl Pramuka, one which had just passed over a railway crossing stopped to haggle with some potential passengers. They were so engrossed in their haggling that they didn't hear the train slam into the coach which had been stranded on the railway lines behind them.

One of the people hanging out of the bus is the "conductor" who, when not collecting fares, spends his time counting a wad of cheesy-red 100 rupiah notes and hollering their destination to the world. Some of their cries have become legendary: *"Blok M"* for example when said at a hundred times a minute becomes *"blemblemblemblemblemblemblem ..."*. It's not uncommon for conductors to leap off the bus and "round up" passengers, some of whom had perhaps no intention of getting on that particular bus. So a hundred metres down the street you will hear either *"kiri pak"* (left here mate) or the sound of a coin tapped on glass, and off they get again. Sometimes the passengers can't make up their minds whether to get off or not; easily decided when the "conductor" shoves them off. The progress of a *metromini* is marked in this way; stopping and starting, stopping and starting, all done as hastily as possible.

Sometimes the bus takes a totally different route, depending on the traffic ahead. If the bus is stuck in a jam, or word comes through that the area ahead is *macet total* (badly jammed) the driver might endeavour to do a three-point turn in the middle of the madness. Naturally, this only adds to the confusion and disappointment of those passengers who had hoped to get to the destination displayed on the front of the bus.

The pollution emitted by most buses is immoral. You do not want to be behind one of these monsters if you are travelling in a *bajaj* or even a taxi where, although spared the brunt of the thick, black exhaust smoke, a ton still gets through the car's AC system, though somewhat chilled.

Many of Jakarta's buses are a truly sad sight: string holding the doors closed, headlamps missing, wiring like spaghetti and tyres like boiled eggs. Re-cutting the tread on tyres is standard practice in Jakarta, but often even that gets bypassed. Sometimes repairs are carried out with the bus still in motion. The conductor removes a panel from the floor of the bus and gets everyone to step over him as he climbs down into the undercarriage for a look. The bus may stall, or simply conk out, leaving the conductor with no option but to jump off and start pushing. Sometimes the passengers join in, sometimes not. Either way, bump-starting a bus full of passengers is no mean task.

The government regularly attempts to clean up the bus service. In 1994 it introduced a strict table of conditions with which buses were expected to comply. Buses producing too much smoke were threatened with massive fines, far beyond the pocket of any *metromini* driver. And because nearly every bus on the street failed to meet these conditions, the implementation of these laws became an impossibility, and a year later nothing had changed, although a lot of drivers were missing their licenses. Another new law was aimed at cutting down the number of people on a single bus (after a glut of death-by-falling-out-a-bus-in-motion reports), and stated that buses had to be able to close their doors. The way round this was simply to cram the usual amount of people in and then shutting the door. This of course resulted in perhaps the single most uncomfortable bus ride of all time.

Of a similar price and standard as a *metromini* is the *bis tingkat*. Run by the government *PPD*, these are old Volvo and British Leyland double-deckers obtained apparently "on loan" from Singapore and never given back. These drivers receive a fixed salary and are therefore under less pressure to pick up passengers. The ride is slightly less hectic.

Not all bus rides are hellish. For a theoretically more comfortable ride take the "clean" and "modern" *Patas* service. These offer space, piped music and relative comfort. Also a government-owned service, it costs twice the price of a *tingkat* while the air-conditioned version, *Patas A.C.* is some five times more. In 1998, following the economic crisis which gripped the country, the *Patas A.C.* was indefinitely scrapped because it had "failed to live up to its operating slogan — fast with limited passengers." Other services

229

were hit too: an estimated 30% of the city's 70,000 buses began indefinitely gathering dust somewhere, the spare parts needed being too expensive for the average bus crew to afford. Completion of the gigantic bus terminal at Blok M Mall has helped to take some of the strain out of Jakarta's utterly mad bus service, and reduce the traffic jams that buses incur, but with buses in general some 30% more crowded, a journey on a Jakarta bus is still a long, long ride.

TAXIS

Taxis are abundant in Jakarta and come in a variety of colours. While many are clean and efficient taxis with polite and honest drivers, many more are absolute Taxis From Hell, roaming the streets of the capital in search of another mug. As a rough guide, you'd be wise sticking to the blue ones. *Bluebird* is a generally reliable service, only just eclipsed by *Kosti Jaya*. Both are blue and pride themselves on customer care.

Not only should a *Bluebird* or *Kosti Jaya* give efficient service, it should also smell good. Since Jakarta's streets are no perfume-garden, many vehicles are equipped with powerful air fresheners, the resulting scent of which is often more overpowering than the smells outside. Taxis in hot countries tend to keep their windows wound up to allow the AC to circulate, and of course germs to spread.

Coming a close third in reliability terms are *Express* (white), *Ratax* (gray) and perhaps *Koperasi* (green). One of the oldest taxi firms operating in the city is *President* (red and yellow). *President Taxis* have a bad reputation. While it's true that grinding their way round Jakarta are a number of barely-functioning examples, it would be unfair to label every *President* a complete waste of time. The owners have made efforts to dispel this unsavoury image of late by putting newer vehicles onto the streets. But this is not the issue when you consider that *President* is often the only taxi to operate throughout the night. Just when you think you have to walk the ten miles home through a *kampung* you don't know, out of nowhere appears a *President*. At three in the morning you are unlikely to complain that the AC isn't working and that it has cockroaches in the back.

On the other extreme is *Silverbird*. A spin-off in the *Bluebird* line, this taxi is a black limo affair with darkened windows, decorous drivers and a higher starting fee. It's the height of luxury.

In practical terms you are usually expected to tip the driver. Rp 500 is a standard sum as they rarely seem to have change below Rp 1000. There's an initial starting fee which inevitably increases from year to year (in 1990 it was Rp 500, five years later it had doubled), and a charge for every kilometre covered. The length of time spent with the taxi is also a factor; witness how the meter continues to rise even when busy going nowhere in a traffic jam.

It's best if you know where you are going. If you don't, you should at least try and sound as if you know where you are going. It helps if you can beat the driver to the punch and tell him which way you want to go before he asks. For example, if you were travelling from Pasar Minggu to Blok M you could *"lewat* (go via) *Kapten Tendean"*, or you could just as well *"lewat Kemang"*. If in doubt you should state that you just want to go there *"langsung"* (directly).

Obvious problems arise when the driver refuses to use the meter, or seems to be deliberately going the wrong way. You are better off leaving the taxi altogether in these circumstances. Occasionally it becomes clear, after being in the taxi for a few minutes, that the driver has never driven before; that he is *baru* (new) to the job and doesn't actually know where he is going. More than likely he's a visiting relative who has agreed to give the taxi's regular driver a day off. Most drivers are pleased to receive a foreign customer and inevitably have all sorts of questions to ask. Prepare to talk.

But all in all, taxis are an inexpensive way to travel about the city and the next best thing to having your own chauffeur. You might be asked to leave the taxi if the driver thinks a particular area is too jammed (*macet)* or flooded (*banjir*), while on a bad day they refuse to even stop.

CARS

Cars are conspicuously expensive in Jakarta. At one point it was quite possible to buy a second-hand car and sell it on a couple of years later at profit. In 1996 *PT Timor Putra Nasional* astounded the public by retailing a car at the comparatively low price of Rp 36 million. To great fanfare the *Timor* was trumpeted as Indonesia's "first national car". The reality was less precise. It soon transpired that the vehicle was an imported Korean car fitted out with a few local bits and pieces. Nothing regarding its manufacture actually occurred in Indonesia — it came ready-made on a big boat. People began joking that Indonesia had obtained a 28th province which officials were tentatively calling "South Korea" for the time being.

At the time, however, it did provoke a minor price war among Indonesian car makers. Yet the farcical nature of the whole affair angered everyone, particularly the USA which took Indonesia to the World Trade Office for "violation of international rules" — and won. The rest of Asia was just as indignant. It seems the government, in a generous gesture to highlight the introduction of its national car policy, had granted the manufacturer of the *Timor* a number of hefty tax concessions. To prove the point, the manufacturer's brother (who didn't get any breaks) put out an almost identical car priced some $3,000 more at Rp 41 million. When it was revealed that the company was being controlled by ex-President Suharto's youngest son, Hutomo Mandala Putra, the preferential treatment made more sense. And when, during the furore, the government hurriedly issued a decree stating that wholly Indonesian-owned companies which bore Indonesian trademarks were free to import foreign car parts tariff-free, it made even more sense, especially as the *Timor* was the only company to meet such a qualification.

Other locally-produced, or partially locally-produced cars include the *Kijang* and *Mobil Rakyat*. Although the majority of cars on the streets are manufactured abroad some, like the *Suzuki Adinegoro*, are "half-and-half". The bodies are produced locally, while the engines and parts are made elsewhere, usually Japan. Presumably, it's the massive import taxes on getting foreign vehicles into Indonesia that account for the unfathomably high prices of cars in Indonesia. If cars were more affordable, everyone would have one, and no one would be able to move anywhere at any time; gridlock indeed.

There are some unusual specimens crawling the streets of Jakarta. One such specimen is the mutant Morris Minor service of north Jakarta. Here, Morris Minors, which have been chopped up, lengthened and converted into something else entirely, work the streets like old warhorses. While many of Jakarta's taxis are typically the *Corona* brand, some particularly clapped-out *Holdens* are used in the *4848* service to Bandung.

An upwardly mobile Jakartan family owns at least a *Kijang* (check its "Full Pressed Body"), equivalent in size and capacity to a Ford Transit. Land Rover-style vehicles are also popular, but recent years have seen a shift away from "passenger-vans" towards more sedan-type cars. The point with cars is that if you can afford to buy and run vehicles like these, you can probably afford to pay someone to drive them for you. People with any sense do not drive themselves — they have it done for them. Many companies provide employees with transport in just this shape: *Kijang* and driver. A sure sign of affluence in Jakarta — of having "made it" — is being able to keep a driver hanging around for hours on end.

On the OPEC notice board, Indonesia is a big word. And in Jakarta petrol prices are good and cheap. Heavily leaded, totally crude and shamelessly monopolized by the Suharto family, mind you, but good and cheap nonetheless. Motor repairs are reasonable too: stop at any *bengkel* (garage) and point out your problem. Workmanship is good and when spare parts are lacking, expect some ingenious, though efficient, bodging. Get your car washed the authentic way: park it in the shallow of the local river and get it washed. "Dirty car, sir? No thanks, I've already got one."

An international driving licence is strongly recommended for foreign drivers in Indonesia. Driving without a licence is a serious offence, although the *polisi* are very understanding upon the appearance of a little *ma'af* (apology) money. The youngest you may drive in Indonesia is 18. At the very least you should bring your local licence, and then apply for the Indonesian licence. The SIM (*Surat Izin Mengemudi*) is obtained from the Police headquarters, *Polda Metro Jaya* at the Semanggi intersection, just across from the Hilton Hotel. The process is a hot and seemingly complicated one, the place invariably crowded and the red tape apparently endless. You may want to take someone with you who is more familiar with the process, and used to queuing up. Alternatively, there are on-site helpers to ease you through, although you need to settle on a price beforehand. After completing the initial form, you may be asked to produce a copy of your passport, a letter (in Indonesian) confirming your employment, a doctor's letter verifying good health, your "blue book" (STMD police book), your international or home licence, and of course, some money. About Rp 150,000 will get you a licence and should cover all interim expenses. After your application, you need to take a written test. Ironically, there is no actual driving test necessary to get a driving licence in Indonesia.

BECAK

Sadly, there are hardly any *becak* left in Jakarta. A 1991 story in the *Jakarta Post* illustrates why: *"ARTIFICIAL REEFS GOOD FOR FISH*

'Artificial reefs made out of mounds of pedicabs and old buses thrown into the waters of Jakarta Bay will not pollute the area,' says the head of City Fishery Agency. He said the reef area was the meeting place of sea currents that make the area a good place for fish to multiply." It's true, folks.

A *becak* is a three-wheeled pedicab; two at the front (over which passengers are seated) and one at the back where drivers work their sinewy legs. There are still a few *becak* operating in Ancol, and the occasional pocket of resistance in back street areas of Bintaro, but on the whole they are a thing of the past. The plan to eradicate them originated in the '70s under the instruction of Governor Ali Sadikin. He restricted them to limited zones and made licence renewal difficult. It came to a head under Governor Suprapto in *Visit Indonesia Year '91* when a mammoth police clean-up operation went into effect, finally ridding the city of *becak*. It had been decided that *becak* were inhumane and that death among *becak* drivers from expanded heart and lung was high. It was decided also that *becak* didn't do much to enhance the modern face of Jakarta. Far too *kampungan* (unrefined) apparently.

One particular "cleanup" witnessed in the streets of Bendungan Hiliar had police and soldiers forcibly removing *becak* from drivers, piling them up in a truck and throwing them in the sea where the authorities could pretend they had always lain. A lot of jobs were lost. Some found work driving *bajaj,* some opted to quit the city for good and *pulang kampung* (go home), while many more became responsible for the million *ojek* (motorbike) that currently fulfil the continuing demand for cheap short distant travel around Jakarta. For the best *becak* in the land go to Yogyakarta, the *becak* capital of the world.

BAJAJ

Bajaj, on the other hand, are cheap taxis. Three-wheeled and orange, *bajaj* (pronounced, "badge-eye") are the two-stroke motorized rickshaws which get you from A to B for a modest fee.

They are the cockroaches of Jakarta transport: the noisiest, hottest and possibly the dirtiest things on the roads. Get stuck behind one in a traffic jam and watch your vehicle slowly fill up with nauseating blue *bajaj* smoke.

Bajaj are not permitted on big roads like Thamrin; restricted (like *becak*) to working one area. Drivers may refuse to go somewhere if they think it's too close, or too far, or they think it might be *macet* (jammed) ahead. You can get two people comfortably inside, up to four if pushed. Ensure you have agreed on the price beforehand; some hard bargaining may be required. Tip the driver enough and he may even let you drive.

Since *bajaj* don't have any air-conditioning, they can get very hot. There's the story of a man wearing plastic shoes while stuck in the back of one for over an hour in a traffic jam. When he finally arrived he found his shoes had melted to the floor of the vehicle, and he had to be cut free.

Bajaj first appeared in the early '70s and were an instant success. Television adverts at the time warned pregnant women to think twice before using one, due to the extremely potholed condition of Jakarta's back streets, not to mention the bouncing, trampoline-style bridges in certain parts of town. The risk of whacking your head on the roof of the *bajaj* every time it hits a pothole is high. Suspension, like AC, is not part of the design.

The competition on the streets is fierce; while the bulk of Jakarta's *bajaj* are run by several cooperatives (mainly *PT Kopaja*), many are privately-owned. Some drivers customize their *bajaj* with pictures of Iwan Fals or pin-ups of *dangdut* singers. A new *bajaj* would cost about 5 million rupiah to buy.

Variations on the traditional orange design have emerged in recent years. Yellow, bigger and quieter, the main design fault is a lack of division between the passenger and the driver, which means you are more likely than ever to end up wrapped around the driver when he brakes suddenly.

The bajaj: it gets you from A to B.

The government had hoped to rid Jakarta of all its *bajaj* by 1995, just like it did in 1991 with *becak*, but like *becak*, which took 20 years to be eradicated, *bajaj* are going to be around for a while longer yet.

AIRPORTS

Jakarta has two major airports, *Halim Perdanakusuma* in the east, and *Soekarno-Hatta International* in the northwest. *Halim* is predominantly the domain of the Air Force, *Bandar Udara,* although it still handles domestic flights to Sumatra and places. *Orang asing* (foreigners) coming to Indonesia invariably arrive at *Soekarno-Hatta* Airport. Jakarta is served by a number of international airlines: Qantas, Cathay Pacific, KLM, and more. Direct flights to Bali are also available. Generally speaking, *Garuda Indonesia Airways* takes care of international flights, while domestic business is squabbled over by three other local carriers: *Merpati Nusantara,*

237

Man∂ala and *Sempati*. An airport tax is charged, and for those lucky enough to have stayed more than six months, a massive fiscal is charged, and an exit permit required.

An uncertain time is had by most first time visitors to Jakarta, but this need not be the case. *Soekarno-Hatta* is a modern, spacious, air-conditioned airport, tastefully built in red brick. It has sufficient amenities, adequate information services, money changing facilities (in the baggage hall) and clean-ish toilets. Terminal 1 is domestic and terminal 2, international. It's not a bad airport, not as swish as Singapore or Kuala Lumpur, but hardly a *gubuk bambu* (bamboo hut) either.

The madness starts when you leave Customs. If you are being met, here is where they will be. Porters are available to help you, but need paying. Expect repeated offers of transport to Jakarta centre ("Taxi, mister?"), which might well be genuine, but no guarantees can be made. Post-flight, you are probably in no mood for much debate should the deal turn out to be less than fair, and you are much better off taking a taxi from the taxi queue. If possible, take one from the more reputable firms, like *Bluebir∂* or *Koʃti Jaya*. In theory, you are safe from rip-off drivers at the airport, as all taxi passengers are given a card detailing the taxi's make and number, as well as toll-road charges the passenger must pay.

The airport is a fair way (25 km) from the centre and linked by a fast toll road. From the airport to Blok M, for example, you are looking at a comparatively high fare, but which should include the airport surcharge and a couple of toll-road fees. A far more cost-effective way to the city centre is the *Damri* bus service which leaves every half an hour for Blok M, Kemayoran, Gambir and Rawamangun. To catch the *Damri* back to the airport, go to the Panglima Polim side of Blok M Plaza.

Jakarta's *Soekarno-Hatta* airport is significant because with it passes any illusion that you are in the "mystical east". For, soon after leaving the airport, as you head along the toll road, you pass through a gateway, two large Balinese Hindu-style constructions, and think to yourself "ah, the mystical east" only to be struck soon after by the terrifying truth that is Jakarta and the rest.

VISAS AND IMMIGRATION

If you come from America, Australia, Austria, Britain, Belgium, Brunei, Canada, Denmark, Finland, France, Germany, Greece, Holland, Iceland, Ireland, Italy, Japan, Liechtenstein, Luxembourg, Malaysia, Malta, New Zealand, Norway, Philippines, Singapore, South Korea, Spain, Sweden, Switzerland, Taiwan or Thailand then you probably do not need a visa to come to Indonesia, providing you don't stay over 60 days, have an ongoing ticket, and can prove that you have sufficient funds to remain for the duration. At the airport immigration desk a stamp is thumped into your passport (which must have at least 6 months left on it). This is your tourist visa, and probably the first of many.

You cannot work on a tourist visa, and it's notoriously difficult to change to another visa without first leaving the country. This usually entails a trip to Singapore if you are in Jakarta. Visas are needed for people intending to work or study in Indonesia and are definitely best left to be arranged by your employer. The immigration department is a notoriously "difficult" one to make much headway with. Consequently, it's better a "fixit" man from your place of employment acts on your behalf by greasing the relevant palms.

If you do stay beyond two months, you are advised to bring a passport with a good many blank pages left. After only a short time in Indonesia you accumulate lots of stamps, each one filling a whole page of the passport. One of the visas currently in use include Business Visas (*Visa Kunjungan*) which are issued at the airport and give you 2 months, although theoretically you are not allowed to work on it. A better option is a Multiple-Entry Business

Visa which is valid for 12 months and must be applied for at an consular outside Indonesia. Again, you are not supposed to work on one and are required to leave the country every four months. The same is true for a Social/Cultural Visit Visa (*Visa Usaha/Social Budaya*) which permits a stay of six months. During this time the processing towards a *KIM/S* can begin. The *Kartu Izin Masuk Sementara* is a one-year, temporary-admission identity card with your photo and fingerprints on it. In theory it should be carried with you everywhere. While many foreigners hold the *KIM/S*, its use is being superseded by the *KITAS* visa (*Kartu Izin Tinggal Terbatas*). This offers the best security for foreigners in Indonesia and is a must for admission to international schools.

Don't forget, however, now that you have overstepped the "tourist" status of 60 days you (or hopefully your sponsor) are liable to pay a couple of extra things. The first is *Pajak Bangsa Asing*, or foreigner's tax, which is made on all foreigners who reside longer than 90 days in Indonesia. The second liability is the fiscal needed to get out of the country. Fiscal cannot be paid, however, without first obtaining an Exit Visa. And as with most visa/tax obligations, little prior notice is given and overdue payments invariably result in a fine.

Inevitably all this is a nightmare should you attempt to do it yourself. Best have a word with that "fixit" man. Jakarta's immigration offices, resembling a cross between a benefit office and a Turkish bath, are not the best places to spend the afternoon.

Immigration officials at *Soekarno-Hatta* are known on occasion to be rather awkward concerning the particulars of a foreigner's passport. If you are taken to a room for "a closer look" at your passport, and assuming you are not a smuggler, there's no reason why you should have to make any payoffs, unless it becomes clear you really have no other option. Try asking for an official receipt, this should determine if their charges are legitimate or not. While you can, just say no.

SOME FOREIGN EMBASSIES IN JAKARTA

Visa regulations and prices inevitably vary from time to time, so if in doubt contact one of the embassies in Jakarta. Alternatively, obtain a copy of the Diplomatic and Consular List published by the Department of Foreign Affairs.

America: Jl Merdeka Selatan 5. Tel: 360360

Australia: Jl Rasuna Said Kav 15-16. Tel: 5227111

Austria: Jl Diponegoro 44. Tel: 338090

Belgium: Wisma BCA, Jl Sudirman, Kav 22-23. Tel: 5710510

Britain: Jl Thamrin 75. Tel: 330904

Brunei: Wisma BCA, Jl Sudirman, Kav 22-23. Tel: 5712180

Canada: Lantai 5, Wisma Metropolitan 1, Jl Sudirman, Kav 29. Tel: 5250709

Denmark: Wisma Bina Mulia, Lantai 4, Jl Rasuna Said, Kav 10. Tel: 5204350

Finland: Wisma Bina Mulia, Lantai 10, Jl Rasuna Said, Kav 10. Tel: 5207408

France: Jl Thamrin 20. Tel: 3142807

Germany: Jl Raden Saleh 54-56. Tel: 3849547

Holland: Jl Rasuna Said, Kav S-3. Tel: 511515

India: Jl Rasuna Said 51. Tel: 5204152

Italy: Jl Diponegoro 45. Tel: 337445

Japan: Jl Thamrin 24. Tel: 324308

Malaysia: Jl Rasuna Said Kav X/6/1-3. Tel: 5224947

New Zealand: Jl Diponegoro 41. Tel: 330680

Norway: Wisma Bina Mulia, Lantai 4, Jl Rasuna Said, Kav 10. Tel: 5251990

Pakistan: Jl Teuku Umar 50. Tel: 3144009

Papua New Guinea: Lantai 6, Panin Bank Centre, Jl Sudirman 1. Tel: 7251218

Philippines: Jl Imam Bonjol 6-8. Tel: 3100345

Poland: Jl Diponegoro 65. Tel: 3140509

Russia: Jl Thamrin 13. Tel: 327007

Singapore: Jl Rasuna Said, Block X, Kav 2, No. 4. Tel: 5201489

South Korea: Jl Gatot Subroto 57. Tel: 5201915

Spain: Jl Agus Salim 61. Tel: 331414

Sri Lanka: Jl Diponegoro 70. Tel: 3161886

Sweden: Wisma Bina Mulia. Jl Rasuna Said, Kav 10. Tel: 5201551

Switzerland: Jl Rasuna Said, B-1, Kav X-3. Tel: 516061

Thailand: Jl Imam Bonjol 74. Tel: 3904055

Vietnam: Jl Teuku Umar 25. Tel: 3100357

INDONESIAN EMBASSIES AROUND THE WORLD

America: 2020 Massachusetts Ave NW, Washington DC 20036. Tel: (202) 7755200

Australia: 8 Darwin Ave, Yarralumla, ACT 2600. Tel: (06) 2733222

Belgium: Avenue de Turvueren 294, 1150 Brussels, Belgium. Tel: (02) 7715060

Britain: 38 Grosvenor Square, London W1X 9AD. Tel: (0171) 4997661

Brunei: KG Sungai Hanching Baru, Simpang 528, Lot 4494, Jl Muara, Bandar Seri Begawan. Tel: 330180

Canada: 287 Maclaren St, Ottawa, Ontario K2P OL9. Tel: (613) 2367403

Denmark: Orehoj Alle 12900, Hellerup, Copenhagen. Tel: (624422)

France: 47-49 Rue Cortambert 75116, Paris. Tel: (1) 45.03.07.60)

Germany: 2 Bernakasteler Strasse, 5300 Bonn 2. Tel: (228) 382990)

Holland: 8 Tobias Asserlaan, 2517 KC Den Haag. Tel : (070) 3108100

India: 50-A Chanakyapuri, New Delhi. Tel: 602348

Italy: 53 Via Campania, Rome 00187. Tel: 4825951

Japan: 9-2 Higashi Gotanda 5 Chome, Shinagawa-ku, Tokyo.
Tel: (03) 34414201

Luxembourg: Ave Guillame 62, L-1650 Luxembourg. Tel: (455858)

Malaysia: 233 Jl Tun Razak, Kuala Lumpur. Tel: (03) 9842011

New Zealand: 70 Glen Rd, Kelburn, Wellington. Tel: (04) 4758669

Norway: Inkonitogata 8, Oslo 2. Tel: (2) 441121

Papua New Guinea: 1 & 2/140, Kiroki St, Sir John Guise Drive, Waigoani,
Port Moresby. Tel: 253116, 253118, 253544)

Philippines: 185/187 Salcedo St, Legaspi Village, Makati, Manila.
Tel: (2) 855061 to 7

Singapore: 7 Chatsworth Rd. Tel: 7377422

Spain: 13 C. del Cinca, Madrid. Tel: 4130294

Sweden: Strandvagen 47/V, 11456, Stockholm. Tel: (08) 6635470

Switzerland: 51 Elfenauweg, 3006 Bern. Tel: 440983

Thailand: 600-602 Petchburi Rd, Bangkok. Tel: 2523135 to 40

Chapter Twelve

METHOD IN THE MADNESS

CORRUPTION

"If you have knowledge of good and bad, then logically you know that corruption is bad. But in Indonesia sometimes corruption is considered a good thing ..." —Emha Ainun Najib, poet

They won't like you saying so, but the place runs on bribes. This doesn't mean that people need to bribe their maids in order to have their homes cleaned or need to bribe hairdressers into cutting their hair. But bigger things, any kind of official paperwork or documentation, is most definitely speeded up by the simple introduction of a white envelope. Think of your day-to-day bribes as an unofficial tax on living in Indonesia.

The giving and taking of bribes may well be a way of life in Indonesia, but it's not necessarily a sordid affair. Bribes can generally be made in a very casual, unspoken manner, and not without a certain dignity. The reference isn't to a "bribe" itself but to something like *uang rokok* (cigarette money) or *uang kopi* (coffee money) to take the edge off.

But it's not good. It seems at times that Indonesia has become a culture of corruption. Even though umpteen surveys have Indonesia as the number one place in Asia for corruption, it has got to the point, within the country, where people don't even consider it to be especially wrong. At worst, bribery is just considered a bit of innocent "hanky panky" that everyone gets involved in at some point in order to keep the wheels in motion. Even the guidebooks have picked up on it: *"You can take this boat to this place after this time if you keep a few packets of cigarettes handy"* or *"Pak so-and-so will let you stay if you slip him a few extra rupiah ..."*

A testimony to how commonplace bribery has become is the fact every large office employs a resident "fixit" man: someone whose sole job is to get in with the right people and grease the relevant palms. Any company or business person who wants to make headway in Indonesia these days is wise to budget accordingly for the bribes they can end up paying. Journalists, for example, at press launches for eager new businesses are routinely bribed by way of twee envelopes of cash in their press-pack; thus hopefully insuring a good write-up from the press — and hopefully better business. On a more sinister level it's theoretically possible to bribe your way in or out of any situation, no matter how criminal. But don't bank on it.

A definite etiquette is employed when giving and receiving bribes; you should wait to be asked to make the bribe. The bull-in-a-china-shop approach, much favoured by whingeing Westerners who seem to be genetically programmed to complain the instant they realize things are not running exactly as advertised, doesn't work here.

Take the case of foreigners queuing up for visa applications at the Indonesian Embassy in Singapore. One Westerner is already getting hot under the collar. The officials are still not back from lunch yet and it is already two minutes after. When, one by one, the people in the queue behind him are called up to collect their passports, he can only fume with rage. The irate man can't understand what is going on. Feeling cheated, he lashes out at the officials. His passport is put to the bottom of the pile.

By rights, the man was correct. He queued. He paid. He complained when it was late. The problem? He didn't play the game. Compare his tragic plight with the man who'd been told by his Jakarta office exactly how to collect a visa. He waits his turn at the desk, and states his request. They say it won't be ready till tomorrow, but the man has a connecting flight later that after-noon. "Oh dear," says the man in a somewhat measured and wistful tone, "What *am* I going to do?" The embassy official behind the glass is approached by a second man who whispers over-loudly that "Maybe he should try the express service." "Oh yes," says the wide-eyed foreigner, "that would be ever so useful." The whole process takes half an hour at twice the price — game played.

Sometimes no words are even spoken; an empty folder or book may simply be placed in front of the requester. The dodgy handshake is another way of getting where you want; several thousand rupiah are easily concealed this way. And then, as if to give the dealing an official seal of approval, and perhaps the illusion that no "hanky-panky" was in any way involved, a little shiny stamp known as a *materai* will be stuck on the bottom of every document. *Materai* come in a variety of colours and prices, but their absence is enough to render any transaction invalid. With a couple of these and a number of "official" stamps thwacked everywhere, the "official" picture is complete.

But some people don't like corruption; some people know it's bleeding the country to death. And some don't like other people knowing this. One Jakarta journalist suffered an appalling incident: clubbed to death in his own home by an unknown intruder and dying two days later. It transpired he had been investigating corruption — high level corruption.

LOCAL GOVERNMENT

Away from the auspicious heavy hand of Big Brother, the people of Jakarta's backstreets and *kampung* turn a blind eye to the actions of the "real" government. The average person, it seems, prefers relating to something more down-to-earth. Perhaps because the actual system of government is too much to take in at once, a system of local government is the preferred way to keep an eye on things.

At the most fundamental, domestic level of government is the *Rukun Tetangga*. Literally, the "peace keeper", he is known more commonly to his clientele as *"Pak RT"*. For he is the Domestic President; the Man In The Know; the Trusted One. *Pak RT* is the reason people sleep well at night in Indonesia.

The *RT* is aware exactly who is living on his allotted patch: who is visiting, who is dying, who is getting born, and all that. Apart from organizing rubbish disposal for some thirty houses, he provides neighbourhood security in the form of night patrols, known as *hansip*. They make their presence known by whacking a stick against your gate every hour, on the hour. This sort of defeats the object of a "good night's sleep" but for the average Indonesian, this racket-making is a subconscious message that all is well, thus they sleep even better.

The *RT* (pronounced "air-tay") is elected by the people of the neighbourhood and is unpaid — most *RT* have day jobs. If the neighbours are happy with a particular *RT*, he will be voted back into "office" time and again. The importance of his job is immense. He's a vital means of communication between the government and the common people. The *RT* is a focal point for the neigh-bourhood: people know there's always someone to go to if there's a problem. Neighbourhood protection of this kind was introduced during the Japanese occupation of the country, and is something lacking in most Western countries. Indonesians have greater peace of mind knowing their area is protected.

It's possible to run into trouble with your *RT*, depending how liberal your lifestyle is. He might read you the riot-act: no friends of the opposite gender after 10 p.m. and no more than four guests at once. Expect all overnight guests to get his clearance first. Strictly speaking, if you choose to sleep at an address which is different to that stated on your identity card, you must report to the police, as well as to your *RT*. You may then want to break a minor law and sweeten your *RT*'s disgust at your Western ways by plying him with small but regular gifts, particularly if you live in an area which gets shut off at night with a security barrier.

Put eight *RT* together and you have an *RW* (*Rukun Warga*). Twenty *RW* are a *kelurahan* and twenty of these, a *kecamatan*. And there is more; put a few *kecamatan* together and you have one of the five municipalities that make up Jakarta. Each of these is headed by a *walikota*, or mayor, who is in turn responsible to the Governor of Jakarta. The rest is Big Boys' stuff and best left that way.

VIGILANTES

While there are a great many fear-evoking police in the city, the "eye for an eye" approach is still much preferred in settling minor cases of burglary and other domestic crime. Should a *maling* (thief) be caught red-handed, he will be dragged screaming to the local security man's office and systematically beaten up by everyone in the neighbourhood. Naturally, the first to join in is the thief's victims. Only then is the thief taken to the police station for further questioning.

Sometimes, however, this free-for-all system of revenge goes too far. There is the story of a woman in Jakarta who bought a TV on hire-purchase. One day, after she had forgotten to keep up with the repayments, a man arrived to repossess it. Infuriated as she was, she decided to shout *"maling!"* as he was on his way out. Hearing this alarm call, the local *kampung* boys (and there is never a shortage) appeared in force and set about putting to right what they believed was a serious misdeed. The man died later that day from his injuries.

After a while in Jakarta, you start to get the feeling that you ought to be careful what you say to people; careful that you don't upset anyone ... because if you do, there is every chance a couple of their relatives will come and get you one night while you sleep.

GETTING INTO TROUBLE

Ideally, you do not want to get into trouble when in Jakarta, for a number of good reasons. First is the fact that you are foreign. While much of the time this is to your advantage, imagine how much more attention you draw to yourself by getting somehow involved in a fight, for example. Second is the ever-present mob tendency in Indonesia. Actions are very rarely undertaken on an individual basis in this country, and you should be prepared to be amazed at just how quickly a crowd, in the case of a road accident or other dispute, can appear from nowhere. Should you be unfortunate enough to be involved in a minor accident, it's recommended you remain calm, polite, apologetic and get ready to make an on-the-spot payment. If necessary, you should locate a policeman — but don't try to run away.

PANCASILA

Pancasila is the guiding star in Indonesia. It's the basis of the Indonesian outlook — the very bedrock of Being Indonesian. *Pancasila* holds the show together. But some say it's nothing more than brainwashing; a doctrine that has got out of hand. Indonesians couldn't imagine life without it. But do people really live their lives by it? Sort of.

It's everywhere: every conscientious household has a metal plaque of the *Pancasila* symbols nailed above the front door. Every office, reception and workplace, apart from the obligatory President and vice-president portrait shots, should have details of *Pancasila* somewhere on display. It's on the curriculum in every school and stays there through university. In the free elementary schools, little else is taught. Buy a cassette of children's songs and find a least two songs espousing its virtues: "*Whose picture is this? Why, it's Pak Harto! The one who made this country great, the one who gave us* Pancasila, *the way to be great!*" are typical sing-song lyrics for your child to learn off by heart.

The learning process is a continuous one; refresher courses in this five-point way of thinking are part of the package in any situation. Prior to their employment, civil servants are given the "P-4 treatment" — intensive training in *Pancasila*. Following the riots in Jakarta and elsewhere in the country in late July '96, members of the press were summoned to the President's Palace for a 10-day seminar on the subject, as well as a firm reminder on how to report the news in Indonesia.

It hasn't always been around; it came into effect with President Sukarno in 1945 in his determined attempt to give the disparate islands of Indonesia a common ground. If young Indonesians were raised under the same ideology, he reasoned, and taught to think in the same way, the chances of developing a unified nation were that much better. Sukarno stressed there was unity in Indonesia's diversity, that this was the country's strength. And if everyone in the land agrees with each other, only unity can follow. This was his vision: a world of mutual assistance, mutual consensus and collectivism. It was chosen in favour of the more Western-style parliament favoured by his political rivals at the time.

The five principles of *Pancasila* have had a sweeping effect on the way life is lived in Indonesia. The five *sila-sila* (points) are represented by symbols. Top left on the coat of arms is the striking and aggressive image of the buffalo head, as adopted by the *PDI (Parti Demokratik Indonesia)*, and which represents national unity: to be proud of being Indonesian, to be patriotic, to dispel regional suspicions. *Pancasila* teaches people to be Indonesian first and foremost. Regional differences come a close second. Every home is expected to possess a flag to fly on independence day.

Top right is the banyan tree. Adopted by the functioning government party, *Golkar*, and symbolic of national consciousness, it sounds a lot like the one before but with hidden political overtones. It's a convoluted way of stating the accepted method of politics in Indonesia — the one which gives the President the final say every time. Any individual steps forward can only be made with the consensus of all.

Bottom right is the chain. It represents, rather dramatically, the unbroken chain of human generations, with Indonesia a mere link in the larger chain of events.

Bottom left are the sprays of cotton and rice, the basics of life. Every citizen has the right to expect these basics of their society. Yes indeed; social justice no less. Black and white proof that all is fair and equal in Indonesia.

In the centre is the star, or rather God. Indonesians are proud of their religious tolerance. What everyone forgets is that there is no choice in the matter. Everyone has to believe in God. This is the underlying principle of *Pancasila*: a belief in "the one and only God". Under the constitution, an individual is free to embrace the religion of their choice. But get married in Indonesia and you find that a marriage can only be registered under five religions: Islam, Hinduism, Protestantism and Catholicism. Confucianism, as practised by the many Chinese in Indonesia, is not accepted.

ISLAM

To be Indonesian is to be religious. By definition, an *orang Indonesia* believes in God. While it's true the constitution is "tolerant" to all religions, it is Islam that dominates almost every aspect of Indonesian life. Followers of other religions are in the minority: Christians and then Hindus being the next largest groups. Declaring yourself Atheist or Agnostic, or something more obscure like an Orangeman or Druid, is to equate yourself with Communism, and is generally a poorly received notion.

Islam is all-prevailing. It accounts for some 90% of Indonesia's practised religions. And in Indonesia, a lot of religion is practised. The official line on religion is that Indonesia is not a Muslim country; under Islamic law it is not. Yet in many situations, continued preference is given to Muslims — parliament is over-whelmingly Muslim, as is the military. It is said that a Muslim boss is more likely to hire a fellow Muslim than he is a non-Muslim; non-Muslim civil servants complain of limited promotion prospects and life-long prejudice in their careers. But then, civil servants would say that.

To be a Muslim in Indonesia is to be part of the picture. Islam is the umbrella of national identity; an indispensable element of sameness for most people. It's always good form, where possible, to show your Islamic allegiance. One way for Jakarta's readily anonymous celebrities to win sure-fire public approval (and thus curb criticism of their apparent affluence) is to advertise an Islam-related product, especially during Ramadan, the fasting month. That's partly why Islamic car-stickers are so common in the city; to show the world behind that the driver in front is a good Muslim. *"Yes, we are Muslim!"*; *"Muslim family ahead"*; *"Be Muslim or die a sinner!"* And always in English.

If you live and work in Jakarta, you will become accustomed to the actions of Muslims around you. The hours in Jakarta's day are punctuated by the sound of prayer-calls. TV programmes are put on hold. People disappear in mid-sentence, rushing off to get changed and enjoy a respite from the chaos of daily life. Men re-appear in sandals with trousers rolled up; feet washed, ready for prayer. These are the routines of life for a Muslim.

At Ramadan, Muslims abstain from food and drink during daylight hours, waking up very early to break their fast at 3:30 a.m. In Jakarta, groups of appointed local boys work the residential areas shouting *"bangun* (wake up)" very loudly. If that doesn't wake people, a good stick-banging session does the trick. By the end of the month, at what is *Idul Fitri*, people are rightly justified in indulging in all-out, all-night celebrations. Expect no sleep on this night. The mosques, your neighbours and everyone will be playing music, praying, singing, shouting, screaming and laughing. All night long, overloaded trucks of drum-banging youths patrol Jakarta's streets, making sure no one forgets what day it is.

For most of its history, Islam in Indonesia has remained distinctly mystical in approach; only in recent times has the more orthodox variety taken root. By the sixteenth century, a distinctly Javanese form of Islam, incorporating great chunks of Hinduism and regional beliefs alongside the Koran, was in practice. Islam is the most recent of three cultural waves to have washed over Indonesia and, apart from the obvious one about spiritual salvation, has served two important purposes so far.

In the beginning, it would have been a weapon; embraced initially as a weapon-of-force in the power games of colonial rule. By accepting Christianity (being pushed at them from all corners) the anti-Dutch resistors would have been submitting to colonial values. Thus, in an all-encompassing example of passive resistance, Islam was welcomed with open arms. The resistance continued into three years of Japanese rule. It was they who granted permission for the setting up of a bureau of Islamic affairs in Jakarta, unaware that local freedom fighters would use its facilities to communicate messages under the convoluted guise of "prayer". That same bureau became what is today's Ministry of Religion.

And for the Indonesian plucked from his thousand-year-old *kampung* and transmigrated to a far-flung corner of the archipelago, Islam serves its current purpose: that of filling the void of being uprooted; giving the people something in common, something to cling to.

In truth, a relaxed form of Islam is practised in Indonesia. Although living examples of the pious do exist, it's more often than not a case of going through the motions. The routines of Islam are second nature for the average person, and not necessarily given much earnest consideration. Many people, for example, drink beer, and those who don't are not offended if you do. But then again, perhaps they are offended. All signs indicate that Islam in Indonesia is growing in intensity. More and more people make the pilgrimage to Mecca (a real career move in Indonesia); more and more schoolgirls wear the *cilubub* (veil); and more and more pressure is placed on the government by *Nahdlatul Ulama* (an independent body of influential Islamic scholars) to adopt a fundamentalist way of thinking.

Aceh, where it's agreed Islam first entered the country, is one "special territory" where Islamic law prevails. Aceh has never been keen on Jakarta and its administration's reluctance to make things all-Islamic in Indonesia, even declaring "war" on the capital in 1953. The government, meanwhile, argues that Islamic law would be impractical in Indonesia, that it would be at odds with too many of the traditional values still employed in much of the country. President Suharto himself played a clever balancing game throughout his office, gently marginalizing the importance of Islam while simultaneously maintaining a continued display of his own loyalty to the faith.

Indonesia is the world's largest Muslim nation, until now it has also been regarded as the easiest going of all. Only time will tell what will happen.

IDUL FITRI AND OTHER RELIGIOUS HOLIDAYS

Those employed in established, reputable companies will find the Indonesian calendar usually offers a generous number of national holidays, or *tanggal merah* ("red dates") as people like to call them. They can vary from year to year, and the most common are described below. But for the great masses of self-employed and under-employed, the concept of "holidays", much like the concept of "weekends", means little other than another day spent slogging the streets. But at least once a year there is the one big holiday that everyone gets to celebrate together: *Idul Fitri* (or *Lebaran*).

This holiday is very much a "holy" day (or three) because it marks the end of the Muslim fasting month of Ramadan. For those who adhere to the Islamic faith (and this is most people in Indonesia) *Lebaran* is a particularly significant time; a time to celebrate that every human temptation has been held at arm's length — during daylight hours at least — for an entire month. In the build up to *Lebaran*, you will notice a gradual slowdown in the general pace of life in Jakarta. The number of beggars in the city seems to increase, however, as do the number of sly requests to bump up any tips you are giving. *Lebaran* in fact becomes an all-round excuse for all manner of delays: letters take longer to come, anything vaguely "official" takes forever, and just when you start to get bored of the excuse, it's time for the next one.

Lebaran is significant for Jakartans because it's the time when you realize just how many people in the capital actually come from somewhere else in Indonesia. In what has become a traditionally frenetic exodus from the city, people throw abandon to the wind (as well as seemingly all that famous Indonesian reserve) in their fight to gain their place as one of Jakarta's *Lebaran* escapees. Shedding fresh light on the concept of "packed like sardines", public transport is pushed to its limit and beyond. Anyone who doesn't need to travel by coach or train out of Jakarta during this time is advised to make alternative plans.

Following this mass departure from the city, streets, shops and restaurants suddenly seem to cease all activity, and, when all the drums have stopped beating, you feel that you can breathe a sigh of relief. Then you notice the shop shelves seem empty because the shelf-fillers have all gone home too. More than likely your *pembantu*, if you have one, will be among the sardines, leaving you to either enjoy the relative privacy for a few weeks, or go bananas because you have forgotten what the word "housework" means.

But with the experience of your first Indonesian *Lebaran* under your belt, you will be all the more prepared when it comes round next year. Being based on the lunar *Hijrah* calendar, they do come round sooner than you think; coming around ten days earlier each year. It's possible, then, to experience more *Lebaran* than the actual number of years you might spend in Jakarta.

Aside from *Lebaran*, there are other significant Islamic holidays. *Idul Adha* (or *Lebaran Haji*) poses similar shocking scenes for those with no experience of living with Islam. You may have wondered, in the week before the celebration, why so many goats can be seen tied up together around the city. You are advised not to get emotionally involved; in a ceremony symbolic of Abraham's willingness to sacrifice his own son, so the sacrifice of animals is undertaken; predominantly goats and chickens, and the meat distributed to the poor. *Idul Adha* falls on the tenth day of the eleventh month in the *Hijrah* calendar. On the twenty-seventh day of the seventh month comes the *Isra Miraj* holiday; and on the twelfth day of the third month is *Maulud Nabi Muhammad SAW;* the birthday of the prophet Mohammed, again a national holiday.

Other *Hari Raya* (or "Big Days" as national holidays are also called) are more "traditional": *Tahun Baru* (New Year's Day); *Jum'at Agung* (Good Friday); *Hari Raya Paskah* (Easter Sunday); and *Hari Raya Kebangkitan* (Ascension Day). Yet other *Hari Raya* are more mystifying; the Balinese New Year, or *Hari Raya Nyepi* (Day of Silence), is a holiday which traditionally sees people taking a vow of silence for the day. Strictly speaking, followers of the Hindu faith should not eat, speak to anyone, use anything electrical, make any journeys or light any fires for a solid twenty-four hours. Certain parts of Bali will be in temporary blackness on *Hari Nyepi*. The evening before, however, is the complete opposite. People intentionally make as much racket as they can: in doing this, the malingering sprits of the land will be roused into curiosity, but when they find the island in absolute silence the next day, will hopefully panic and flee the island. That at least is the belief. And accompanying the racket on the day before *Nyepi* is a parade of *ogah,* which are demonic mannequins designed again to scare off evil spirits. Traditionally they are representations of generic villain-types, but in recent times they have become an outlet for wider social comment: effigies of presidents, both home and away, are cropping up more and more.

Buddhism also gets its token mention on *Hari Raya Waisak,* a day which celebrates the Lord Buddha's birth, death and enlightenment. Celebrations are held during a full moon in April or May of every year to a somewhat surreal fanfare in Central Java's magnificent Borobudur temple.

Despite the number of Chinese-descended Indonesians in the country, the historical links with China, and the fact that so much of the country's business is tied up with Chinese tycoons, there is no official celebration of *Imlek,* or the Chinese New Year. However, particularly in North Jakarta's "Chinatown", many stores close for the day as the owners take an unofficial day off to celebrate.

OTHER NATIONAL HOLIDAYS

With Indonesia's religious obligations taken care of, there are still a number of other national holidays which are likely to be granted. The first, on April 21, is *Hari Raya Kartini* which commemorates the birthday of Raden Ajeng Kartini, the founder of the movement for the emancipation of Indonesian women. Next, on June 22, is *Hari Ulang Tahun Jakarta,* the official birthday of Jakarta.

On August 17 is *Hari Kemerdekaan RI* (Independence Day). Naturally, this is a "big one", with celebrations occurring throughout the archipelago — parades, street-parties and recitals of the original Proclamation of Independence made in Jakarta by Sukarno in 1945. To celebrate the introduction of the state philosophy, *Pancasila,* by that same president, is *Hari Pancasila* on October 1. Four days later sees the Army have its turn with *Hari Angkatan Bersenjata RI* (Armed Forces Day), and all the attendant (and televised) military muscle-flexing that this entails. Lastly, on November 10, the nation's many heroes, past and present, are honoured in *Hari Pahlawan* (Hero's Day). This day is a kind of New Year's Honours List where the "ordinary" people can be awarded by the President himself for their charitable work, or other outstanding achievements for which they will have been nominated.

On these Indonesian national holidays it is expected that every home will have a national flag to fly. If not, the *RT* may be round for a chat. It is not compulsory, and certainly not illegal, but your address may well be noted and your name branded, albeit in a manner unspoken, a "radical". Obviously *orang asing* (foreigners) are generally forgiven such faux pas the first time around, but don't be surprised when your *pembantu* eventually asks you to invest in a flag and requisite pole.

POLITICS

For the "average" person, the politics of their country has been engineered to remain a mystery, an unquestioned mish-mash of half-truth and trickery. Closer investigation reveals a system that expects its population to let the powers-that-be run the show for them, i.e. to systematically shove them down and keep them there. Investigate too closely, however, and you may never see the light of day again. The world's press brand this a "regime", a military government of power games and mystery disappearances. Yet within the country the "official" political picture is complete: a glowing success story, one of "courage", "self-sufficiency" and "freedom". Whichever side you believe one thing is certain: the "average" person has probably never had it so bad.

To be ignorant of politics therefore is nothing to be particularly ashamed of in Indonesia. In fact, it's a far safer bet to simply do what everyone around you does than say, organize a petition against the government. Imagine the embarrassment of declaring yourself a Beatles fan when everyone else in the *kampung* turns out to be a Rolling Stones fan. This is the kind of thinking that the Indonesian system has encouraged. The only political role people are expected to play is that prescribed by the "floating mass" policy: that of doing your bit for the country, of knuckling down to the task of developing this proud land to its full potential, i.e., shutting up and getting on with it.

However, as we shall find out, such thinking has faced increasing resistance, not only from the outside world but more worryingly, from the young people in Indonesia.

THE SYSTEM

Under the system that ex-President Suharto established, Indonesia's leader will have the final say every time. The country's first president, however, Achmad Sukarno, began his office with a far more democratic parliament, but rapidly grew dissatisfied with it, believing it inherently *tidak cocok* (unsuitable) to the Indonesian way of things. Hence, the introduction of the state ideology *Pancasila* and a system of reaching agreement on a small scale through general consensus — as traditionally achieved in the *kampung*.

With general elections held to great fanfare every five years in Indonesia, there was always assumed to be a certain degree of democracy in play somewhere. Yet this facade belied the true restrictions of the New Order government. Under the system, only three parties were allowed: the ruling party *Golongan Karya* (Golkar), *Partai Persatuan Pembangunan* (PPP) which represents Islamic politics, and *Partai Demokrasi Indonesia* (PDI) which had always been the political troublemaker. However, the politics and leadership of any party remained the sole discretion of the government. When, for example, in 1996, the President thought PDI had become too vocal for its own good, he merely removed its leader (one Megawati Sukarnoputri, daughter of Sukarno) and installed one of his own carefully-vetted subjects. Adding to the facade of democracy were the restrictions placed on political campaigning. Under the law, should more than ten people have gathered in one place to discuss politics, the meeting became a political rally, which was illegal and had to be stopped.

Vote-rigging was never a problem, mainly because the electoral process had been orchestrated to work in the President's favour every time. ABRI (the Armed Forces) had a block vote in every election, while the cabinet itself remained the sole choice of the President. In the run-up to the elections of May '97, government experts reckoned *Golkar* would win with a 70.02% majority. When all the votes had been counted it was found *Golkar* had won with a 70.02% majority. This then, was not "democracy" in any recognizable form, but a tightly-controlled pretence at democracy. Under Suharto, elections were never supposed to be about democracy or change for the better; they were solely about maintaining the status quo and changing as little as possible. Which is partly why, a year later, Suharto suddenly found he was no longer the President of Indonesia.

SUHARTO AND HIS FAMILY

When President Suharto relinquished power after thirty-two years, he was, by Indonesian standards, an old man. In many ways, he had done tremendous things for Indonesia; he was there as the country blossomed in its first flushes of independence. Under his leadership, Indonesia became self-sufficient in food. It was under his leadership that Indonesia remained stable — up to a point anyway.

But he was also there when a number of terrible things were brushed under the carpet. Suharto was there when Indonesia was still fighting the Dutch; he was one of the "old brigade", a man with a history. The first thing he did after stepping in to assist the ailing Sukarno led to the death of several hundred thousand people.

Having instilled a level of fear in the populace which was to last three decades, his second big move was less bloody, though no less ambitious: to take out a massive mortgage on the country in the form of foreign loans, mainly Yen and US dollars. To this day, some 40% of Indonesia's annual earnings are put aside for the repayments. By the end of his marathon length in office, Suharto had seen some amazing changes occur, whilst simultaneously amassing a personal fortune for himself and his family.

While there are other wealthy, well-connected families in Indonesia, none have been afforded the privileges that the Suharto family have enjoyed. At the peak of their powers, they seemed to actually own Jakarta — so plainly were their names written over the nation's economy. The country's toll-roads, for example, belonged to the eldest daughter, while the youngest son had the *Timor*, the country's first "all-Indonesian" car. In addition, they also controlled the country's petrol supplies, an airline, a TV station, a taxi company, the Hyatt Hotel complex, besides having the monopolies on plastics, paper, timber, banking, shipping, fishing, mining and telecommunications. They seemed to have at least 10% on every business transaction in the country, and it was common knowledge that without the nod of approval from one of the Suharto family, foreign businesses could make little headway in Indonesia. Perhaps the most amazing fact was that they had managed to get away with it for so long.

CRISIS TIME

But then, in 1998, it all went pear-shaped as they say. It all seemed to happen at once for Indonesia — everything bad that could happen happened. Everything an ageing President Suharto had accomplished over three decades seemed to have been unravelled in a few short months. Yet forecasters had long been predicting a "crash" of sorts — that trouble had been bubbling under the surface for years. The process was a gradual one.

The years previously had certainly been touch and go in a number of respects. There was the "problem" of East Timor; the United Nations' refusal to accept it as an Indonesian province, and the West's obligation to be appalled, while struggling with the "dilemma" of honouring escalating arms requests. But on the whole, scenarios like these, like the sporadic street violence, or the embarrassment of the Busang fiasco (the site of what had been touted the world's biggest gold mine, but which turned out to be a complete hoax), were viewed as localized problems which could be partially forgotten about by most of the world.

But there was an international outcry when it was revealed that various parts of Indonesia, as well as certain parts of Malaysia, were burning out of control. The resulting smog at one point affected Indonesia, Malaysia, Brunei, Singapore, Thailand, Philippines, and seemed poised to affect the whole planet. The international firefighters were called in, and the traditionally imperious Suharto government had to admit that yes, there was a problem (they declared a national disaster, and Malaysia, a state of emergency) and yes, they would appreciate a hand in solving it. And by the way — sorry.

Jakarta was almost embarrassingly unaffected by the choking smog. As a diversion, the capital suddenly found itself hosting *Pekan Olahraga Nasional '97* (National Sports Week) to great fanfare and, when the wind was blowing in the right direction, pretending that the trouble was somewhere else entirely. But no matter, Jakarta had trouble of its own brewing.

Indonesia became a demon of all things anti-environmental. With the continuing spread of the fires and the realization that they couldn't so easily be extinguished, came accusations that Indonesia was going for broke. Its developers were accused of monumental greed: for example, in order to catapult Indonesia to the rank of number one rice producer, vast areas of Sumatran rainforest were cleared to be turned into paddies. That the land turned out to be totally unsuitable for rice production only added to the irony of their over-ambition. The press had a field day. In defence, Suharto's business crony, Mohammed "Bob" Hassan, appeared on TV saying that perhaps Western countries were jealous of Indonesia's breakneck economy, and asking why, for example, they didn't go and look at countries in Africa if they wanted to criticize developing nations' affairs. Few were convinced. The focus of the blame was pointed at the Suharto family and that, allegedly, most of the companies responsible for the land-clearance which had resulted in the fires, could be linked back to a member of the Suharto family, or at least to one of their cronies.

To rub salt further into the wound, three major accidents were then attributed, though of course never officially, to the smog. A Garuda Airbus flying from Jakarta to Medan lost visibility and flew into a mountain-side, killing all 234 aboard and making this Indonesia's worst ever air disaster. Days later, two cargo ships in the Malacca Straits collided, killing 28. And then, soon after leaving Jakarta, a Silkair plane bound for Singapore went down. Meanwhile, the orangutan, long a favourite of ecological documentary makers, were filmed rolling out of the blazing forests; confused and smouldering — and straight into the hands of the poachers.

So with eco-disasters, the horrors of the East Timor atrocities still fresh in the mind, plane-crashes, outbursts of rioting, drought and starvation in Irian Jaya, and the increasingly worrying question of what would happen after Suharto, the last thing the Jakarta administration wanted was for the economy to crash. But that is exactly what happened.

"DOLLAR NAIK/RUPIAH TURUN"

Thailand, Japan and Korea experienced it first. And then it happened to Indonesia. At first, prices appeared to be doubling and tripling on a weekly basis, then doubling and tripling daily.

There was panic buying of the most fundamental things like rice, oil and powdered milk. Realizing this potential, many suppliers withheld the *sembako* (staples) and held out for the highest bidder. Bus, train and plane services were slashed. Banks were closed, and the bankers ordered not to leave the country. The airport fiscal was raised from Rp 250,000 to Rp 1,000,000. Imported goods tripled in price. Debts went unpaid. Work on construction sites halted. Great expanses of land which had been ear-marked for real-estate development lay empty, while the folk displaced from their land were left to stare back in confusion. Jobs were lost — millions of jobs.

Those hardest hit were those who had to struggle hardest to make ends meet; those who have to sweat out an impossible human task for their basic bread and butter. *Kaki lima* street-vendors began offering two prices: one for their regulars and one for non-regulars. The number of *pemeulang* visibly increased; those who pick over the city's rubbish in the hope of finding something worth recycling. Unicef stepped in, advising people of ways to give children nourishment when food and money were so scarce. *Tajin* (the thick water from boiled rice) was reluctantly accepted as a poor substitute for milk.

Those fortunate enough to be paid in dollars, however, were less affected. And tourists coming to Indonesia suddenly had more rupiah than ever. But for the "ordinary", modern-day Jakartan family, this was a nightmare they had hoped would never come true. The threat of poverty had always been two steps away for such a family — perhaps a couple in their 30s with the proverbial two-point-four children; a couple who both worked diligently fifty hours a week in some white-collar office to bring home just enough to sustain the illusion of being "middle class". Now that same middle class had to be content with dropping a few rungs down the ladder, while the poor had to be content with a meal or two less. The corporate elite, on the other distant hand, continued limping by on borrowed time, but with their empires tied up in the massive debts that had caused the crash, theirs was an uncertain future too.

The rupiah was renowned for its tendency to reflect the general state of affairs in Indonesia. Indeed, the mere mention of a presidential illness was enough to see it drop a few points, but few really expected it to crash so completely. People were genuinely confused by the new terminology emerging: "CBS", "IMF", "Debt rescheduling". Reduced to a simple phrase, it was *dollar naik* (dollar up) and *rupiah turun* (rupiah down) that sounded loudest for most people. A strange sense of denial set in — disbelief that the city was being eaten from the inside out.

With morale so low the government embarked on another of its famous propaganda campaigns. TV and billboard slogans this time imbued "*Saya cinta rupiah — saya cinta produk Indonesia*" (I love rupiah, and I love Indonesian products) or "*Mari, pakai rupiah di dalam bisnis anda*" (Come on, use the rupiah in your business). In addition, TV coverage was made of government ministers and members of the upper classes donating gold, dollars, and even entire year's salaries (although it was the private sector and not the state which was bankrupt). The notion was that if the country stuck together, it could pull through. If there was ever a time for national consciousness, it was now.

Loans were promised, outstanding debts put on hold, and the government cornered into a bargaining liaison with the International Monetary Fund. Help would be given, it transpired, but only on certain conditions. Here was perhaps a chance for the long-standing corruption that defined much of the system to be wiped clean. But the government was obviously reluctant to comply with any reform measures and, despite some half-hearted attempts, much of the reform package was rejected on "unconstitutional" grounds.

On the street level this didn't translate so well. With powdered baby milk costing a week's wages for the poor of Indonesia, the protesters suddenly had what seemed like a valid excuse for protesting. They suddenly had good reason to prove right what they had been saying all along was a rip-off. Even with the government providing subsidized foods for the poor, exploding violence as a consequence of the crash, had never seemed closer.

ACTS OF REBELLION

"Morally they are right. Whether politically they are right, they don't seem to care."
   —Sarwono Kusumaatmadja, former Environment Minister

Student protests were the headache that the Suharto government couldn't get rid of. They had a tried and tested method of containing any outbursts, however, in the shape of several hundred tons of military hardware purchased from the West. This time around though, it wasn't just the youngsters who were brave enough to stand up and make a stand. It was like that scene in *2001: A Space Odyssey* when the first ape-man dares to reach out and touch the monolith from outer space. When he realizes it can be done without instant reprimand, the others one by one follow suit, and before they know what's happened, they have become a force of their own.

The mood was infectious. TV celebrities came out to make their protests public. Letters to the newspapers called for Suharto to step down. Comparisons were made with Sukarno's presidency; that it had been good at the beginning, but tired and worn out at the end. There were, however, three distinct strands of opposition which eventually culminated in the downfall of President Suharto. The most vocal were the middle-class students — mostly educated, middle-class kids with hopes and career plans suddenly on the line. The most violent were the urban masses of *orang kampung*, those who did most of the looting. But the most significant, were the ones from within — Suharto's own ministers and ex-ministers.

In the very short time since independence, the gap between rich and poor has widened beyond everyone's imaginings. Dissatisfaction has grown, and corruption seemingly permeated every aspect of the Indonesian way of life. Yet for the older generation, a generation still reeling from the massacres of the late-'60s, it had always been too painful to contemplate questioning why their land was not theirs, or why they didn't earn enough money. But not for this new generation.

The widespread thinking of those over the age of forty, those who remembered that life hadn't always been so rosy, was that people in Jakarta would simply have to find a way to manage. It was Jakarta's *Coca-Cola* generation that was up in arms: for them there seemed no excuse. Things had been going so well for everyone: a piece of the riches of an accelerating economy was seemingly available to everyone if they only worked at it. This new generation, the one born under the gaze of an ageing, yet revered godfather, felt especially cheated. The promise they had grown up to believe was that Indonesia had so very nearly "caught up": all the relevant technologies were in place, all the right attitudes had been practised — all that was left was to tidy up the edges a bit. It seemed so unreasonable that the country's veneer of apparent gloss and modernity could be wiped clean away so abruptly.

And so with a master plan that was apparently failing, and large cracks appearing throughout the entire system, those who weren't prepared to keep their fingers crossed and hope it would get better soon, took to the streets and began ripping the place apart. Or rather, threatening to rip the place apart. For most of the time, the legendary iron-rule of the Indonesian military was sufficient to contain most of the trouble. But not for long.

Perhaps everyone knew that they had too much foreign media interest to back them up should the government decide to jail everyone. Perhaps they just wanted what everyone, secretly or not, had been wishing for all along — a change for the better.

THE WEEK THAT WAS

"They have come to a point of no return. They will stage their demonstrations daily if necessary, until the old man goes forever."
—Amien Rais, Head of Muhammadiyah, 20 May 1998

The Week That Was began on a Tuesday when four students from Tri Sakti University were shot dead, and ended nine days later on a Thursday when President Suharto relinquished power. The days in-between saw unbridled anarchy sweep through Jakarta and the rest of the country. The man himself, however, the man who was ultimately to blame, was out of the country when the chaos erupted. Would he come back, they wondered? Some believed Suharto had written the country off, and had left for good. There was little left to lose.

Thursday and Friday saw the worst of the mayhem. Anything remotely connected to the authorities was attacked; anything of any value was stolen or destroyed; any place worth looting was looted. The rioters singled out their Chinese half-cousins again, and almost the entire area of Glodok was destroyed. To cries of *"Hidup Indonesia!"* (Long Live Indonesia!), they even ended up killing one another when they set the shopping malls on fire, unaware that shop staff and other looters were still inside.

Suharto flew back to a capital city in tatters. The overwhelming calls for his resignation were met with the vague response that he might, after all, consider stepping "aside". The mayhem continued. The international press descended. In a desperate measure to calm the situation, local TV was instructed to broadcast only the "official" news, and food and petrol prices were cut. But still the mayhem continued. Those who could, began to leave. Those who couldn't, stayed at home glued to their TV sets, hoping a truckload of looters wouldn't stop outside.

By Saturday, the atmosphere had calmed a little. A feeling of uncertain quiet came over Jakarta, as people stopped to assess

PDI supporters rally on Jalan Sudirman.

the damage of their burned out city. The worst part was, they were still broke, still hungry, and still under the rule of someone they had decided they no longer wanted.

The students headed for the parliament building. There was a peculiar sense of paranoid confidence, knowing that the world was watching, and that they could be killed at any moment. They put up banners in English, and handed out flowers to the soldiers. Then they climbed on the roof of the parliament building and sat there, protesting. They were to occupy the parliament building for the next five days.

They called for Suharto to stand down, they called for Suharto to stand trial — even for Suharto to be executed. As the days progressed the cries for *"reformasi"* grew louder, although precisely what they had in mind was never fully detailed. All they knew was they wanted "the old man" out — a man who had come to symbolize the reason the country was in economic despair.

269

Riding high on the roller-coaster of support for Suharto's resignation was a vocal little man called Amien Rais, who had come to represent the heroic opposition to a dictatorship. It was Amien who, having been advised that the situation could turn into another Tiananmen Square, cancelled what was, in Senayan the next day, to be the biggest demonstration yet. But as fate would have it, it was the government itself which actually came to the rescue. One by one, Suharto's ministers, past and present, began to publicly turn against him. Suharto appeared unworried, even chuckling, as he announced that he would be holding elections within six months — elections in which he would not be standing. This was not enough. They wanted him out now.

And so the next morning, Thursday, 21 May 1998, in a broadcast to the nation, it was a shuffling old man who, clearing his throat, acknowledged that he had lost the trust of the nation. He begged forgiveness for any mistakes he had made, and, after thirty-two years, stepped down as the President of Indonesia. There was a rapturous response from the students, and then a kind of stunned disbelief that the father of the nation, the Big *Bapak* himself was gone. The next day, after trying to barricade themselves in one final time, the students decided to vacate parliament and go home. The job had been done.

It was a week of madness that saw the true power of the Indonesian people expressed for the first time in three decades.

THE FUTURE

The future of Jakarta (and the rest) could go several ways. It's not going to get any smaller, and it's not going to get any less crowded. It might well implode after all. The traffic might improve if enough roads are built, but there's a limit to how many times a fly-over can actually fly over. The rich will get richer, and the poor will continue to flood the city in hope of work. The middle classes will swell. Relatively rural areas like Bekasi and Tangerang will become part of the bigger picture, swelling to accommodate the residential needs of Jakarta. Whatever it becomes — it will be big.

But it would be foolish to think Indonesia had always been the garish, painted street-picture of a happy president inoculating happy babies. Perhaps it is simply time the elastic snapped and it once more broke up into the thousand mini mad-houses it always was. Perhaps there will be a revolution and everything will turn to chaos. Perhaps there will be a revolution but the authorities will stop it just in time, only to impose a regime of unmitigated military rule, curfew and paranoia. Or perhaps someone fair and honest who can see beyond the charade will come to power and start a whole new ball game of equality, welfare, and re-distribution of the rupiah. Perhaps Indonesia will become an Islamic state after all and shut itself off from the rest of the world. Perhaps the earth will open up and swallow it whole.

Whatever happens, people are getting worried about Indonesia's future. People might say it's as hazy as a Borneo day. People are worried that their options are running out; as some two million new workers enter the labour force each year, and jobs get fewer and fewer. People are worried that the food is going to run out, or become too expensive. People are worried that the unemployed and underemployed will, in turn, become the hungry, the restless and the threatening. And the threatening will turn to more rioting, rock throwing and bloodshed. People are worried for the small Chinese shop-owner whose lifestyle and outlook is as far removed from the Chinese tycoons as the rock throwers, but who, nonetheless, is somehow to blame.

One day Indonesia's natural resources will run out one by one. Judging by the ferocity with which they have been extracted of late, this might not be so far off. With no more "foreign interest"; no more turning a blind eye to the abuses of human rights in exchange for a cut of the winnings, the country would be stuck.

Let's hope not. Let's hope Indonesia opens up to the rest of the world. Let's hope Indonesia can shake off the bad reputation it has developed in recent years. Let's hope *dangdut* makes an impact in the West. Let's hope Americans start queuing up to watch *Warkop* movies. Let's hope *kretek* cigarettes turn out to be the cure for cancer. But above all, let's hope the "common" people (and don't forget, this *is* most people in Indonesia) get a better deal in life.

Perhaps the next best thing to considering the problem of Jakarta is simply being there. Perhaps the only way Jakarta is a vital, happening place is when you are actually there. Living in Jakarta means being submerged in an entire planet of its own where nothing else matters. Where the country can do no wrong; where Busang never happened; where the rainforests are not burned; where life is better than it ever has been; where life could be worse. To be there is to find a place that knows no different.

GLOSSARY

A

ada there is; there are
aduh gosh; blimey; wow
air matang clean, boiled water
air minum drinking water
air putih plain, "white" water
anak child
anda you (polite form)
aneh odd; weird
angkuh arrogant
anjing dog
antik antique; ancient
apa what
apotik chemist; pharmacy
ari-ari placenta; abdomen
arisan social gathering; involves small-scale gambling
Arjuna hero of the *Mahabharata*; also refers to a playboy
asal origins; source; cause

B

babi pig
badut clown
bahagia happy
bahasa language
bahaya danger
bajaj motorized pedicab
baju-baju clothes
bakmi goreng fried noodles
bakso meatballs, usually in soup
banci transvestite
bandar harbour; port
bangun tidur wake up
banjir flood
bapak father; father figure
baru new
basa-basi good manners; courteous small-talk
Batak native of North Sumatra

batik printed pattern
bau smell (often bad smell)
bayi baby
belimbing starfruit
bemo motorized public transport vehicle
bengkel workshop (often for cars)
beras hitam uncooked black rice
beras merah uncooked "red" (or brown) rice
berwarna coloured
besok tomorrow
Betawi person native to Jakarta
biji seed
binatang animal
bingung confused; puzzled; bewildered
bintang star (also brand name of beer)
bir beer
bisa can; be able to; could
bius drugs
bodoh dumb; stupid
bubur porridge; general mush
bukan not; no
bule white person; albino; pale
bumi earth
bunga flower
burung bird

C

campur mixed; blended
cantik pretty
cari look for
cerewet talkative; fussy
cetak print
cewek girl; "chick"
cicak house lizard
cinta love
cium kiss; smell
coba try; attempt
cocok suitable; agreeable
contoh example; specimen

273

cowok boy; "lad"
cuci wash
cuci-mata window-shopping; girl-watching
cukup enough

D

dijual for sale
disini here
djarum needle
doktor umum general practitioner
domestik domestic
dua two
duit money; cash
dulu previously

E

e'ek poo-poo (child talk)
eksperimen experiment
emas gold
ember bucket

G

gabah unhulled raw rice
gado-gado salad with peanut sauce
Gambang Kromong Chinese-influenced, Jakartan *gamelan* music
gamelan orchestra; "classical" Indonesian music
gangguan disturbances; hassle
ganja marijuana
garam salt
gatal itchy
gila mad; crazy; loopy; potty
gila uang money-mad
golok machete
got gutter; drain
gotong-royong mutual cooperation
gudang warehouse; storeroom
gulai ayam chicken curry
gulai kambing lamb curry
guntur thunder
gunung sampah rubbish mountain

H

habis finished; all gone

balilintar lightning
bansip neighbourhood watchman
bantu ghost
Hanuman monkey hero in the *Ramayana* epic
banya only; just
barum nice-smelling; fragrant
bati-bati careful
bidup alive; on
bitam black
bujan rain

I

ibu mother; older woman
ibukota capital city
ikan goreng fried fish
Indomie legendary local brand of instant noodles
ini this
intan diamond
itu that

J

jahat evil; nasty; horrible
jalan road/street; to walk; to function
jam hour; time
jambu air rose-apple fruit
jamu traditional tonic of medicinal herbs
jangan don't
janur palm leaves (usually arranged as wedding decoration)
jauh far
jilbab Islamic female headgear
jongkok squatting; crouching
jorok rude; dirty-minded; slovenly
juice alpukat avocado juice

K

kakak older relative
kaki lima "five-footer", street vendor's cart
kalau if; when
kamar kecil small room; toilet
kambing goat
kampung village; lower-class residential area; slum

274

kampungan uncool; unrefined; countrified

kamu you

kanan right (not left)

kancing button

kantor office; work place

Kapal Api steam boat; name of local coffee brand

kapur sirih lime for chewing with betel nut

karet rubber

kartu card

kasih give; love

kasihan pity; sympathy; mercy

kau you (informal)

kaya rich

kayu manis scented wood; cinnamon

ke to

kebebasan pribadi privacy

kebun garden

kecoa cockroach

kehormatan respect

kemanusiaan humanity

kemarin yesterday; the day before

kenapa why

keriting curly

kerja keras hard work

kerokan painful massage with coin

kesabaran patience

kesehatan health

ketan sticky rice

ketoprak salad with tofu and peanut sauce

kijang antelope; brand name for popular vehicle

kiri left (not right)

kita we (to include the person addressed)

konsultan consultant

kontol penis (very bad word)

kopi coffee

kost room and board

kretek clove cigarette

kroncong Portuguese-influenced popular music

kuat strong

kucing cat

kue cake

kuntilanak evil child-hunting spirit in Javanese folklore

kunyit turmeric

kuping-kuping ears

L

lagi again; more

lagu cinta love song

laki-laki men

lalapan sayur dish of raw vegetables with hot sauce

lampu merah red light; menstrual period (slang)

langsung immediately; straight away

laten latent

layang-layang kite

lecek dishevelled; worn out (Jakartan)

lelucon joke

lem nasi rice glue

lem tikus rat glue

lengkuas ginger plant variant

lewat via; by way of

lihat look

listrik electricity

loe you (very informal; Jakartan)

M

ma'af sorry; excuse me

mabuk drunk; delirious; "out of it"

macet jammed; stuck

madu honey

mainan toy

makan eat

maling thief

malu shy; bashful; reluctant

mandi to bathe

mangga mango

manggis mangosteen

manis sweet

martabak thick crepe (sweet or savoury)

mas older brother/relative; contemporary male (Javanese)

masak cook; ripe

masuk angin "entered wind"; flu-like illness
matahari sun
mau want; desire
mbak older sister/relative (like *mas*); contemporary female
mesjid mosque
metromini mad, orange bus service
mie pangsit ravioli-style noodles
mie rebus boiled, plain noodles
mikrolet another public transport service
minum drink
miskin poor
Monas national monument
monyet monkey
mudah-mudahan hopefully
mungkin maybe; perhaps
musholla small mosque; praying room
musim hujan wet, rainy season
musim kering dry season

N

nanas pineapple
nasi rice
nasi goreng fried rice
nasi pulan well-cooked rice
nasi putih plain rice
nasi rawon beef-stew with rice
nasi uduk coconut-based rice dish
negara state
nenek grandma; any older woman
nggak no (slang — Jakarta)
nyamuk mosquito

O

obat medicine
ojek motorcycle and rider used as public transport
oleh-oleh gift; present
operasi operation
orang person
orang Jawa Javanese person
orang-orang people
oseng-oseng stir-fried dish with chilli

P

pak shorter form of *bapak*
paling most (general superlative form)
Pancasila the state ideology
panggil call; summon
panjang long; lengthy
pantat bottom; bum
Pasaraya grand market; Jakarta's most famous department store
payung umbrella
peci black rimless hat, usually black and worn by male Muslims
pelacur prostitute
pelit mean; stingy
pembantu helper; servant; maid
pemulung rubbish collector; scavenger
pendidikan education
penduduk citizen
penting important
perempuan woman
petani farmer
pinang areca nut
pisang banana
polisi police
polisi tidur sleeping policeman; traffic hump
preman villain
prokem Jakarta street slang
puasa fasting
pulang go home
pulang kampung go home (specifically to place of origin, especially village)
pusing dizzy; lightheaded

R

rajawali large black hawk
rakyat the masses; common populace
rambut hair
rame crowded; busy
rasa taste; feeling; sensation; vibe
Rinso legendary all-round local washing powder
ronggeng performing dancing girl
rujak fruit salad with spicy sauce
Rukun Tetangga (RT) neighbourhood cooperative

Rukun Warga (RW) administrative
  unit one level above RT
rumah house
rumah makan restaurant
rumah sakit hospital

S

sakit flu the common cold; perhaps
  influenza
sakit perut bad stomach
sama the same as; with
sambal terasi pungent fish-paste
sampah rubbish
sampai until
santai relax
saron xylophone-style instrument
  found in *gamelan* music
sarong all-purpose wraparound cloth
sate grilled meat on a stick, usually
  with peanut sauce
satu one
selendang sling; scarf
semampai slender
semangat pemuda spirit of youth; lust
  for life
semeter one metre
senang happy; content; pleased
sendiri on your own
sering kebanjiran prone to flooding
silakan please; go ahead
singkatan abbreviation; acronym
sop ayam chicken soup
sopir driver
sudah already; done
sudah mandi? have you bathed yet?
suka like
sulit difficult; tricky
surya sun
susah difficult; hard
swalayan self-service

T

tadi earlier; just now
tahu goreng fried tofu
tai excrement (bad word)
tanda sign

tanggal date
tanjidor weird Jakartan "brass band"
  music
teh manis sweet tea
telor egg
teman friend; pal
tempe fermented soya-bean cake
terus go on; straight ahead; continue
tetek breast
tidak no
tidak apa-apa it doesn't matter; don't
  worry about it
tidur sleep
tikus rat
tingkat floor; storey; level
tokek gecko
toko shop
tolong please; por favor
tukang tradesman/craftsman (very
  general)
tukang parkir parking assistant
tukang sate sate seller

U

uang money
umbul-umbul Betawi wedding
  decoration
untuk for, e.g. *untuk apa?* (what for?)

W

warung small shop or stall
waspada beware of
wong Londo foreign person (Javanese)

Y

yang the one that/which/who, etc.
yang dingin a cold one; one which is
  cold

FURTHER READING

- An essential book for anyone intending to move to Jakarta long-term is the American Women's Association publication: *Introducing Indonesia — A Guide to Expatriate Living*. Although rather presumptuous in its text, it does contain a wealth of information to cover areas as far apart as the procedure for bringing pets into Indonesia, or what to do should your house-maid die. The AWA also produce that most comprehensive of publications: the *Jakarta Shopper's Guide*. Both books are available at the AWA Center, Jl Gaharu 1, No. 15, Cilandak Barat (South Jakarta), tel: 769-4008.
- For more on the cultural dos and don'ts of living in Indonesia; the social customs, traditions and business/social etiquette, you can do worse than read Cathie Draine and Barbara Hall's *Culture Shock! Indonesia: A Guide to Customs and Etiquette*.
- Gateway Books, based in Jakarta, publish a number of books about business opportunities in Indonesia, as well as about its culture and tourism. Richard Mann's *Business in Indonesia* is a guide to the country's economic strategies and policies. Also available is *The Culture of Business in Indonesia,* and *Economic Crisis in Indonesia: The Full Story,* as well as sector-specific publications such as *The Guide to Industrial Estates in Indonesia* and the *Guide to British Business in Indonesia*. It also makes Indonesian export guides and publishes the official *Guide to Business in Indonesia*. For more information contact: Gateway Books, Dwimitra Tata Sejati, Jl Haji Soleh 1 No. 1G, Jakarta or Tanglin PO Box 414, Singapore 912414.
- Anyone keen on knowing exactly how Jakarta came to be should read Adolf Heuken's *Historical Sights of Jakarta*. Aside

from numerous maps and illustrations, it details a number of little-known historical places of interest.

- The most famous novel about Jakarta is probably *Twilight in Djakarta* by the writer and artist Mochtar Lubis. Twice imprisoned for the "subversive" content of his writing, Lubis continues his quiet resistance to the corruption and abuse of basic human rights. "I have seen the insides of the prisons of both 'orders' [the 'old' order under Sukarno, and Suharto's New Order]," he says, "and I don't like either."

MAPS

A highly recommendable map of Jakarta (and there are many to choose from), and recently expanded to encompass Jabotabek (the areas comprising Jakarta, Bogor, Tangerang and Bekasi) is the *Falk Plan* map. Now in its eleventh edition, the *Falk* map is available as a wall map and a street atlas. Indispensable really.

THE AUTHOR

Derek Bacon was born in 1968 near Heathrow Airport, and has been trying to get as far away as possible ever since. At 21, he arrived in Jakarta as a language teacher, and five years later, had fallen in love and adopted the entire populations of Java and Bali as in-laws. The endless number of "love/hate" relationships he witnessed over the years, between the city and its innumerable visitors, inspired him to write the kind of book that should be read prior to a first visit; the kind of book that made sense of Jakarta.

He currently lives in England, with his Indonesian wife Ratna and their son John Wisnu, where he continues to write and illustrate. He has written numerous articles about Indonesia, and a novel set in Jakarta. He is the illustrator of the WWF children's book *The Last Turtle*, as well as a number of book covers. This is his first book.

INDEX